THE MANY FACES OF GOD

A READER OF
MODERN JEWISH
THEOLOGIES

RIFAT SONSINO, Editor

URJ Press · New York, New York

Library of Congress Cataloging-in-Publication Data

Sonsino, Rifat.
   The many faces of God : a reader of modern Jewish theologies / Rifat Sonsino,
editor.
       p. cm.
   Includes bibliographical references.
   ISBN 0-8074-0854-9 (pbk. : alk. paper)
   1. God (Judaism). 2. Jews—Biography. 3. Judaism—20th century.
I. Sonsino, Rifat, 1938–
   BM610.M283   2004
   296.3´11—dc22

                                                        2004049792

This book is printed on acid-free paper.
Copyright © 2004 by Rifat Sonsino.
Manufactured in the United States of America.
10 9 8 7 6 5 4 3 2 1

Copyright Acknowledgments

BEHRMAN HOUSE: Excerpt from *Choices in Modern Jewish Thought* by Eugene B. Borowitz. © Behrman House, Inc., reprinted with permission, www.behrmanhouse.com; excerpt from *Jewish Spiritual Journeys* ed. by Lawrence A. Hoffman and Arnold J. Wolf. © Behrman House, reprinted with permission, www.behrmanhouse.com.

CCAR: Excerpt from *CCAR Yearbook* 1997. Reprinted by permission of the Central Conference of American Rabbis.

FARRAR, STRAUS AND GIROUX: Excerpt from *God in Search of Man* by Abraham Joshua Heschel. Copyright © 1955 by Abraham Joshua Heschel. Copyright renewed © 1983 by Sylvia Heschel. Reprinted by permission of Farrar, Straus and Giroux, LLC. Excerpts from *Man Is Not Alone* by Abraham Joshua Heschel. Copyright © 1951 by Abraham J. Heschel. Copyright renewed 1979 by Sylvia Heschel. Reprinted by permission of Farrar, Straus and Giroux, LLC.

GEORGE BORCHARDT, INC.: Excerpt from *What Is Judaism?* by Emil Fackenheim. Copyright © 1987 by Emil Fackenheim. Reprinted by permission of Georges Borchardt, Inc., for the author.

HARPERCOLLINS: Excerpt from *Standing Again at Sinai* by Judith Plaskow. Copyright © 1990 by Judith Plaskow. Reprinted by permission of HarperCollins Publishers Inc.; excerpt from *The Art of Loving* by Erich Fromm. Copyright © 1956 by Erich Fromm. Copyright renewed © 1984 by Annis Fromm. Reprinted by permission of HarperCollins Publishers Inc.; excerpt from *For Those Who Can't Believe: Overcoming the Obstacles to Faith* by Harold M. Schulweis. Copyright © 1994 by Harold M. Schulweis. Reprinted by permission of HarperCollins Publishers Inc.; excerpt from Margaret Moers Wenig's "God is a Woman" from *Best Sermons 5*, edited by James W. Cox and Kenneth M. Cox. Copyright © 1992 by HarperCollins Publishers. Reprinted by permission of HarperCollins Publishers Inc.

HEBREW UNION COLLEGE PRESS: Excerpt from *Evil and the Morality of God* by Harold M. Schulweis. Reprinted with permission of Hebrew Union College Press, Cincinnati.

JASON ARONSON: Excerpt from *Paradigm Shift: From the Jewish Renewal Teachings of Reb Zalman Schachter-Shalomi* edited by Ellen Singer. Reprinted by permission of Jason Aronson.

THE JEWISH PUBLICATION SOCIETY: Reprinted from *Renewing the Covenant*, by Eugene Borowitz, © 1991, The Jewish Publication Society with the permission of the publisher, The Jewish Publication Society.

THE JOHNS HOPKINS UNIVERSITY PRESS: Excerpt from *After Auschwitz: History, Theology, and Contemporary Judaism* by Richard L. Rubenstein. © 1992 Richard L. Rubenstein. Reprinted by permission of The Johns Hopkins University Press.

RANDOM HOUSE: Excerpt from *When Children Ask About God* by Harold Kushner, copyright © 1971, 1989 by Harold S. Kushner. Used by permission of Schocken Books, a division of Random House, Inc.; excerpt from *When Bad Things Happen to Good People* by Harold S. Kushner, copyright © 1981 by Harold S. Kushner. Used by permission of Schocken Books, a division of Random House, Inc.; excerpt from *On Judaism* by Martin Buber, edited by Nahum Glatzer, translated by Eva Jospe, translation copyright © 1967 by Schocken Books, a division of Random House, Inc. Used by permission of Schocken Books, a division of Random House, Inc.

THE RECONSTRUCTIONIST PRESS: Excerpt from *The Meaning of God in Modern Jewish Religion* by Mordecai M. Kaplan. Reprinted by permission of The Reconstructionist Press.

RECONSTRUCTIONIST RABBINICAL COLLEGE PRESS: Excerpt from "God to Godliness: Proposal for a Predicate Theology," *The Reconstructionist* (February 1975). Reprinted by permission of the Reconstructionist Rabbinical College Press.

REFORM JUDAISM: Excerpt from "The God Puzzle" by Rabbi Richard Levy used with permission from the Spring 2000 edition of *Reform Judaism* magazine, published by the Union of American Hebrew Congregations, and with the permission of Rabbi Richard N. Levy

ZALMAN SCHACHTER-SHALOMI AND DONALD GROPMAN: Excerpt from *The First Step: A Guide for the New Jewish Spirit*. Copyright © 1983 by Zalman Schachter-Shalomi and Donald Gropman. Reprinted with permission of Brockman, Inc. on behalf of Zalman Schachter-Shalomi and Donald Gropman.

SH'MA: Excerpt from "God: some feminist questions" by Judith Plaskow from *Sh'ma*. Reprinted with permission from *Sh'ma: A Journal of Jewish Responsibility* Jan. 1987. For further information visit ww.shma.com.

SIMON AND SCHUSTER: Reprinted with permission of Simon & Schuster Adult Publishing Group from *Who Needs God?* by Harold S. Kushner. Copyright © 1989 by Harold S. Kushner.

THOMSON PUBLISHING SERVICES: Excerpt from *Between Man and Man* by Martin Buber. Reprinted by permission of Thomas Publishing Services.

TIKKUN: Excerpt from "Facing the Ambiguity of God" by Judith Plaskow from *Tikkun*, vol. 6, no. 5 Sept/Oct 1991. Reprinted by permission of Tikkun.

Editor's Note:

The excerpts in this book have all come from different publishers. Wherever possible, we have chosen to leave Hebrew transliteration and other style issues as they appeared in the source publication.

To my family:

My wife, Ines

My children, Daniel and Gabriela Sonsino

Deborah and Ran Seri

My granddaughter, Ariella Sonsino

My grandson, Abraham Seri

CONTENTS

ACKNOWLEDGMENTS

This book was a labor of love. It was brought to fruition through the efforts of many people. I am very grateful to:

Rabbi Peter C. Knobel of Beth Emeth, The Free Synagogue of Evanston, Illinois, for the initial impetus he gave me to undertake this project;

All the living authors who enthusiastically supplied me with all the information I needed for my work;

Rabbi Hara Person, my editor, who encouraged me to go forward with my work and shepherded the project to the very end with a keen eye, sensitivity, and personal interest;

Debra Hirsch Corman, the copy editor, who meticulously read through the entire manuscript;

Everyone else from the URJ Press who worked carefully and thoughtfully in helping to prepare the manuscript for publication, including Annie Vernon, Liane Broido, Joel Eglash, Lauren Dubin, and the publisher, Ken Gesser;

And all my students who studied with me many of the texts included in this book.

I extend my deepest thanks to all of them. "May God reward your deeds" (Ruth 2:12).

Rifat Sonsino
Needham, Massachusetts

INTRODUCTION

The statement in Deut. 6:4, "Hear, O Israel, YHVH [the Lord] our God, the Lord *echad*," is considered to be the watchword of the Jewish faith. It is usually known simply as "the *Sh'ma*," after the first Hebrew word. However, its meaning is ambiguous and therefore has been historically translated and understood in a variety of ways. For example, the New Oxford Annotated Bible (NRSV, 2001) renders it as "Hear, O Israel: The Lord is our God, the Lord alone," but adds a note at the bottom of the same page with other alternatives: "Or *The Lord our God is one Lord*, or *The Lord our God, the Lord is one*, or *The Lord is our God, the Lord is one*."

The basic problem with Deut. 6:4 is trying to discover its purpose. Does it deal with God's unity or with the quality of Israel's relationship with God? In other words, is the emphasis on *"our* God" or on "one"? Furthermore, what does the word *echad* mean: "one" or "alone"? Commentators have debated these issues for centuries.

I prefer the interpretation that stresses Israel's special bond with God. The statement in Deut. 6:4, therefore, implies that other people may and do serve other divinities, but Israel is expected to worship only YHVH, and no one else (cf. Deut. 4:19–20). The Hebrew Scriptures contain clearer statements about the uniqueness of God, even within the Book of Deuteronomy: "YHVH alone is God; there is none other beside Him" (Deut. 4:35); "The Creator of heaven who alone is God" (Isa. 45:18); "Who is god except YHVH?" (II Sam. 22:32; cf. Ps. 18:32). In Deut. 6:4, the author seems to be more interested in the special covenant that God has with Israel.

I also maintain that in Deut. 6:4 we have an affirmation that God is "alone." "One" (the standard translation of the Hebrew word *echad*) implies not "two" or "three." God is *sui generis*. There is nothing or no one like God. God is unique. As the medieval philosopher Moses Maimonides (1135–1204) writes:

> He is not like a member of a pair, nor a species of a genus, nor a person divided into many discrete elements. Nor is He one in the sense that a simple body is, numerically one but still infinitely divisible. God, rather, is uniquely one.
>
> *Chelek, Sanhedrin,* chap. 10
> Isadore Twersky, *Maimonides Reader*
> (New York: Behrman House, 1972), 417–418.

The belief in God's unity has been the hallmark of Jewish thought. This became clearer as the biblical period evolved and continued through the rabbinic times. Medieval Jewish philosophers who, under Greek and Arab influence, probed the meaning and the existence of God with greater intensity in a more systematic fashion, began with the unity of God as a given and then provided different interpretations of God's nature. In our own time the principle of divine unity is taken for granted, based on the assumption that the universe represents an all-encompassing, orderly structure, very much in line with the modern scientific view of the world as operating within a unified field theory.

Theologians are very much aware that we do not know what God is or looks like. Maimonides reminds us that all talk about God is metaphorical, for our language and understanding of the universe are limited. We are incapable of comprehending God's essence, or in biblical terms, we cannot "see God's face" but can only ponder God's "back" (cf. Exod. 33:23), namely, God's effects. Even mystics who aim for direct experience of the presence of God admit that God's essence is ultimately beyond their understanding. In the words of the Kabbalah, God is at best *Ein Sof* (Without Limit). Through observation, analysis, or intuition, the human mind discovers the divine and then comes up with different conceptions of God.

This volume deals with contemporary Jewish images of God in the twentieth century. In our previous book, *Finding God: Selected Responses* (New York: UAHC Press, 2002), Rabbi Daniel B. Syme and I chose more than a dozen Jewish philosophers, and provided a summary of their thought, with appropriate quotations. During this past century, there has been an enormous flow of creativity in this field by numerous Jewish thinkers, who have provided us with refreshingly new images. I felt the need to give them a greater voice by collecting their most representative passages within one volume. The result is now in your hands.

Each chapter begins with detailed biographical information about the author as well as a brief overview of his/her approach. This is followed by a selection of texts written by the particular thinker on the subject of God and, occasionally, other related topics that are central to his or her ideas.

The selection of the authors and their texts compelled me to make hard decisions. Aware of the fact that my space was limited, I had to choose the most representative thinkers and passages. First, I decided to limit my research to the twentieth century, because the thinkers included here speak our language and deal with topics with which we are struggling at the beginning of a new millennium. Then, I had to select those thinkers who, in my estimation, stood out because of their novel approach. Thus, for example, I went with Buber, and not with Rosenzweig. Similarly, I chose Gittelsohn over Levi Olan, and Zalman Schachter-Shalomi instead of the many Jewish Renewal thinkers. Other contemporary thinkers such as David Hartman, Neil Gillman, Emmanuel Levinas, and William Kaufman have written substantive books on God and deserve more extensive recognition, but I chose to leave them out in part for fear of making the book too unwieldy, and in part because their theologies are, to a certain extent, represented by others prominently featured in the present volume. Furthermore, I realize that not all the thinkers I have added here are, strictly speaking, theologians with extensive treatises on God, but I felt their approaches were fresh and insightful, and, therefore, worthy of inclusion. For the sake of diversity, I have also added those who have written shorter essays on God, because they provide us with new images that are refreshing and thought provoking.

The next problem I confronted was to decide the appropriate order in which to present the thinkers: would I go alphabetically, by the length of their creative work, or, simply, by their birth date? I decided to follow the latter in order to provide a better historical perspective of their work.

My task would have been much easier had I opted to ask living authors to provide me with their own selection of their material on God. I decided against this approach, because ultimately this entire project has a subjective tone to it, and I did not want the thinkers I studied to determine the orientation and content of the book. So, I chose those texts that in my opinion represented each author's most authentic view on God and related matters.

My hope is that by studying the writings of these outstanding thinkers of our time, the reader, Jewish or not, will come to realize the vast diversity of thought on this subject within Judaism. Each of us needs to seek and appropriate a conception of God that will provide us with the best explanation of the mystery of the universe.

· 1 ·

MARTIN BUBER

1878–1965

*I*n the 1800s a philosophical movement that was primarily interested in the individual and the nature of existence began to emerge in Europe; it bore the name "existentialism." Among its prominent founders were the Danish philosopher Soren Kierkegaard (1813–1855) and the German thinker Friedrich Nietzsche (1844–1900). This approach was largely a reaction to the German thinkers, such as Immanuel Kant (1724–1804) and Friedrich Hegel (1770–1831), who viewed philosophy almost like a science with its objective and universal knowledge about the universe. The existentialists, on the other hand, concentrated on personal needs and on the choices that each individual is forced to make in a free world. Among these thinkers, Martin Buber stands as one of the most respected representatives.

Martin (Mordekhai) Buber was born in Vienna in 1878. After the disappearance of his mother when he was young, he went to Lvov, in western Ukraine, to live with his grandfather, Solomon Buber, a wealthy businessman and prominent Judaica scholar, who edited a number of midrashic texts. Martin grew up with a number of languages, including Yiddish, German, Hebrew, French, and Polish, and at an early age was exposed to an intensive Chasidic life. In 1892 he returned to his father's house in Lemberg, and in 1896 he enrolled at the University of Vienna to study philosophy and German literature. Later, he attended the universities of Leipzig, Zurich, and Berlin. His commitment to Judaism led Buber to begin editing the periodical Die Welt *(The World)* in 1901, but soon after he split from Herzl's political Zionism to pursue a more cultural venue.

When he was in his early twenties, Buber concentrated on his studies of Chasidism and published a number of works, including Tales of Rabbi Nachman *and* Legends of the Baal Shem. *These publications earned him a significant reputation among the critics. In the early 1920s, while teaching at the University of Frankfurt, he developed a close friendship with Franz Rosenzweig (1886–1929), the author of* The Star of Redemption *(1921). Working together at Rosenzweig's Frankfurt Lehrhausen, the two began to translate the Bible into German in order to further the education of Jews in Germany. It was around that time that Buber published his masterful little book* Ich und Du *(I and Thou; 1923), in which he synthesized his religious philosophy.*

Buber was not only a chair-bound thinker, but a social activist as well. During World War I, he helped establish the Jewish National Commission to alleviate the plight of Jews in Eastern Europe. After Hitler's rise in 1933, he became the director of the Central Office for Jewish Adult Education. However, in 1938, deprived of the opportunity to lecture, he decided to leave Germany for Israel, where he taught social philosophy at the Hebrew University until his retirement in 1951. Buber also served as the leader of Ichud, a movement that was dedicated to the betterment of the Jewish-Arab relations within a binational state. After World War II, and until his death in 1965, Buber traveled extensively around the world, teaching and lecturing on his unique religious approach.

Buber's influence on his contemporaries and among the modern thinkers is most profound, though it must be said that he is more popular among non-Jews than among Jews, most likely because of his antinomian attitude toward Jewish law and practice.

In his philosophical work, Buber concentrated on the inner needs of the individual. For him, meaning could only be achieved through relationship. Authentic human experience, Buber taught, is based on two types of dialogues: "I and It" and "I and Thou." Where there is judgment, evaluation, and control, the dialogue is "I-It." Here "It" is another person or thing. Our daily life is mostly spent in this area: we measure, define, place. We relate to people or objects by "using" them.

Yet, for Buber, there is a higher level of relationship that is based on total acceptance, one that goes from "subject to subject" and where there is "confirmations of selves." This is called "I-Thou," or "I-You," with "You" being the other person or thing, and ultimately God. However, as soon as we become aware of this unique bond, evaluation and judgment interfere, and the dialogue turns into an "I-It."

In Buber's opinion, one cannot have an "experience" of God. Unlike ordinary objects, God cannot be described or defined. God can only be "met." God, Buber reminds us, is always present; God is "the Eternal You." We, on the other hand, are at times absent. At the end of this "meeting" with the "You," we receive not a mandate or a set of rules but simply a "Presence" as power. One can encounter God, Buber argues, in everyday acts, not only at peak moments of our lives. The Bible is a record of these experiences and forms the basis of our attempt to deal with our own existential challenges.

An "I-You" with a Horse

The basic movement of the life of dialogue is the turning towards the other. That, indeed, seems to happen every hour and quite trivially. If you look at someone and address him you turn to him, of course with the body, but also in the requisite measure with the soul, in that you direct your attention to him. But what of all this is an essential action, done with the essential being? In this way, that out of the incomprehensibility of what lies to hand this one person steps forth and becomes a presence. Now to our perception the world ceases to be an insignificant multiplicity of points to one of which we pay momentary attention. Rather it is a limitless tumult round a narrow breakwater, brightly outlined and able to bear heavy loads—limitless, but limited by the breakwater, so that, though not engirdled, it has become finite in itself, been given form, released from its own indifference. And yet none of the contacts of each hour is unworthy to take up from our essential being as much as it may. For no man is without strength for expression, and our turning towards him brings about a reply, however imperceptible, however quickly smothered, in a looking and sounding forth of the soul that are perhaps dissipating in mere inwardness and yet do exist. The notion of modern man that this turning to the other is sentimental and does not correspond to the compression of life today is a grotesque error, just as his affirmation that turning to the other is impractical in the bustle of this life today is only the masked confession of his weakness of initiative when confronted with the state of the time. He lets it dictate to him what is possible or permissible, instead of stipulating, as an unruffled partner, what is to be stipulated to the state of *every* time, namely, what space and what form it is bound to concede to creaturely existence.

The basic movement of the life of monologue is not turning away as opposed to turning towards; it is "reflexion."

When I was eleven years of age, spending the summer on my grandparents' estate, I used, as often as I could do it unobserved, to steal into the stable and gently stroke the neck of my darling, a broad dapple-grey horse. It was not a casual delight but a great, certainly friendly, but also deeply stirring happening. If I am to explain it now, beginning from the still very fresh memory of my hand, I must say that what I experienced in touch with the animal was the Other, the immense otherness of the Other, which, however, did not remain strange like the otherness of the ox and the ram, but rather let me draw near and touch it. When I stroked the mighty mane, sometimes marvellously smooth-combed, at other times just as astonishingly wild, and felt the life beneath my hand, it was as though the element of vitality itself bordered on my skin, something that was not I, was certainly not akin to me, palpably the other, not just another, really the Other itself; and yet it let me approach, confided itself to me, placed itself elementally in the relation of *Thou* and *Thou* with me. The horse, even when I had not begun by pouring oats for him into the manger, very gently raised his massive head, ears flicking, then snorted quietly, as a conspirator gives a signal meant to be recognizable only by his fellow-conspirator; and I was approved. But once—I do not know what came over the child, at any rate it was childlike enough—it struck me about the stroking, what fun it gave me, and suddenly I became conscious of my hand. The game went on as before, but something had changed, it was no longer the same thing. And the next day, after giving him a rich feed, when I stroked my friend's head he did not raise his head. A few years later, when I thought back to the incident, I no longer supposed that the animal had noticed my defection. But at the time I considered myself judged.

Source: Martin Buber, *Between Man and Man*, trans. Ronald Gregor-Smith (New York: Routledge Classics, 2002), 25–27.

The Holy Way

Faced with the need of measuring Judaism's reality against its truth, we must start with an accusation. For whatever is to be learned here about the hidden relationship of metal and dross cannot be recognized from the outside; it will be disclosed only to him who throws himself into the testing fire. By this crucial test, then, we shall perceive that we Jews, all of us, are renegades. Not because another people's landscape, language, and culture have permeated our soul and our life; even if our own landscape, our own language, our own culture were given back to us, we could not regain that inmost Judaism to which we have become unfaithful. Nor because many of us have renounced the norms of Jewish tradition and the system of rules imposed by this tradition; those of us who have kept these norms and rules inviolate in their yea and nay have not preserved this inmost Judaism any more than those who renounced them. All that is customarily referred to as assimilation is harmlessly superficial compared to the fateful assimilation I have in mind: the assimilation to the Occidental dualism that sanctions the splitting of man's being into two realms, each existing in its own right and independent of the other—the truth of the spirit and the reality of life—an assimilation to the mentality of compromise. All renunciation of the treasures of national culture or religious tradition is trifling compared to the fatal renunciation of the most precious heritage of classical Judaism: its disposition toward realization.

This disposition means that true human life is conceived to be a life lived in the presence of God. For Judaism, God is not a Kantian idea but an elementally present spiritual reality—neither something conceived by pure reason nor something postulated by practical reason, but emanating from the immediacy of existence as such, which religious man steadfastly confronts and nonreligious man evades. He is the sun of mankind. However, it is not the man who turns his back on the world of things, staring into the sun in self-oblivion, who will remain steadfast and live in the presence of God, but only the man who breathes, walks, and bathes his self and all things in the sun's light. He who turns his back on the world comprehends God solely as an idea, and not as a reality; he is aware of Him in some experiences in life *(Erlebnis)*, but he is unaware of Him in life itself.

But even he who turns toward the world and desires to see God in all things does not truly live in His presence. God may be seen seminally within all things, but He must be realized between them. Just as the sun's substance has its being among the stars yet beams its light into the earthly realm, so it is granted to human creatures to behold in their midst the radiance of the ineffable's glory. It glows dimly in all human beings, every one of them; but it does not shine in its full brightness within them—only between them. In every human being there is present the beginning of universal being *(Allsein)*; but it can unfold only in his relatedness to universal being, in the pure immediacy of his giving and taking, which surrounds him like a sphere of light, merging him with the oneness of the world. The Divine may come to life in individual man, may reveal itself from within individual man; but it attains its earthly fullness only where, having awakened to an awareness of their universal being, individual beings open themselves to one another, disclose themselves to one another, help one another; where immediacy is established between one human being and another; where the sublime stronghold of the individual is unbolted, and man breaks free to meet other man. Where this takes place, where the eternal rises in the Between, the seemingly empty space: that true place of realization is community, and true community is that relationship in which the Divine comes to its realization between man and man.

Source: Martin Buber, "The Holy Way," in *On Judaism*, ed. Nahum N. Glatzer (New York: Schocken, 1995), 108–110.

I and Thou

THE EXTENDED LINES OF RELATIONS meet in the eternal *Thou.*

Every particular *Thou* is a glimpse through to the eternal *Thou;* by means of every particular *Thou* the primary word addresses the

eternal *Thou*. Through this mediation of the *Thou* of all beings ful-
filment, and non-fulfilment, of relations comes to them: the inborn
Thou is realised in each relation and consummated in none. It is
consummated only in the direct relation with the *Thou* that by its
nature cannot become *It*.

MEN HAVE ADDRESSED THEIR ETERNAL *Thou* with many
names. In singing of Him who was thus named they always had the
Thou in mind: the first myths were hymns of praise. Then the names
took refuge in the language of *It*; men were more and more strongly
moved to think of and to address their eternal *Thou* as an *It*. But all
God's names are hallowed, for in them He is not merely spoken about,
but also spoken to.

Many men wish to reject the word God as a legitimate usage, because
it is so misused. It is indeed the most heavily laden of all the words used
by men. For that very reason it is the most imperishable and most indispensable. What does all mistaken talk about God's being and works
(though there has been, and can be, no other talk about these) matter in
comparison with the one truth that all men who have addressed God had
God Himself in mind? For he who speaks the word God and really has
Thou in mind (whatever the illusion by which he is held), addresses the
true *Thou* of his life, which cannot be limited by another *Thou*, and to
which he stands in a relation that gathers up and includes all others.

But when he, too, who abhors the name, and believes himself to be
godless, gives his whole being to addressing the *Thou* of his life, as a
Thou that cannot be limited by another, he addresses God.

IF WE GO ON OUR WAY and meet a man who has advanced towards
us and has also gone on *his* way, we know only our part of the way, not
his—his we experience only in the meeting.

Of the complete rational event we know, with the knowledge of life
lived, our going out to the relation, our part of the way. The other part
only comes upon us, we do not know it; it comes upon us in the meeting. But we strain ourselves on it if we speak of it as though it were
some thing beyond the meeting.

We have to be concerned, to be troubled, not about the other side
but about our own side, not about grace but about will. Grace concerns

us in so far as we go out to it and persist in its presence; but it is not our object.

The *Thou* confronts me. But I step into direct relation with it. Hence the relation means being chosen and choosing, suffering and action in one; just as any action of the whole being which means the suspension of all partial actions, and consequently of all sensations of actions grounded only in their particular limitation, is bound to resemble suffering.

This is the activity of the man who has become a whole being, an activity that has been termed doing nothing: nothing separate or partial stirs in the man any more, thus he makes no intervention in the world; it is the whole man, enclosed and at rest in his wholeness, that is effective—he has become an effective whole. To have won stability in this state is to be able to go out to the supreme meeting.

To this end the world of sense does not need to be laid aside as though it were illusory. There is no illusory world, there is only the world—which appears to us as twofold in accordance with our twofold attitude. Only the barrier of separation has to be destroyed. Further, no "going beyond sense-experience" is necessary; for every experience, even the most spiritual, could yield us only an *It*. Nor is any recourse necessary to a world of ideas and values; for they cannot become presentness for us. None of these things is necessary. Can it be said what really is necessary?—Not in the sense of a precept. For everything that has ever been devised and contrived in the time of the human spirit as precept, alleged preparation, practice, or meditation, has nothing to do with the primal, simple fact of the meeting. Whatever the advantages in knowledge or the wielding of power for which we have to thank this or that practice, none of this affects the meeting of which we are speaking; it all has its place in the world of *It* and does not lead one step, does not *take* the step, out of it. Going out to the relation cannot be taught in the sense of precepts being given. It can only be indicated by the drawing of a circle which excludes everything that is not this going out. Then the one thing that matters is visible, full acceptance of the present.

To be sure, this acceptance presupposes that the further a man has wandered in separated being the more difficult is the venture and the more elemental the turning. This does not mean a giving up of, say, the *I*, as mystical writings usually suppose: the *I* is as indispensable to this, the supreme, as to every relation, since relation is only possible between *I* and *Thou*. It is not the *I*, then, that is given up, but that false self-asserting instinct that makes a man flee to the possessing of things before the unreliable, perilous world of relation which has neither density nor duration and cannot be surveyed.

EVERY REAL RELATION with a being or life in the world is exclusive. Its *Thou* is freed, steps forth, is single, and confronts you. It fills the heavens. This does not mean that nothing else exists; but all else lives in *its* light. As long as the presence of the relation continues, this its cosmic range is inviolable. But as soon as a *Thou* becomes *It*, the cosmic range of the relation appears as an offence to the world, its exclusiveness as an exclusion of the universe.

In the relation with God unconditional exclusiveness and unconditional inclusiveness are one. He who enters on the absolute relation is concerned with nothing isolated any more, neither things nor beings, neither earth nor heaven; but everything is gathered up in the relation. For to step into pure relation is not to disregard everything but to see everything in the *Thou*, not to renounce the world but to establish it on its true basis. To look away from the world, or to stare at it, does not help a man to reach God; but he who sees the world in Him stands in His presence. "Here world, there God" is the language of *It*; "God in the world" is another language of *It*; but to eliminate or leave behind nothing at all, to include the whole world in the *Thou*, to give the world its due and its truth, to include nothing beside God but everything in him—this is full and complete relation.

Men do not find God if they stay in the world. They do not find Him if they leave the world. He who goes out with his whole being to meet his *Thou* and carries to it all being that is in the world, finds Him who cannot be sought.

Of course God is the "wholly Other"; but He is also the wholly Same, the wholly Present. Of course He is the *Mysterium Tremendum* that appears and overthrows; but He is also the mystery of the self-evident, nearer to me than my *I*.

If you explore the life of things and of conditioned being you come to the unfathomable, if you deny the life of things and of conditioned being you stand before nothingness, if you hallow this life you meet the living God.

MAN'S SENSE OF *Thou*, which experiences in the relations with every particular *Thou* the disappointments of the change to *It*, strives out but not away from them all to its eternal *Thou*; but not as something is sought: actually there is no such thing as seeking God, for there is nothing in which He could not be found. How foolish and hopeless would be the man who turned aside from the course of his life in order to seek God; even though he won all the wisdom of solitude and all the power of concentrated being he would miss God. Rather is it as when a man goes his way and simply wishes that it might be the way: in the strength of his wish his striving is expressed. Every relational event is a stage that affords him a glimpse into the consummating event. So in each event he does not partake, but also (for he is waiting) does partake, of the one event. Waiting, not seeking, he goes his way; hence he is composed before all things, and makes contact with them which helps them, though everything now meets him in the one event. He blesses every cell that sheltered him, and every cell into which he will yet turn. For this finding is not the end, but only the eternal middle, of the way.

It is finding without seeking, a discovering of the primal, of origin. His sense of *Thou*, which cannot be satiated till he finds the endless *Thou*, had the *Thou* present to it from the beginning; the presence had only to become wholly real to him in the reality of the hallowed life of the world.

God cannot be inferred in anything—in nature, say, as its author, or in history as its master, or in the subject as the self that is thought in it. Something else is not "given" and God then elicited from it; but God is the Being that is directly, most nearly, and lastingly, over against us, that may properly only be addressed, not expressed.

WHAT IS THE ETERNAL, primal phenomenon, present here and now, of that which we term revelation? It is the phenomenon that a man does not pass, from the moment of the supreme meeting, the same being as he entered into it. The moment of meeting is not an "experience" that stirs in the receptive soul and grows to perfect blessedness; rather, in that moment something happens to the man. At times it is like a light breath, at times like a wrestling bout, but always—it *happens*. The man who emerges from the act of pure relation that so involves his being has now in his being something more that has grown in him, of which he did not know before and whose origin he is not rightly able to indicate. However the source of this new thing is classified in scientific orientation of the world, with its authorised efforts to establish an unbroken causality, we, whose concern is real consideration of the real, cannot have our purpose served with subconsciousness or any other apparatus of the soul. The reality is that we receive what we did not hitherto have, and receive it in such a way that we know it has been given to us. In the language of the Bible, "Those who wait upon the Lord shall renew their strength." In the language of Nietzsche, who in his account remains loyal to reality, "We take and do not ask who it is there that gives."

Man receives, and he receives not a specific "content" but a presence, a Presence as power. This Presence and this power include three things, undivided, yet in such a way that we may consider them separately. First, there is the whole fulness of real mutual action, of the being raised and bound up in the relation: the man can give no account at all of how the binding in relation is brought about, nor does it in any way lighten his life—it makes life heavier, but heavy with meaning. Secondly, there is the inexpressible confirmation of meaning. Meaning is assured. Nothing can any longer be meaningless. The question about the meaning of life is no longer there. But were it there, it would not have to be answered. You do not know how to exhibit and define the meaning of life, you have no formula or picture for it, and yet it has more certitude for you than the perceptions of your senses. What does the revealed and concealed meaning purpose with us, desire from us? It does not wish to be explained (nor are we able to do that) but only to be done by us. Thirdly, this meaning is not that of "another life," but that of this life of ours, not one of a world "yonder" but that of this world of ours, and it desires its confirmation in this life and in relation with this world. This meaning can be received, but not experienced; it cannot be experienced but it can be done, and this is its purpose with us. The assurance I have of it does not wish to be sealed within me, but it wishes to be born by me into the world. But just as the meaning itself does not permit itself to be transmitted and made into knowledge generally current and admissible, so confirmation of it cannot be transmitted as a valid Ought; it is not prescribed, it is not specified on any tablet, to be raised above all men's heads. The meaning that has been received can be proved true by each man only in the singleness of his being and the singleness of his life. As no prescription can lead us to the meeting, so none leads from it. As only acceptance of the Presence is necessary for the approach to the meeting, so in a new sense is it so when we emerge from it. As we reach the meeting with the simple *Thou* on our lips, so with the *Thou* on our lips we leave it and return to the world.

That before which, in which, out of which, and into which we live, even the mystery, has remained what it was. It has become present to us and in its presentness has proclaimed itself to us as salvation; we have "known" it, but we acquire no knowledge from it which might lessen or moderate its mysteriousness. We have come near to God, but not nearer to unveiling being or solving its riddle. We have felt release, but not discovered a "solution." We cannot approach others with what we have received, and say "You must know this." We can only go, and confirm its truth. And this, too, is no "ought," but we can, we *must*.

This is the eternal revelation that is present here and now. I know of no revelation and believe in none whose primal phenomenon is not precisely this. I do not believe in a self-naming of God; a self-definition of God before men. The Word of revelation is *I am that I am*. That which reveals is that which reveals. That which is *is*, and nothing more. The eternal source of strength streams, the eternal contact persists, the eternal voice sounds forth, and nothing more.

THE ETERNAL *Thou* can by its nature not become *It*; for by its nature it cannot be established in measure and bounds, not even in the measure of the immeasurable, or the bounds of boundless being; for by its nature it cannot be understood as a sum of qualities, not even as an infinite sum of qualities raised to a transcendental level; for it can be found neither in nor out of the world; for it cannot be experienced, or thought; for we miss Him, Him who is, if we say "I believe, that He is"—"He" is also a metaphor, but "Thou" is not.

And yet in accordance with our nature we are continually making the eternal *Thou* into *It*, into some thing—making God into a thing. Not indeed out of arbitrary self-will; God's history as a thing, the passage of God as Thing through religion and through the products on its brink, through its bright ways and its gloom, its enhancement and its destruction of life, the passage away from the living God and back again to Him, the changes from the present to establishment of form, of objects, and of ideas, dissolution and renewal—all are one way, are *the* way.

What is the origin of the expressed knowledge and ordered action of the religions? How do the Presence and the power of the revelation (for all religions necessarily appeal to some kind of revelation, whether through the medium of the spoken word, or of nature, or of the soul: there are only religions of revelation)—how do the Presence and the power received by men in revelation change into a "content"?

The explanation has two layers. We understand the outer psychical layer when we consider man in himself, separated from history, and the inner factual layer, the primal phenomenon of religion, when we replace him in history. The two layers belong together.

Man desires to possess God; he desires a continuity in space and time of possession of God. He is not content with the inexpressible confirmation of meaning, but wants to see this confirmation stretched out as something that can be continually taken up and handled, a continuum unbroken in space and time that insures his life at every point and every moment.

Man's thirst for continuity is unsatisfied by the life-rhythm of pure relation, the interchange of actual being and of a potential being in which only our power to enter into relation, and hence the presentness (but not the primal Presence) decreases. He longs for extension in time, for duration. Thus God becomes an object of faith. At first faith, set in time, completes the acts of relation; but gradually it replaces them. Resting in belief in an *It* takes the place of the continually renewed movement of the being towards concentration and going out to the relation. The "Nevertheless I believe" of the fighter who knows remoteness from as well as nearness to God is more and more completely transformed in the certainty of him who enjoys profits, that nothing can happen to him, since he believes that there is One who will not let anything happen to him.

Source: Martin Buber, *I and Thou*, trans. Ronald Gregor-Smith (New York: Scribner, 2000), 77–81; 104–107.

· 2 ·

MORDECAI M. KAPLAN

1881–1983

Mordecai M. Kaplan was the founder of Reconstructionism, which came to be the fourth major Jewish movement in America, alongside Orthodox, Conservative, and Reform. Kaplan was born in Lithuania in 1881 and immigrated to the United States at the age of nine. Though he grew up as an Orthodox Jew, by the time he reached secondary school he was interested in a more liberal approach to the study of Bible and religion in general. Kaplan attended the City College of New York and thereafter the Jewish Theological Seminary (JTS; Conservative), from which he received his rabbinic ordination in 1902. His first pulpit was at Kehillat Jeshurun, an Orthodox congregation in New York. After a brief tenure there, Solomon Schechter appointed him in 1909 to be the dean of the newly founded Teachers Institute of the JTS. He also taught homiletics, midrash, and philosophy of religion in the rabbinical school. After his retirement in 1963, Kaplan went to the Hebrew University in Jerusalem and returned to the United States in 1983, just before his death at the age of 102.

Kaplan was influenced not only by traditional rabbinic writings, but also by various thinkers of the Haskalah (Enlightenment) movement in Judaism (c. 1770–1880), which tried to bridge the gap between the religious and the secular world. From his nonrabbinic studies he drew insights from American philosophical pragmatism, scientific methods, and the new sociological approaches, especially those espoused by the famous French-Jewish sociologist, Émile Durkheim (1858–1917). Kaplan published extensively on various scholarly topics, including a translation of Moses Hayyim Luzzatto's Mesillat Yesharim (1937). However, most of his writings are dedicated to his new philosophy of Judaism based on peoplehood and naturalistic theology.

Kaplan was a scholar and a man of action. In 1918, in response to the need of the Jewish community, he set up the first Jewish center in New York City in order to promote cultural and social activities for young people. In 1922, he established the Society for the Advancement of Judaism, which later on, in 1935, became the Jewish Reconstructionist Foundation. The Reconstructionist Rabbinical College (RRC) was founded mostly through his personal efforts in 1968. This school has since ordained both men and women to the rabbinate. Kaplan's influence on other Jewish thinkers was profound and continues even today among many liberal theologians. His commitment to women's rights also led him to create and officiate at the first bat mitzvah—of his own daughter, Judith, in 1922.

Kaplan set up to reconstruct Judaism because he believed traditional norms were not satisfactory to meet the scientific mind of the modern age. By defining Judaism as an "evolving religious civilization" that includes culture, land, language, arts, mores, and sacred paths, Kaplan changed the center of gravity from religion to peoplehood and maintained that religion too must evolve in response to people's needs. Science, he noted, views the universe as one whole; therefore, God too must be One and is intuitively known by individuals. In keeping with his religious naturalism, Kaplan argued that because nature urges us to realize our potential, God is the combination of powers, the forces, or the processes, conceived impersonally, that enables us to reach our goals in life. In his words, "God is the Power that makes for salvation" (The Meaning of God, p. 40), where "salvation" basically means "self-realization." Kaplan's God is not personal or supernatural, does not choose one among peoples, and is not even omnipotent. The evil we experience in the universe is chaos still unconquered by the creative energy that sustains us all. Yet, life is full of possibilities and moves us toward the ultimate fulfillment of our ideals.

The Idea of Salvation

The salvation that the modern man seeks in this world, like that which his fathers sought in the world to come, has both a personal and a social significance. In its personal aspect it represents the faith in the possibility of achieving an integrated personality. All those natural impulses, appetites and desires which so often are in conflict with one another must be harmonized. They must never be permitted to issue in a stalemate, in such mutual inhibition as leaves life empty and meaningless, without zest and savor. Nor must they be permitted to issue in distraction, in a condition in which our personality is so pulled apart by conflicting desires that the man we are in certain moments or in certain relations looks with contempt and disgust at the man we are in others. When our mind functions in such a way that we feel that all our powers are actively employed in the achievement of desirable ends, we have achieved personal salvation.

This personal objective of human conduct cannot, however, be achieved without reference to a social objective as well. Selfish salvation is an impossibility, because no human being is psychologically self-sufficient. We are impelled by motives that relate themselves to the life of the race with as imperative an urge as by any that relate themselves to the preservation of our individual organism. "Love is strong as death" [Cant. 8:6], and frequently sacrifices life itself for the object of love. Although to every individual the achievement of personal salvation is his supreme quest and responsibility, it is unattainable without devotion to the task of social salvation. The thought, "If I am not for myself, who will be for me?" in this striving for salvation always carries with it the implication, "If I am but for myself, what am I?" [*Pirkei Avot* 1:14] because we cannot even think of ourselves except in relation to something not ourselves.

In its social aspect, salvation means the ultimate achievement of a social order in which all men shall collaborate in the pursuit of common ends in a manner which shall afford to each the maximum opportunity for creative self-expression. There can be no personal salvation so long as injustice and strife exist in the social order; there can be no social salvation so long as the greed for gain and the lust for domination are permitted to inhibit the hunger for human fellowship and sympathy in the hearts of men. There is a sense in which it is still true that salvation is of the world to come, for its attainment is clearly not of today or of tomorrow. That it will ever be attained can never be demonstrated, but faith must assume it as the objective of human behavior, if we are not to succumb to the cynical acceptance of evil, which is the only other alternative.

The goal to be reached need not necessarily be conceived as a static and final goal. Life can always be depended upon to create new wants that call for satisfaction and give birth to new ideals. But the measure of our self-fulfillment as individuals and as a society will ever be the extent to which our lives are oriented to valid ideals. In this sense the center of gravity of our lives remains in the world to come, for it is ever the potentialities of the future that redeem the efforts of the present from futility, and that save our souls or ethical personalities from frustration. The self-indulgent sensualist who spiritually lives a hand-to-mouth existence can never find self-fulfillment, because such a life does not begin to bring into play all the latent faculties and powers that inhere in human nature. Only the individual whose purposes in life relate themselves to objectives that lie in the future can experience that sense of well-being and aliveness which comes when all our powers are enlisted in the pursuit of some desired end.

In the light of all that, *salvation must be conceived mainly as an objective of human action, not as a psychic compensation for human suffering.* Though it is absurd to charge religion as such with being an opiate, the truth is that otherwordly religion did function as an opiate. But this fact by itself does not count even against other-worldly religion. In the two thousand years preceding the Enlightenment, religion had to function as an opiate, for so acutely aware had man become of evil which seemed to him irremediable that he might have been driven into despair, had he not been able to hope for salvation in the hereafter. By preserving the ideal of salvation, so to speak, in heaven, man could bring that ideal down to earth as soon as he learned enough about himself and the world he lived in to be able to improve both. But religion owes a genuine debt to those who have called attention to the danger in our own day of drugging the human with the opiate of other-worldliness. The effect of such an opiate at the present time is to keep us from the attainment of salvation on earth. This is equally true whether we think in terms of personal salvation or of social salvation.

Source: Mordecai M. Kaplan, *The Meaning of God in Modern Jewish Religion* (Detroit, Mich.: Wayne State University Press, 1994), 53–55.

Belief in God

To the modern man, religion can no longer be a matter of entering into relationship with the supernatural. The only kind of religion that can help him live and get the most out of life will be the one which will teach him to identify as divine or holy whatever in human nature or in the world about him enhances human life. Men must no longer look upon God as a reservoir of magic power to be tapped whenever they are aware of their physical limitations. It was natural for primitive man to do so. He sought contact with his god or gods primarily because he felt the need of supplementing his own limited powers with the external forces which he believed were controlled by the gods. He sought their aid for the fertility of his fields, the increase of his cattle, and the conquest of his foes. In time, however—and in the case of the Jewish people early in their history—men began to seek communion with God not so much as the source of power but rather as the source of goodness, and to invoke His aid to acquire control not over the external forces but over those of human nature in the individual and in the mass. With the development of scientific techniques for the utilization of natural forces, and with the revision of our world-outlook in a way that invalidates the distinction between natural and supernatural, it is only as the sum of everything in the world that renders life significant and worthwhile—or holy—that God can be worshiped by man. Godhood can have no meaning for us apart from human ideals of truth, goodness, and beauty, interwoven in a pattern of holiness.

To believe in God is to reckon with life's creative forces, tendencies and potentialities as forming an organic unity, and as giving meaning to life by virtue of that unity. Life has meaning for us when it elicits from us the best of which we are capable, and fortifies us against the worst that may befall us. Such meaning reveals itself in our experiences of unity, of creativity, and of worth. In the experience of that unity which enables us to perceive the interaction and interdependence of all phases and elements of being, it is mainly our cognitive powers that come into play; in the experience of creativity which we sense at first hand, whenever we make the slightest contribution to the sum of those forces that give meaning to life, our cognitive powers come to the fore; and in the experience of worth, in the realization of meaning, in contrast to chaos and meaninglessness, our emotional powers find expression. Thus in the very process of human self-fulfillment, in the very striving after the achievement of salvation, we identify ourselves with God, and God functions in us. This fact should lead to the conclusion that when we believe in God, we believe that reality—the world of inner and outer being, the world of society and of nature—is so constituted as to enable man to achieve salvation. If human beings are frustrated, it is not because there is no God, but because they do not deal with reality as it is actually and potentially constituted.

Our intuition of God is the absolute negation and antithesis of all evaluations of human life which assume that consciousness is a disease, civilization a transient sickness, and all our efforts to lift ourselves above the brute only a vain pretense. It is the triumphant exorcism of Bertrand Russell's dismal credo: "Brief and powerless is man's life. On him and all his race the slow sure doom falls pitiless and dark." It is the affirmation that human life is supremely worthwhile and significant, and deserves our giving to it the best that is in us, despite, or perhaps because of, the very evil that mars it. This intuition is not merely an intellectual assent. It is the "yea" of our entire personality. "That life is worth living is the most necessary of assumptions," says Santayana, "and were it not assumed, the most impossible of conclusions." The existence of evil, far from silencing that "yea," is the very occasion for articulating it. "The highest type of man," said Felix Adler, "is the one who *in articulo mortis* can bless the universe."

The human mind cannot rest until it finds order in the universe. It is this form-giving trait that is responsible for modern scientific theory. That same need is also operative in formulating a view of the cosmos, which will support the spiritual yearnings of the group and make their faith in the goals and objectives of their group life consistent with the totality of their experience as human beings. Out of this process of thought there arise traditional beliefs as to the origin of the world, man's place in it, his ultimate destiny, the role of one's own particular civilization in the scheme of human history, and all those comprehensive systems of belief that try to bring human experience into a consistent pattern.

But there is one underlying assumption in all these efforts at giving a consistent meaning to life, whether they are expressed in the naïve cosmologies of primitive peoples or in the most sophisticated metaphysical systems of contemporary philosophers, and that is the assumption that life is meaningful. Without faith that the world of nature is a cosmos and not a chaos, that it has intelligible laws which can be unravelled, and that the human reason offers us an instrument capable of unravelling them, no scientific theorizing would be possible. This is another way of saying that science cannot dispense with what Einstein has appropriately named "cosmic religion," the faith that nature is meaningful and hence divine. And just as our inquiry into natural law demands the validation of cosmic religion, so also does our inquiry into moral law and the best way for men to live. It implies the intuition that life inherently yields ethical and spiritual values, that it is holy. The God idea thus expresses itself pragmatically in those fundamental beliefs by which a people tries to work out its life in a consistent pattern and rid itself of those frustrations which result from the distracting confusion of ideals and aims, in a word, beliefs by which it orients itself and the individuals that constitute it to life as a whole.

The purpose of all education and culture is to socialize the individual, to sensitize him to the ills as well as to the goods of life. Yet the more successful we are in accomplishing this purpose, the more unhappiness we lay up for those we educate. "As soon as high consciousness is reached," says A. N. Whitehead, "the enjoyment of existence is entwined with pain, frustration, loss, tragedy." Likewise, the more eager we are to shape human life in accordance with some ideal pattern of justice and cooperation, the more reasons we discover for being dissatisfied with ourselves, with our limitations, and with our environment. If, therefore, culture and social sympathy are not to break our hearts, but to help us retain that sureness of the life-feeding which is our native privilege, they must make room for religious faith which is needed as a tonic to quicken the pulse of our personal existence.

Faith in life's inherent worthwhileness and sanctity is needed to counteract the cynicism that sneers at life and mocks at the very notion of holiness. Against such a cheapening of life's values no social idealism that does not reckon with the cosmos as divine is an adequate remedy. How can a social idealist ask men to deny themselves immediate satisfactions for the sake of future good that they may never see in their lifetime, when he leaves them without any definite conviction that the universe will fulfill the hopes that have inspired their sacrifice, or is even able to fulfill them? If human life does not yield some cosmic meaning, is it not the course of wisdom to pursue a policy of "Eat, drink and make merry, for tomorrow we die"?

Belief in God as here conceived can function in our day exactly as the belief in God has always functioned; it can function as an affirmation that life has value. It implies, as the God idea has always implied, a certain assumption with regard to the nature of reality, the assumption that reality is so constituted as to endorse and guarantee the realization in man of that which is of greatest value to him. If we believe that assumption to be true, for, as has been said, it is an assumption that is not susceptible of proof, we have faith in God. No metaphysical speculation beyond this fundamental assumption that reality assures both the emergence and the realization of human ideals is necessary for the religious life.

Source: Mordecai M. Kaplan, *The Meaning of God in Modern Jewish Religion* (Detroit, Mich.: Wayne State University Press, 1994), 25–29.

Can God Create Miracles?

The mere fact that we cannot accept as historical the record of miraculous events in the Bible and elsewhere does not imply that we regard the miracle stories as of no significance in our thinking about God and human life. The question raised, however, does pose a general difficulty which has to be met. Disbelief in the traditional account of the miracles has, undoubtedly, created a religious void. How is that void to be filled?

To fill that void we must put ourselves, first of all, in the position of those who lived at a time when belief in miracles was not questioned. In those days people lacked all understanding of natural law. They had no way of realizing that inner necessity which compels things to be what they are, at the same time that they are subject to immutable laws of cause and effect. Whatever occurred in nature or in human life was to them the manifestation of some personal will. That personal will was a projection of their inner purposive drives, magnified to a cosmic scale. They accepted literally the notion that God was a king whose kingdom was the world. In that kingdom He was conceived as enacting the laws whereby all things in heaven and on earth were governed. Everything that took place was regarded as fulfillment of those laws. On rare occasions, however, for the sake of His chosen People, or of any individual whom He loved, He would suspend the laws by which the entire universe was governed. Such personal decrees were conceived not figuratively but literally; they were thought to emanate from God as they would from a king.

All of this is completely out of gear with the thinking of the average intelligent person at the present time. We can hardly expect him to accept as literally true the traditional accounts of miraculous events. This is what has caused the religious vacuum.

The modern-minded person must be made to realize that the purely naturalistic approach to reality is true as far as it goes, but does not go far enough. From the standpoint of salvation, or making the most of human life, the strictly scientific account of reality can help us only *in providing the conditions* necessary to our achieving that goal. But the very notion of salvation, in any sense whatever, is entirely beyond its scope. It cannot even justify our striving for that goal, much less assure that it is attainable. All values or ideals, though they do not deny natural law as understood by scientists, do point to a phase of reality, of which natural law does not take account.

To believe in God means to accept life on the assumption that it harbors conditions in the outer world and drives in the human spirit which together impel man to transcend himself. To believe in God means to take for granted that it is man's destiny to rise above the brute and to eliminate all forms of violence and exploitation from human society. In brief, God is the Power in the cosmos that gives human life the direction that enables the human being to reflect the image of God.

That conception of God does not require our believing in miracles, which imply the suspension of natural law. Does that mean, then, that we can afford to ignore the tradition which affirms such miracles? Not at all. On the contrary, we need that tradition to realize that we have come upon our present idea of God after considerable groping and searching for the truth. That tradition records the gropings and searchings which went on in the consciousness of our ancestors. Would we want to forget our own childish notions? Are they not essential to our experiencing our personal identity? Likewise, our tradition is indispensable as a means to our experiencing our continuity with our ancestry and our Jewish People. If we study that tradition carefully, we are bound to discover nuances and anticipations of attitudes toward life that are not only tenable but well worth cultivating. Those are the permanent values in our tradition, which we cannot afford to ignore.

Source: Mordecai M. Kaplan, *Judaism without Supernaturalism*
(New York: The Reconstructionist Press, 1958), 110–112.

What Is Evil?

Historically considered, however, rabbinic teaching on the subject of evil is to be viewed as intended primarily to counter the religions that affirmed a dualistic conception of reality. According to that conception, the evil in the world was not intended as a means to the good or as part of a unitary plan in which it was subservient to the good. The dualistic religions regarded evil as coordinate in power with the good, as being the manifestation of a principle no less divine than goodness. By proclaiming its God as the author of both good and evil, the Jewish religion did not solve the question of evil, but it took an important step in the direction of a truer conception of God whereby He is identified solely with the good. *The duty which Jewish religion imposes upon the Jew to bless God for the evil as well as for the good should be interpreted as implying that it is our duty so to deal with the evil in life as not to permit it to negate our belief in God.* We should so identify ourselves with the divine in the world as to greet in the evil an occasion for reaffirming the reality of the divine. *Evil is chaos still uninvaded by the creative energy, sheer chance unconquered by will and intelligence.* So far as our power permits, such an attitude toward evil would of necessity impel us to transform the situation in which it inheres, so that it be eliminated. And where such elimination is impossible, as is the case with the fact of death, we would be impelled to acquire the capacity of transcending it. But in no instance would we confront evil in a spirit either of terror or of desperation. To be sure, this is no theoretic solution of the problem of evil, but it is the only way in which the human being will ever learn to adjust himself to it *creatively*.

It must not be assumed that traditional Jewish religion presents us with consistent and unvarying patterns of its main teachings. This is scarcely the case with anything that has come down from the past. But it is in its dealing with the problem of evil that traditional Jewish religion has most often swerved from the line of consistency. This is illustrated by its occasional lapses into a kind of microcosmic dualism. Though the Jewish religion managed to suppress all dualistic conceptions of the macrocosm, it failed to do so in its interpretation of human nature. Instead of treating the natural instincts and impulses in man as in need of being controlled and coordinated, it hypostatized the desires and hungers of men as the Evil *Yezer*, as the tool through which Satan sought to undo the work of God. The serpent that tempted Eve attained the status of a demigod. In the Kabalah, he is the great enemy. Life in accordance with the law of God is conceived as a struggle against a host of inner enemies that beset the soul. The passage in Deuteronomy which contains ordinances pertaining to war is reinterpreted as applying to the war against the Evil *Yezer*. Throughout the days of penitence the Jews read the twenty-seventh Psalm to avow their confidence in God, despite the hosts with which the enemy besieged them. Again "enemy" is a metaphor for the hostile forces that prevent man from attaining his purpose in life. The Evil *Yezer* became a sort of rival to God, contesting for the possession of the soul of man.

Thus even the Jews have not yet realized the full implications of their own monotheistic teachings. It should be noted, however, that certain of the rabbinic dicta pertaining to the Evil *Yezer* show an awareness of the dualism implied in the concept, and seek to resolve the paradox of the dualism of man's nature by the thought that even those aspects of human character which are considered as the prompt-ings of the Evil *Yezer* may be made to serve God. Such, for example, is the interpretation of the verse, "Thou shalt love the Lord thy God with all thy heart" [Deut. 6:5], to mean "with thy two *Yezarim*, the Evil *Yezer* as well as the Good *Yezer*" [*Sifrei*]. To appreciate the originality of this conception try to imagine a Christian theologian urging his people to serve the Lord with the "Old Adam" in them as well as with the Divine Grace. Whether the author of this Midrash perceived the implication of his teaching or not, it unquestionably points to the idea that even that aspect of human nature which is self-regarding rather than altruistic and which, consequently, is responsible for any anti-social behavior may, nevertheless, be turned to good, if given its prop-er place in an integrated personal and social ideal.

In general, however, the Jews in the past yielded to the dualistic ten-dency which had led religion to evolve the idea of other-worldliness; for, other-worldliness is based on the despair of, and contempt for, this world. This dualism has also bred in religion the contempt for, and despair of, human nature, so that men came to believe that only a mir-acle, only the manifestation of supernatural grace, could redeem their nature from the dangers to which it was exposed. Instead of aiming to achieve the harmonious functioning of all the powers with which man is endowed, he has been treated as the battlefield of contending forces. A strife-torn mind must needs breed intolerance, truculence and sadism.

It may appear that dualism in religion is no longer a vital issue. But we must remember that certain errors are so inbred as to take on a new guise each time there is a change in men's thinking. The modern ver-sion of ancient dualistic religion finds expression in the popular inter-pretation of the facts about the struggle for existence which have become common knowledge. "Ethical nature," wrote Thomas H. Huxley, "may count upon having to reckon with a tenacious and pow-erful enemy as long as the world lasts." That enemy was to him cos-mic nature. Cosmic nature is only a new name for the old Satan, and man considers himself once again in opposition to world forces that are bent upon his destruction. In reality, however, it is incorrect to assume that cosmic nature is "red in tooth and claw," and that the ethical strivings of man lie outside nature and constitute as it were a world by themselves. If there is any metaphysical significance to the doctrine of the unity of God, it is that the ethical and spiritual strivings should be considered as belonging to the same cosmos as the one in which there is so much that is evil and destructive of the good.

For purposes of religion, we need not undertake to account for the existence of evil and suffering by proving them in detail to be serving some good. All that religion calls upon us to believe is that the element of helpfulness, kindness and fair play is not limited to man alone but is diffused throughout the natural order. It asks us to obey the moral law in order that we may call to our aid those forces in the world which make for human life and its enhancement. We cannot claim to comprehend why evil should be necessary in the process of world making and development. *But in affirming the existence of God, we deny to evil the nature of absoluteness and finality.* The very tendency of life to overcome and transcend that evil points to the relativity of evil. As life progresses, the tendency is increasingly reinforced and organized, resulting in the growth of man's power to eliminate, transform or negate the evil in the world. Even in regarding God as the author of evil, the Rabbis realized that "the divine attribute which confers goodness excels the attribute which sends punishment" [*Yoma* 46a]. But for anticipation of what must needs be the modern conception of God, we have to refer to the following less frequent type of dictum, "The Holy One, blessed be He, does not associate His name with evil, but only associates it with that which is good" [*B'reishit Rabbah* 3:6].

The modern man cannot possibly view earthquakes and volcanic eruptions, devastating storms and floods, famines and plagues, noxious plants and animals, as "necessary" to any preconceived plan or purpose. They are simply that phase of the universe which has not yet been completely penetrated by godhood. Of course, this involves a radical change in the traditional conception of God. It conflicts with that conception of God as infinite and perfect in His omniscience and omnipotence. But the fact is that God does not have to mean to us an absolute being who has planned and decreed every twinge of pain, every act of cruelty, every human sin. *It is sufficient that God should mean to us the sum of the animating, organizing forces and relationships which are forever making a cosmos out of chaos. This is what we understand by God as the creative life of the universe.* Religion is the endeavor to invoke these animating and organizing forces and relationships and to get us to place ourselves in rapport with them.

Source: Mordecai M. Kaplan, *The Meaning of God in Modern Jewish Religion* (Detroit, Mich.: Wayne State University Press, 1994), 72–76.

· 3 ·

ERICH FROMM

1900–1980

Erich Fromm was one of the most renowned Jewish-German psychoanalysts and social philosophers of the twentieth century. He was born in 1900 in Frankfurt, into an Orthodox family that had a long list of rabbis on both his mother's and father's sides. He received a strong traditional education, was active in Zionist groups, and was highly influenced by his teachers, Rabbis Nehemiah Nobel and Salman Baruch Rabinkow, who instilled in him a love of Judaism but also the humanistic values of the Jewish tradition. During his teen years, he became interested in social studies and, through philosophy, in psychoanalysis. After earning his doctorate at the University of Heidelberg, he trained at the University of Munich and the Psychoanalytic Institute of Berlin.

After Hitler's rise to power, Fromm moved to the United States and became an American citizen. He lectured all over the country and in many parts of the world. In 1949 he moved to Mexico City because of his wife's poor health but continued to write and lecture. In the 1950s, concerned with the proliferation of technology, he focused on warning his readers about the possibility of turning people into robots. Since childhood, Fromm was a pacifist, and in 1957 he helped organize the "National Committee for a Sane Nuclear Policy" (SANE), the name of which comes from his book, The Sane Society *(1955), where* he argued that in the twentieth century the major problem is not that God is dead but that man is dead—that fear is self-alienation and emotional slavery. In 1974 Fromm moved to Switzerland to continue his work. He died of a heart attack in his home in Muralto at the age of eighty.

Fromm was interested in the relationship of the individual to society. He subscribed to a socialist humanism that stressed each person's connection to another on the basis of mutuality, rather than subservience and domination. He defined religion as any "system of thought and action shared by a group of people which gives the individual a frame of orientation and an object of devotion" (Psychoanalysis of Religion, p. 21) and argued that this would make all of us religious, with the question being whether one subscribes to an authoritarian religion or a humanistic religion. He recommended that we opt for the latter, which furthers human development within a free society.

For Fromm, God is not a symbol of power over a person but stands for the highest value, the most desirable good. In his system, God is not a reality but an idea, the image of every human being's higher self, a symbol of what a person potentially is or ought to become. He called his position "nontheistic mysticism." Tracing the development of the God idea in Judaism, he noted that it went through various stages: an absolute ruler, a partner in covenant, a deity of history rather than nature, a God who is nameless (cf. Ehyeh, "I am/shall be" in Exodus 3:14), a supreme being about whom nothing is known or only known through negative attributes (e.g., "God is not imperfect"—cf. Maimonides).

The logical consequence of Jewish monotheism, Fromm argues, is the absurdity of theology. If God's essence is not known, then there is little that can be said about God. Many Jewish teachers have already emphasized that God "is" means God "acts." The imitation of God's deeds has replaced the knowledge of God's essence. Our role in society, therefore, has to be to act as godly as we can and, primarily, to eliminate idol worship, which in our time can include worship of honor, fame, production, and the state. Instead, we can find oneness with the world by the full development of our human qualities of love and reason.

Definition of Religion

Any discussion of religion is handicapped by a serious terminological difficulty. While we know that there were and are many religions outside of monotheism, we nevertheless associate the concept religion with a system centered around God and supernatural forces; we tend to consider monotheistic religion as a frame of reference for the understanding and evaluation of all other religions. It thus becomes doubtful whether religions without God like Buddhism, Taoism, or Confucianism can be properly called religions. Such secular systems as contemporary authoritarianism are not called religions at all, although psychologically speaking they deserve this name. We simply have no word to denote religion as a general human phenomenon in such a way that some association with a specific type of religion does not creep in and color the concept. For lack of such a word I shall use the term religion in these chapters, but I want to make it clear at the outset that I understand by religion *any system of thought and action shared by a group which gives the individual a frame of orientation and an object of devotion.*

There is indeed no culture of the past, and it seems there can be no culture in the future, which does not have religion in this broad sense of our definition. We need not, however, stop at this merely descriptive statement. The study of man permits us to recognize that the need for a common system of orientation and for an object of devotion is deeply rooted in the conditions of human existence. I have attempted in *Man for Himself* to analyze the nature of this need, and I quote from that book:

> Self-awareness, reason, and imagination have disrupted the "harmony" which characterizes animal existence. Their emergence has made man into an anomaly, into the freak of the universe. He is part of nature, subject to her physical laws and unable to change them, yet he transcends the rest of nature. He is set apart while being a part; he is homeless, yet chained to the home he shares with all creatures. Cast into this world at an accidental place and time, he is forced out of it, again accidentally. Being aware of himself, he realizes his powerlessness and the limitations of his existence. He visualizes his own end: death. Never is he free from the dichotomy

of his existence: he cannot rid himself of his mind, even if he should want to; he cannot rid himself of his body as long as he is alive—and his body makes him want to be alive.

Reason, man's blessing, is also his curse; it forces him to cope everlastingly with the task of solving an insoluble dichotomy. Human existence is different in this respect from that of all other organisms; it is in a state of constant and unavoidable disequilibrium. Man's life cannot "be lived" by repeating the pattern of his species; *he* must live. Man is the only animal that can be *bored*, that can be *discontented*, that can feel evicted from paradise. Man is the only animal for whom his own existence is a problem which he has to solve and from which he cannot escape. He cannot go back to the prehuman state of harmony with nature; he must proceed to develop his reason until he becomes the master of nature, and of himself.

The emergence of reason has created a dichotomy within man which forces him to strive everlastingly for new solutions. The dynamism of his history is intrinsic to the existence of reason which causes him to develop and, through it, to create a world of his own in which he can feel at home with himself and his fellow men. Every stage he reaches leaves him discontented and perplexed, and this very perplexity urges him to move toward new solutions. There is no innate "drive for progress" in man; it is the contradiction in his existence that makes him proceed on the way he set out. Having lost paradise, the unity with nature, he has become the eternal wanderer (Odysseus, Oedipus, Abraham, Faust); he is impelled to go forward and with everlasting effort to make the unknown known by filling in with answers the blank spaces of his knowledge. He must give account to himself of himself, and of the meaning of his existence. He is driven to overcome this inner split, tormented by a craving for "absoluteness," for another kind of harmony which can lift the curse by which he was separated from nature, from his fellow men, and from himself. . . .

The disharmony of man's existence generates needs which far transcend those of his animal origin. These needs result in an imperative drive to restore a unity and equilibrium between himself and the rest of nature. He makes the attempt to restore this unity and equilibrium in the first place in thought by constructing an all-inclusive mental picture of the world which serves as a frame of reference from which he can derive an answer to the question of where he stands and what he ought to do. But such thought-systems are not sufficient. If man were only a disembodied intellect his aim would be achieved by a comprehensive thought-system. But since he is an entity endowed with a body as well as a mind he has to react to the dichotomy of his existence not only in thinking but also in the process of living, in his feelings and actions. He has to strive for the experience of unity and oneness in all spheres of his being in order to find a new equilibrium. Hence any satisfying system of orientation implies not only intellectual elements but elements of feeling and sense to be realized in action in all fields of human endeavor. Devotion to an aim, or an idea, or a power transcending man such as God, is an expression of this need for completeness in the process of living. . . .

Because the need for a system of orientation and devotion is an intrinsic part of human existence we can understand the intensity of this need. Indeed, there is no other more powerful source of energy in man. Man is not free to choose between having or not having "ideals," but he is free to choose between different kinds of ideals, between being devoted to the worship of power and destruction and being devoted to reason and love. All men are "idealists" and are striving for something beyond the attainment of physical satisfaction. They differ in the kinds of ideals they believe in. The very best but also the most satanic manifestations of man's mind are expressions not of his flesh but of his "idealism," of his spirit. Therefore a relativistic view which claims that to have some ideal or some religious feeling is valuable in itself is dangerous and erroneous. We must understand every ideal including those which appear in secular ideologies and expressions of the same human need and we must judge them with respect to their truth, to the extent to which they are conducive to the unfolding of man's powers and to the degree to which they are a real answer to man's need for equilibrium and harmony in his world. [*Man for Himself*, pp. 40–41, 46–47, 49–50]

What I have said about man's idealism holds true equally for his religious need. There is no one without a religious need, a need to have a frame of orientation and an object of devotion; but this statement does not tell us anything about a specific context in which this religious need is manifest. Man may worship animals, trees, idols of gold or stone, an invisible god, a saintly man or diabolic leaders; he may worship his ancestors, his nation, his class or party, money or success; his religion may be conducive to the development of destructiveness or of love, of domination or of brotherliness; it may further his power of reason or paralyze it; he may be aware of his system as being a religious one, different from those of the secular realm, or he may think that he has no religion and interpret his devotion to certain allegedly secular aims like power, money or success as nothing but his concern for the practical and expedient. The question is not *religion or not* but *which kind of religion*, whether it is one furthering man's development, the unfolding of his specifically human powers, or one paralyzing them.

Curiously enough the interests of the devoted religionist and of the psychologist are the same in this respect. The theologian is keenly interested in the specific tenets of a religion, his own and others, because what matters to him is the truth of his belief against the others. Equally, the psychologist must be keenly interested in the specific contents of religion for what matters to him is what human attitude a religion expresses and what kind of effect it has on man, whether it is good or bad for the development of man's powers. He is interested not only in an analysis of the *psychological roots* of various religions but also in their *value*.

The thesis that the need for a frame of orientation and an object of devotion is rooted in the conditions of man's existence seems to be amply verified by the fact of the universal occurrence of religion in history. This point has been made and elaborated by theologians, psychologists, and anthropologists, and there is no need for me to discuss it any further. I only want to stress that in making this point the adherents of traditional religion have often indulged in a fallacious bit of reasoning. Starting out with so broad a definition of religion as to include every possible religious phenomenon, their concept has remained associated with monotheistic religion, and thus they proceed to look upon all nonmonotheistic forms as precursors of or deviations from the "true" religion and they end demonstrating that the belief in God in the sense of the Western religious tradition is inherent in man's equipment.

Source: Erich Fromm, *Psychoanalysis and Religion* (New Haven: Yale University Press, 1958), 21–27.

Authoritarian and Humanistic Religions

The essential element in authoritarian religion and in the authoritarian religious experience is the surrender to a power transcending man. The main virtue of this type of religion is obedience, its cardinal sin is disobedience. Just as the deity is conceived as omnipotent or omniscient, man is conceived as being powerless and insignificant. Only as he can gain grace or help from the deity by complete surrender can he feel strength. Submission to a powerful authority is one of the avenues by which man escapes from his feeling of aloneness and limitation. In the act of surrender he loses his independence and integrity as an individual but he gains the feeling of being protected by an awe-inspiring power of which, as it were, he becomes a part.

In Calvin's theology we find a vivid picture of authoritarian, theistic thinking. "For I do not call it humility," says Calvin, "if you suppose that we have anything left. . . . We cannot think of ourselves as we ought to think without utterly despising everything that may be supposed an excellence in us. This humility is unfeigned submission of a mind overwhelmed with a weighty sense of its own misery and poverty; for such is the uniform description of it in the word of God" [*Institutes of the Christian Religion* (Presbyterian Board of Christian Education, 1928), p. 681].

The experience which Calvin describes here, that of despising everything in oneself, of the submission of the mind overwhelmed by its own poverty, is the very essence of all authoritarian religions whether they are couched in secular or in theological language. In authoritarian religion God is a symbol of power and force, He is supreme because He has supreme power, and man in juxtaposition is utterly powerless.

Authoritarian secular religion follows the same principle. Here the Führer or the beloved "Father of His People" or the State or the Race or the Socialist Fatherland becomes the object of worship; the life of the individual becomes insignificant and man's worth consists in the very denial of his worth and strength. Frequently authoritarian religion postulates an ideal which is so abstract and so distant that it has hardly any connection with the real life of real people. To such ideals as "life after death" or "the future of mankind" the life and happiness of persons living here and now may be sacrificed; the alleged ends justify every means and become symbols in the names of which religious or secular "elites" control the lives of their fellow men.

Humanistic religion, on the contrary, is centered around man and his strength. Man must develop his power of reason in order to understand himself, his relationship to his fellow men and his position in the universe. He must recognize the truth, both with regard to his limitations and his potentialities. He must develop his powers of love for others as well as for himself and experience the solidarity of all living beings. He must have principles and norms to guide him in this aim. Religious experience in this kind of religion is the experience of oneness with the All, based on one's relatedness to the world as it is grasped with thought and with love. Man's aim in humanistic religion is to achieve the greatest strength, not the greatest powerlessness; virtue is self-realization, not obedience. Faith is certainty of conviction based on one's experience of thought and feeling, not assent to propositions on credit of the proposer. The prevailing mood is that of joy, while the prevailing mood in authoritarian religion is that of sorrow and of guilt.

Inasmuch as humanistic religions are theistic, God is a symbol of *man's own powers* which he tries to realize in his life, and is not a symbol of force and domination, having *power over man.*

Source: Erich Fromm, *Psychoanalysis and Religion*
(New Haven: Yale University Press, 1958), 35–37.

The Love of God

It has been stated above that the basis for our need to love lies in the experience of separateness and the resulting need to overcome the anxiety of separateness by the experience of union. The religious form of love, that which is called the love of God, is, psychologically speaking, not different. It springs from the need to overcome separateness and to achieve union. In fact, the love of God has as many different qualities and aspects as the love of man has—and to a large extent we find the same differences.

In all theistic religions, whether they are polytheistic or monotheistic, God stands for the highest value, the most desirable good.

Hence, the specific meaning of God depends on what is the most desirable good for a person. The understanding of the concept of God must, therefore, start with an analysis of the character structure of the person who worships God.

The development of the human race as far as we have any knowledge of it can be characterized as the emergence of man from nature, from mother, from the bonds of blood and soil. In the beginning of human history man, though thrown out of the original unity with nature, still clings to these primary bonds. He finds his security by going back, or holding on to these primary bonds. He still feels identified with the world of animals and trees, and tries to find unity by remaining one with the natural world. Many primitive religions bear witness to this stage of development. An animal is transformed into a totem; one wears animal masks in the most solemn religious acts, or in war; one worships an animal as God. At a later stage of development, when human skill has developed to the point of artisan and artistic skill, when man is not dependent any more exclusively on the gifts of nature—the fruit he finds and the animal he kills—man transforms the product of his own hand into a god. This is the stage of the worship of idols made of clay, silver or gold. Man projects his own powers and skills into the things he makes, and thus in an alienated fashion worships his prowess, his possessions. At a still later stage man gives his gods the form of human beings. It seems that this can happen only when he has become still more aware of himself, and when he has discovered man as the highest and most dignified "thing" in the world. In this phase of anthropomorphic god worship we find a development in two dimensions. The one refers to the female or male nature of the gods, the other to the degree of maturity which man has achieved, and which determines the nature of his gods and the nature of his love of them.

Let us first speak of the development from mother-centered to father-centered religions. According to the great and decisive discoveries of Bachofen and Morgan in the middle of the nineteenth century, and in spite of the rejection their findings have found in most academic circles, there can be little doubt that there was a matriarchal phase of religion preceding the patriarchal one, at least in many cultures. In the matriarchal phase, the highest being is the mother. She is the goddess, she is also the authority in family and society. In order to understand the essence of matriarchal religion, we have only to remember what has been said about the essence of motherly love. Mother's love is unconditional, it is all-protective, all-enveloping; because it is unconditional it can also not be controlled or acquired. Its presence gives the loved person a sense of bliss; its absence produces a sense of lostness and utter despair. Since mother loves her children because they are her children, and not because they are "good," obedient, or fulfill her wishes and commands, mother's love is based on equality. All men are equal, because they all are children of a mother, because they all are children of Mother Earth.

The next stage of human evolution, the only one of which we have thorough knowledge and do not need to rely on inferences and reconstruction is, the patriarchal phase. In this phase the mother is dethroned from her supreme position, and the father becomes the Supreme Being, in religion as well as in society. The nature of fatherly love is that he makes demands, establishes principles and laws, and that his love for the son depends on the obedience of the latter to these demands. He likes best the son who is most like him, who is most obedient and who is best fitted to become his successor, as the inheritor of his possessions. (The development of patriarchal society goes together with the development of private property.) As a consequence, patriarchal society is hierarchical; the equality of the brothers gives way to competition and mutual strife. Whether we think of the Indian, Egyptian or Greek cultures, or of the Jewish-Christian, or Islamic religions, we are in the middle of patriarchal world, with its male gods, over whom one chief god reigns, or where all gods have been eliminated with the exception of the One, *the* God. However, since the wish for mother's love cannot be eradicated from the hearts of man, it is not surprising that the figure of the loving mother could never be fully driven out from the pantheon. In the Jewish religion, the mother aspects of God are reintroduced especially in the various currents of mysticism. In the Catholic religion, Mother is symbolized by the Church, and by the Virgin. Even in Protestantism, the figure of Mother has not been entirely eradicated, although she remains hidden. Luther established as his main principle that nothing that man *does* can procure God's love. God's love is Grace, the religious attitude is to have faith in this grace, and to make oneself small and helpless; no good works can influence God—or make God love us, as Catholic doctrines postulated. We can recognize here that the Catholic doctrine of good works is part of the patriarchal picture; I can procure father's love by obedience and by fulfilling his demands. The Lutheran doctrine, on the other hand, in spite of its manifest patriarchal character carries within it a hidden matriarchal element. Mother's love cannot be acquired; it is there, or it is not there; all I can do is to have faith (as the Psalmist says, "Thou hadst let me have faith into my mother's breasts" [Ps. 22:9]) and to transform myself into the helpless, powerless child. But it is the peculiarity of Luther's faith that the figure of the mother has been eliminated from the manifest picture, and replaced by that of the father; instead of the certainty of being loved by mother, intense doubt, hoping against hope for unconditional love by *father*, has become the paramount feature.

I had to discuss this difference between the matriarchal and the patriarchal elements in religion in order to show that the character of the love of God depends on the respective weight of the matriarchal and the patriarchal aspects of religion. The patriarchal aspect makes me love God like a father; I assume he is just and strict, that he punishes and rewards; and eventually that he will elect me as his favorite son; as God elected Abraham-Israel, as Isaac elected Jacob, as God elects his favorite nation. In the matriarchal aspect of religion, I love God as an all-embracing mother. I have faith in her love, that no matter whether I am poor and powerless, no matter whether I have sinned, she will love me, she will not prefer any other of her children to me; whatever happens to me, she will rescue me, will save me, will forgive me. Needless to say, my love for God and God's love for me cannot be separated. If God is a father, he loves me like a son and I love him like a father. If God is mother, her and my love are determined by this fact.

This difference between the motherly and the fatherly aspects of the love of God is, however, only one factor in determining the nature of this love; the other factor is the degree of maturity reached by the individual, hence in his concept of God and in his love for God.

Since the evolution of the human race shifted from a mother-centered to a father-centered structure of society, as well as of religion, we can trace the development of a maturing love mainly in the development of patriarchal religion. In the beginning of this development we find a despotic, jealous God, who considers man, whom he created, as his property, and is entitled to do with him whatever he pleases. This is the phase of religion in which God drives man out of paradise, lest he eat from the tree of knowledge and thus could become God himself; this is the phase in which God decides to destroy the human race by the flood, because none of them pleases him, with the exception of the favorite son, Noah; this is the phase in which God demands from Abraham that he kill his only, his beloved son, Isaac, to prove his love for God by the act of ultimate obedience. But simultaneously a new phase begins; God makes a covenant with Noah, in which he promises never to destroy the human race again, a covenant by which he is bound himself. Not only is he bound by his promises, he is also bound by his own principle, that of justice, and on this basis God must yield to Abraham's demand to spare Sodom if there are at least ten just men. But the development goes further than transforming God from the figure of a despotic tribal chief into a loving father, into a father who himself is bound by the principles which he has postulated; it goes in the direction of transforming God from the figure of a father into a symbol of his principles, those of justice, truth and love. God *is* truth, God *is* justice. In this development God ceases to be a person, a man, a father; he becomes the symbol of the principle of unity behind the manifoldness of phenomena, of the vision of the flower which will grow from the spiritual seed within man. God cannot have a name. A name always denotes a thing, or a person, something finite. How can God have a name, if he is not a person, not a thing?

The most striking incident of this change lies in the Biblical story of God's revelation to Moses. When Moses tells him that the Hebrews will not believe that God has sent him, unless he can tell them God's name (how could idol worshipers comprehend a nameless God, since the very essence of an idol is to have a name?), God makes a concession. He tells Moses that his name is "I am becoming that which I am becoming." "I-am-becoming is my name." The "I-am-becoming" means that God is not finite, not a person, not a "being." The most adequate translation of the sentence would be: tell them that "my name is nameless." The prohibition to make any image of God, to pronounce his name in vain, eventually to pronounce his name at all, aims at the same goal, that of freeing man from the idea that God is a father, that he is a person. In the subsequent theological development, the idea is carried further in the principle that one must not even give God any positive attribute. To say of God that he is wise, strong, good implies again that he is a person; the most I can do is to say what God is *not*, to state negative attributes, to postulate that he is *not* limited, not unkind, not unjust. The more I know what God is *not*, the more knowledge I have of God.

Following the maturing idea of monotheism in its further consequences can lead only to one conclusion: not to mention God's name at all, not to speak *about* God. Then God becomes what he potentially is in monotheistic theology, the nameless One, an inexpressible stammer, referring to the unity underlying the phenomenal universe, the ground of all existence; God becomes truth, love, justice. God is I, inasmuch as I am human.

Quite evidently this evolution from the anthropomorphic to the pure monotheistic principle makes all the difference to the nature of the love of God. The God of Abraham can be loved, or feared, as a father, sometimes his forgiveness, sometimes his anger being the dominant aspect. Inasmuch as God is the father, I am the child. I have not emerged fully from the autistic wish for omniscience and omnipotence. I have not yet acquired the objectivity to realize my limitations as a human being, my ignorance, my helplessness. I still claim, like a child, that there must be a father who rescues me, who watches me, who punishes me, a father who likes me when I am obedient, who is flattered by my praise and angry because of my disobedience. Quite obviously, the majority of people have, in their personal development, not overcome this infantile stage, and hence the belief in God to most people is the belief in a helping father—a childish illusion. In spite of the fact that this concept of religion has been overcome by some of the great teachers of the human race, and by a minority of men, it is still the dominant form of religion.

Inasmuch as this is so, the criticism of the idea of God, as it was expressed by Freud, is quite correct. The error, however, was in the fact that he ignored the other aspect of monotheistic religion, and its true kernel, the logic of which leads exactly to the negation of this concept of God. The truly religious person, if he follows the essence of the monotheistic idea, does not pray for anything, does not expect anything from God; he does not love God as a child loves his father or his mother; he has acquired the humility of sensing his limitations, to the degree of knowing that he knows nothing about God. God becomes to him a symbol in which man, at an earlier stage of his evolution, has expressed the totality of that which man is striving for, the realm of the spiritual world, of love, truth and justice. He has faith in the principles which "God" represents; he thinks truth, lives love and justice, and considers all of his life only valuable inasmuch as it gives him the chance to arrive at an ever fuller unfolding of his human powers—as the only reality that matters, as the only object of "ultimate concern"; and, eventually, he does not speak about God—nor even mention his name. To love God, if he were going to use this word, would mean, then, to long for the attainment of the full capacity to love, for the realization of that which "God" stands for in oneself.

Source: Erich Fromm, *The Art of Loving*
(New York: Perennial Classics, 2000), 59–66.

Nontheistic Mysticism

Words and concepts referring to phenomena related to psychic or mental experience develop and grow—or deteriorate—with the person to whose experience they refer. They change as he changes; they have a life as he has a life.

If a six-year-old boy says to his mother, "I love you," he uses the word "love" to denote the experience he has at the age of six. When the child has matured and developed into a man, the same words spoken to a woman he loves will have a different meaning, expressing the wider range, the greater depth, the larger freedom and activity that distinguish the love of a man from that of a child. Yet while the experience to which the word "love" refers is different in the child and in the man, it has a common core, just as the man is different from the child and yet the same.

There is simultaneously permanence and change in any living being; hence, there is permanence and change in any concept reflecting the experience of a living man. However, that concepts have their own lives, and that they grow, can be understood only if the concepts are not separated from the experience to which they give expression. If the concept becomes alienated—that is, separated from the experience to which it refers—it loses its reality and is transformed into an artifact of man's mind. The fiction is thereby created that anyone who uses the *concept* is referring to the substratum of *experience* underlying it. Once this happens—and this process of the alienation of concepts is the rule rather than the exception—the idea expressing an experience has been transformed into an *ideology* that usurps the place of the underlying reality within the living human being. History then becomes a history of ideologies rather than the history of concrete, real men who are the producers of their ideas.

The foregoing considerations are important if one wants to understand the concept of God.

They are also important in order to understand the position from which these pages are written. I believe that the concept of God was a historically conditioned expression of an inner experience. I can understand what the Bible or genuinely religious persons mean when they talk about God, but I do not share their thought concept; I believe that the concept "God" was conditioned by the presence of a socio-political structure in which tribal chiefs or kings have supreme power. The supreme value is conceptualized as analogous to the supreme power in society.

"God" is one of many different poetic expressions of the highest value in humanism, not a reality in itself. It is unavoidable, however, that in talking about the thought of a monotheistic system I use the word "God" often, and it would be awkward to add my own qualification each time. Hence, I wish to make my position clear at the outset. If I could define my position approximately, I would call it that of a nontheistic mysticism.

Source: Erich Fromm, *You Shall Be as Gods*
(New York: Henry Holt and Co., 1991), 17–19.

· 4 ·

ABRAHAM JOSHUA HESCHEL

1907–1972

*A*braham Joshua Heschel was an outstanding expositor of prophetic and mystical traditions of Judaism in the twentieth century. He was born in Warsaw, Poland, in 1907 to a devoted Chasidic family, originally from Medzibozh in Podolia, Ukraine. After receiving a thorough religious education, he studied at the Universities of Vilna and Berlin, from which he obtained his doctorate in 1935 with a thesis on prophetic consciousness. He taught at the Hochschule für die Wissenschafts des Judentums and, along with Martin Buber, at the Lehrhaus in Frankfurt. After his deportation by the Nazis in 1938, he was able to get a teaching position at the Warsaw Institute for Jewish Studies. In 1940, upon his arrival in the United States, he became a member of the faculty at the Hebrew Union College in Cincinnati, Ohio, and, until his death in 1972, at the Jewish Theological Seminary as professor of Jewish ethics and mysticism.

Heschel was an observant Jew and a social activist. During the early days of the Civil Rights movement, he marched alongside Martin Luther King Jr. in Selma, Alabama. In 1965, he founded the "Clergy and Laity Concerned about Vietnam," a peace movement that fought against the Vietnam War. He also played an active role in Jewish-Christian dialogue, particularly in the preparation of the Vatican's 1965 historic "Nostra Aetate" document, which established a more positive relationship with non-Jews and eliminated many layers of anti-Jewish teachings from Church manuals.

Heschel's early writings were in Yiddish, but he also wrote in Hebrew, German, and Polish. After his arrival in the United States, he quickly mastered the English language and wrote in a poetic prose style that was admired by many.

Starting with his contention that religion is an answer to our ultimate questions, Heschel maintains that we are all born with a sense of the sublime, what he called "radical amazement," which generates the idea of the divine and to which we must respond positively. Reason alone, adds Heschel, cannot bring us to God, just as reverence, love, prayer, and faith remain beyond the workings of the mind.

Heschel argued for a God-centered approach, insisting that the beginning point is God and not humanity. This view was in conflict with the one advocated by his mentor and then colleague, Martin Buber, who had founded his own theology on a dialogue with God, the so-called "I-Thou" meeting. Heschel also disagreed with Mordecai Kaplan, who maintained that ethnicity is at the core of Judaism. For Heschel, however, God stands at the center and is known intuitively, emerging out of deep religious insights and in confrontation with our existential realities. He called this approach "depth theology."

For Heschel, awareness of the divine begins with wonder, with a sense of awe. This leads us to faith. The certainty of God does not come to us as a result of logical thinking. On the contrary, once we realize the grandeur of the mystery of being, we become overwhelmed by God's presence, and this brings us to the awareness of God's existence. God, for Heschel, is a being beyond which no other exists or is possible. Furthermore, for many Greek thinkers, such as Aristotle, and quite a few medieval Jewish philosophers, including Maimonides, God has no feelings but represents pure thought. Heschel found this idea unsatisfactory. God, he argued, is not aloof, but displays "divine pathos." Like human beings, if not more so, God is alive, has feelings, and has certain demands of us. This approach establishes the foundation for Heschel's neo-traditional approach to Jewish law and practice.

About the Meaning of God

In undertaking an inquiry, we must from the beginning possess a minimum of knowledge of the meaning of that about which we are trying to inquire. No inquiry starts out of nothing. In asking the first question, we must anticipate something of the nature of that which we ask about, because otherwise we would not know in what direction to proceed or whether the result of our inquiry will be an answer to the question we ask.

We ask about God. But what is the minimum of meaning that the word God holds for us? It is first the idea of *ultimacy*. God is a Being beyond which no other exists or is possible. It means further One, unique, eternal. However, all these adjectives are auxiliary to the noun to which they are attached. In themselves they do not express the essence. We proclaim, God is One; it would be intellectual idolatry to say, the One is God. What, then, is the meaning of the noun to which ultimacy or oneness is attached? Is it the concept of the absolute? Is it the concept of a first cause?

To say that our search for God is a search for the idea of the absolute is to eliminate the problem which we are trying to explore. A first cause or an idea of the absolute—devoid of life, devoid of freedom—is an issue for science or metaphysics rather than a concern of the soul or the conscience. An affirmation of such a cause or such an idea would be an answer unrelated to our question. The living soul is not concerned with a dead cause but with a living God. Our goal is to ascertain the existence of a Being to whom we may confess our sins, of a God who loves, of a God who is not above concern with our inquiry and search for Him; a father, not an absolute.

We must see clearly from the beginning that the minimum of meaning we associate with the word God is that He is alive, or, to put it negatively, He is not inferior to us in the order of being. A being that lacks the attributes of personal existence is not our problem.

This, then, is the minimum of meaning which the word God holds for us: *God is alive.* To assume the opposite, namely that the word God means a Being devoid of life and freedom—inferior to us in the order of being and more finite than ourselves—would immediately invalidate the problem we are concerned with in the same way as the premise that the universe is more finite than our own body would invalidate any effort to explore the meaning of the universe.

Indeed, there are essentially only two ways to begin: to think of God in terms of free and spontaneous being or in terms of inanimate being; either He is alive or devoid of life. Both premises are beyond demonstration, and yet the second premise in the form of saying, God is the great unknown, appears to most people to be more respectable. Let us examine the latter premise.

The statement "God is the great unknown," meaning that He has never become known and can never become known, is an absolute assertion based upon the theory that God remains eternally mysterious. Such a theory, however, is a dogma entailing a contradiction. For by attributing eternal mysteriousness to the ultimate being, we definitely claim to know it. Thus the ultimate being is not an unknown but a known God. In other words: a God whom we know but one who does not know, the great Unknower. We proclaim the ignorance of God together with our knowledge of His being ignorant!

This seems to be a part of our pagan heritage: to say, the Supreme Being is a total mystery, and even having accepted the idea of a first cause and its power of bringing the universe into being, we still cling to the assumption that the power that can make possible the world's coming into being has never been able to make itself known. Yet why should we assume that the absolute power is absolutely powerless? Why should we *a priori* exclude life and freedom from the ultimate being?

Thinking of God as a speculative problem may perhaps start out with the premise of God's absolute mysteriousness. Thinking of God as a religious problem which begins with wonder, awe, praise, fear, trembling and radical amazement cannot proceed one step if tied to the assumption that God is devoid of life. We cannot utter words and deny at the same time that there are words, and we cannot in religious thinking say God and deny at the same time that He is alive. If God is dead, then worship is madness.

The problem of religious thinking is not only whether God is dead or alive, but also whether we are dead or alive to His realness. A search for God involves a search of our own measure, a test of our own spiritual potential. To be sure, there are levels of thinking where we can comfortably maintain that God is not alive: on the level of conceit and callousness to the grandeur and mystery of living. In moments when we carry the load of radical amazement we know that to say God is alive is an understatement.

Yet there seems to be a third possibility: God is neither alive nor devoid of life but a *symbol*. If God is defined "as a name for that which concerns man ultimately," then He is but a symbol of man's concern, the objectification of a subjective state of mind. But as such God would be little more than a projection of our imagination.

As the acceptance of God and the rejection of idols are indicated in the first two of the Ten Commandments, the rejection of the symbol is implied in the third commandment: "Thou shalt not take the name of God in vain."

Certainly God is more than "a name for that which concerns man ultimately." Only saints are ultimately concerned with God. What concerns most of us ultimately is our ego. The Biblical consciousness begins not with man's but with *God's concern*.

Source: Abraham Joshua Heschel, *God in Search of Man*
(New York: Noonday Press, Farrar, Straus and Giroux, 2000) 125–127.

One Is Not God

God is one, but one is not God. Some of us are inclined to deify the one supreme force or law that regulates all phenomena of nature, in the same manner in which primitive peoples once deified the stars. Yet, to refer to the supreme law of nature as God or to say that the world came into being by virtue of its own energy is to beg the question.

For the cardinal question is not what is the law that would explain the interaction of phenomena in the universe, but why is there a law, a universe at all. The content and operation of the universal law may be conceived and described, but the fact that there is such a law does not lose its ineffable character by the knowledge we may acquire about the scope of its operation.

To instill scientific explanations of nature in a soul astir with the holy terror of the ineffable is like trying to plant artificial flowers in the midst of blossoms in a garden. Unless we betray what we sense, unless we succumb to intellectual narcissism, how can we regard the known as the ultimate?

As noted above, it is not nature's order and wisdom which are manifest in time and space, but the indicativeness within all order and wisdom of that which surpasses them, of that which is beyond time and space which communicates to us an awareness of the ultimate questions. The world is replete with such indicativeness; wherever we go it is the ineffable we encounter, with our sense too feeble and unworthy to grasp it. If the universe is an immense allusion and our inner life an anonymous quotation, the discovery of one universal law dominating empirical reality would not answer our essential question. The ultimate problem is not a problem of syntax, of trying to learn how the various parts of nature are collocated and arranged in their relations to one another. The problem is: What does reality, what does unity stand for? Universal laws one attempts to describe by relations within the given, within the known, but in facing our ultimate question we are carried beyond the known, to the presence of the divine.

From the empirical plurality of facts and values, we would not infer *one* design which would dominate both the realm of facts and the realm of norms, nature and history. It is only in the mirror of a divine unity, in which we may behold the unity of all: of necessity and freedom, of law and love. It alone gives us an insight into the unity that transcends all conflicts, the brotherhood of hope and grief, of joy and fear, of tower and grave, of good and evil. Unity as a scientific concept is only a reflection of a transcendent idea, embracing not only time and space but also being and value, the known and the mystery, the here and the beyond.

God cannot be distilled to a well-defined idea. All concepts fade when applied to His essence. To the pious man knowledge of God is not a thought within his grasp, but a form of thinking in which he tries to comprehend all reality. It is the untold secret of the soil in which all knowledge becomes a seed of sense, a secret by which we live and which we never truly understand; a soil from which the roots of all values derive perpetual vitality. Over and against the split between man and nature, self and thought, time and timelessness, the pious man is able to sense the interweaving of all, the holding together of what is apart, the love that hovers over acts of kindness, mountains, flowers, which shine in their splendor as if looked at by God.

How do we identify the divine?

Divine is a message that discloses unity where we see diversity, that discloses peace when we are involved in discord. God is He who holds our fitful lives together, who reveals to us that what is empirically diverse in color, in interest, in creeds—races, classes, nations—is one in His eyes and one in essence.

God means: No one is ever alone; the essence of the temporal is the eternal; the moment is an image of eternity in an infinite mosaic. God means: *Togetherness of all beings in holy otherness.*

God means: What is behind our soul is beyond our spirit; what is at the source of our selves is at the goal of our ways. He is the heart of all, eager to receive and eager to give.

When God becomes our form of thinking we begin to sense all men in one man, the whole world in a grain of sand, eternity in a moment. To worldly ethics one human being is less than two human beings, to the religious mind if a man has caused a single soul to perish, it is as though he had caused a whole world to perish, and if he has saved a single soul, it is as though he had saved a whole world [*Mishnah Sanhedrin* 4:5].

If in the afterglow of a religious insight I can see a way to gather up my scattered life, to unite what lies in strife; a way that is good for all men as it is for me—I will know it is His way.

Source: Abraham Joshua Heschel, *Man Is Not Alone*
(New York: Noonday Press, Farrar, Straus and Giroux, 1997), 107–109.

Faith

"Canst Thou by Searching Find Out God?"

Thinking about the ultimate, climbing toward the invisible, leads along a path with countless chasms and very few ledges. For all our faith, we are easily lost in misgivings which we can't fully dispel. What could counteract the apprehension that it is utter futility to crave for understanding of God?

Man in his spontaneity may reach out for the hidden God and with his mind try to pierce the darkness of His distance. But how will he know whether it is God he is reaching out for or some value personified?

How will he know where or when God is found? In moments of meditation we may encounter His presence. But does God encounter us? We may deeply, wholeheartedly adore His glory. But how do we know that He takes notice of our adoration?

"Canst thou by searching find out God?" (Job 11:7). Job admits freely: "God is great, beyond our knowledge" (36:26). "The "Almighty—we cannot find Him; He is great in power and justice, and abundant righteousness He will not violate" (37:23). All Abraham could achieve by his own power was wonder and amazement; the knowledge that there is a living God was given him by God.

There is no substitute for faith, no alternative for prophecy, no surrogate for tradition.

No Faith at First Sight

There is no faith at first sight. A faith that comes into being like a butterfly is ephemeral. He who is swift to believe is swift to forget. Faith does not come into being out of nothing, inadvertently, unprepared, as an unearned surprise. Faith is preceded by awe, by acts of amazement at things that we apprehend but cannot comprehend. In the story of the Red Sea we read: "Israel *saw* the great works which the Lord did . . . and the people *feared* the Lord . . . and they *believed in the Lord*" (Exodus 14:31). We must learn how to see "the miracles which are daily with us"; we must learn how to live in awe, in order to attain the insights of faith.

"The thoughtless believes every word, but the prudent looks where he is going" (Proverbs 14:15). The will to believe may be the will to power in disguise, yet the will to power and the will to believe are mutually exclusive. For in our striving for power we arrogate to ourselves what belongs to God and suppress the claim of His presence. We must learn how to let His will prevail. We must understand that our faith is not only our concern but also His; that more important than our will to believe is His will that we believe.

It is not easy to attain faith. A decision of the will, the desire to believe, will not secure it. All the days of our lives we must continue to deepen our sense of mystery in order to be worthy of attaining faith. Callousness to the mystery is our greatest obstacle. In the artificial light of pride and self-contentment we shall never see the splendor. Only *in His light shall we see light.*

Man's quest for God is not a quest for mere information. In terms of information little was attained by those countless men who strained their minds to find an answer. Only in terms of responsiveness, as an answer to Him who asked, much was achieved and much can be achieved by every one of us. In the realm of science, a question may be asked and an answer given by one man for all men. In the realm of religion, the question must be faced and the answer given by every individual soul.

God is of no importance unless He is of supreme importance. We cannot leave it uncertain whether or not there is a living God who is concerned with the integrity of man. We cannot leave it uncertain whether or not we know what He requires of us. The answer to these questions cannot be found off-hand. According to Maimonides, "It is well known and quite evident that the love of God cannot strike deep root in the heart of man unless it occupies his mind constantly so that nothing in the world matters to him but this love of God" [*Mishneh Torah, T'shuvah* 10:6]. What applies to the love of God applies to some degree to faith in God.

Faith Is Attachment

Faith is not the same as belief, not the same as the attitude of regarding something as true. When the people of Israel worshiped a golden calf, forty days after Sinai, their belief in the event was surely present. Faith is an act of the whole person, of mind, will, and heart. Faith is *sensitivity, understanding, engagement,* and *attachment;* not something achieved once and for all, but an attitude one may gain and lose.

The generation that went out of Egypt and witnessed the marvels at the Red Sea and Sinai did not attain faith completely. At the end of forty years in the wilderness Moses summoned all Israel and said to them: "*You have seen* all that the Lord did before your eyes in the land of Egypt, to Pharaoh and to all his servants and to all his land; the great trials which *your eyes saw,* the signs, and those great wonders. But to this day *the Lord has not given you a mind to understand or eyes to see, or ears to hear*" (Deuteronomy 29:1–3).

"Marvelous things did He in the sight" of Israel. "For all this they sinned still, and believed not in His wondrous works" (Psalm 78:14–32).

The Embarrassment of Faith

Faith in the living God is, we repeat, not easily attained. Had it been possible to prove His existence beyond dispute, atheism would have been refuted as an error long ago. Had it been possible to awaken in every man the power to answer His ultimate question, the great prophets would have achieved it long ago. Tragic is the embarrassment of the man of faith. "My tears have been my food day and night, while they say unto me all the day, where is thy God?" (Psalm 42:4). "Where are all His marvelous works which our father told us of?" (Nehemiah 6:13; see Psalm 44:2). "How long, O Lord, wilt Thou hide Thyself perpetually?" (Psalm 89:47). "My God, my God, why hast Thou forsaken me?" (Psalm 22:2).

Why, we often ask in our prayers, hast Thou made it so difficult to find Thee? Why must we encounter so much anguish and travail before we can catch a glance of Thy presence? What a sad spectacle are the honest efforts of the great minds to prove Thy existence! And why dost Thou permit faith to blend so easily with bigotry, arrogance, cruelty, folly and superstition?

> O Lord, why dost Thou make us err from thy ways
> And harden our heart, so that we fear Thee not?
>
> Isaiah 63:17

There must be a profound reason for this fact, for man's supreme misery. The reason, perhaps, is that God in His relation to us follows not only the path of compassion but also the path of justice, and that His compassion is concealed by His justice, as His justice is concealed by His compassion.

Source: Abraham Joshua Heschel, *God in Search of Man*
(New York: Noonday Press, Farrar, Straus and Giroux, 2000), 152–155.

The Divine Pathos

HOW CAN we define the prophetic consciousness in relation to God? The prophetic consciousness was, of course, a consciousness about the world, but the prophets did not see the world as a superficial succession of causes and effects in the world; they saw it rather as a meaningful relation among events. History revealed the work of God and therefore needed interpretation. To the prophet God is never an object; He is always a person, a subject. The prophet does not think of God as of something absolute in the sense of unrelated; he thinks of Him primarily as of One who takes a direct part in the events of the world.

The prophets never ask: "*What* is God?" They are interested only in His activity and influence in human affairs. Even their views of what we would call basic principles took the form of concrete aims and tasks. It is from this point of view that we must try to answer the questions: What is typically prophetic theology like? What attitude to God defines the meaning of prophecy? Which aspect of the monotheism they affirmed had the most decisive influence upon their thought and feeling?

To the prophet, as we have noted, God does not reveal himself in an abstract absoluteness, but in a specific and unique way—in a personal and *intimate* relation to the world. God does not simply command and expect obedience; he is also moved and affected by what happens in the world and he *reacts* accordingly. Events and human actions arouse in Him joy or sorrow, pleasure or wrath. He is not conceived as judging facts so to speak "objectively," in detached impassivity. He reacts in an intimate and subjective manner, and thus determines the value of events. Quite obviously in the biblical view man's deeds can move Him, affect Him, grieve Him, or, on the other hand, gladden and please Him. This notion that God can be intimately affected, that he possesses not merely intelligence and will, but also feeling and *pathos*, basically defines the prophetic consciousness of God.

Pathos is not, however, to be understood as mere feeling. Pathos is an act formed with intention, depending on free will, the result of decision and determination. The divine *pathos* is the theme of the prophetic mission. The aim of the prophet is to reorient the people by communicating to them the divine *pathos* which, by impelling the people to "return," is itself transformed. Even "in the moment of anger" (Jer. 18:7), what God intends is not that His anger should be executed but that it should be appeased and annulled by the people's repentance.

The divine *pathos* is not merely intentional; it is also transitive. The gods of mythology are self-centered, egoistic. Their passions— erotic love, jealousy, envy—are determined by considerations of self. *Pathos*, on the other hand, is not a self-centered and self-contained state; it is always, in prophetic thinking, directed outward; it always expresses a relation to man. It is therefore not one of God's attributes as such. It has not a reflective, but rather a transitive character. Hence, whereas in the mythological genealogy of the gods man plays no part, the "history" of God cannot be separated from the history of the People Israel: the history of the divine *pathos* is embedded in human affairs.

In primitive religion, God's anger is something arbitrary, and unrelated to any conditions. The prophetic thought that human actions bring about divine *pathos*, emphasizes the unique position that man occupies in his relation to God. The divine *pathos* rooted though it is in God's free will, emerges in the context of conditions which are quite clearly human conditions.

The prophets know two different kinds of divine *pathos:* from the point of view of man, the *pathos* of redemption and that of affliction; from the point of view of God, the *pathos* of sympathy and that of rejection. But the fact that rejection seems to occur more frequently in the biblical account should not be taken to prove that wrath is inherently one of God's chief attributes. On the contrary, prophecy aims at the annulment of the *pathos* of affliction and rejection. The prophets experience God's wrath as suffering which He receives at the hand of man. It is the incredible disloyalty of His people which arouses in Him the *pathos* which afflicts. God's word comes as an appeal and a warning to His people not to arouse His anger.

The basic features emerging from the above analysis indicate that the divine *pathos* is not conceived as an essential attribute of God. The *pathos* is not felt as something objective, as a finality with which man is confronted, but as an expression of God's will; it is a functional rather than a substantial reality. The prophets never identify God's *pathos* with His essence, because it is for them not something absolute, but a form of relation. Indeed, prophecy would be impossible were the divine *pathos* in its particular structure a necessary attribute of God. If the structure of the *pathos* were immutable and remained unchanged even after the people had "turned," prophecy would lose its function, which is precisely so to influence men as to bring about a change in the divine *pathos* of rejection and affliction.

God's *pathos* is obviously not to be understood as a powerful wave of emotion which overwhelms and sweeps everything away since for the prophets justice is a basic feature of God's ways. *Pathos* and *ethos* do not simply exist side by side, opposing one another; they pass into each other. Because God is the absolute source of value, his *pathos* is always ethical. The divine *pathos* is a form of expression of God's absolute value.

Pathos is not something created arbitrarily. Its inner law is the moral law, for *ethos* is immanent in *pathos*. God is concerned about the world and shares in its fate. How could His *ethos* express itself more deeply and more immediately than by this intimate and emotional participation? But to identify God with the moral idea would be contrary to the very meaning of prophetic theology. God is not the appointed guardian of the moral order. He is not an intermediary between a transcendental idea of the good and man. The prophet does not think of Him as a being whose function it is to supervise the moral order and to bring about the realization of an autonomous morality. Morality is the norm, not the structure of the relation between God and man. As love cannot be identified with the values found in it, so the relation between God and man cannot be associated simply with the value of the moral idea. The *pathos*-structure of divine *ethos* [is] implied and follows from the unlimited sovereignty of God. If the moral law were something absolute and final, it would represent a destiny to which God Himself would be subject. Far from being sovereign, God would then fall into dependence on rigid, objective norms.

The subjection of the moral idea to the divine *pathos* is the indispensable assumption of prophetic religion. Mercy, repentance, forgiveness, would be impossible if moral principle were held to be superior to God. God's call to man, which figures so frequently in the writings of the prophets, presupposes subjective ethics. God's repenting a decision which was based on moral grounds clearly shows the supremacy of *pathos*. Let us take the idea of retaliation as an example. Whereas in Hindu religion retaliation is automatic, punishment following crime; in prophetic religion, it is seen not as a blind movement of mechanical power, but as directed by the *pathos* of conscience and will. This is why it was only in Biblical religion that the powerful and paradoxical idea could be developed.

A comparison with other theological systems can help to reveal the uniqueness of the prophetic idea of God. The Stoics considered *pathos* to be unreasonable and unnatural emotion, whereas apathy—the subduing and the overcoming of the emotions—was taken to be the supreme moral task. Spinoza held feeling to be "confused ideas." Laotse's *Tao* (the "divine way") is the eternal silence, the overlasting calm and the unchangeable law of the cosmic order. In accordance with *Tao*, man is to rid himself of desire and sympathy, greed and passion, and humbly and quietly become like *Tao*. Zeal and unrest are to be avoided. To live according to *Tao* means to live passively. The God of the prophets, however, is not the Law, but the Lawgiver. The order emanating from Him is not a rigid, unchangeable structure, but a historic-dynamical reality. Aristotle's god ever rests in itself. Things long for it and thus are set into motion; it is in this sense the "prime mover," but is itself immovable. Aristotle's god knows no feeling or suffering; it is simply pure thought thinking itself. The prophet's God is concerned with the world, and His thoughts are about it. He is the God of the fathers, the God of the covenant. The divine *pathos* expresses itself in the relation between God and His people. God is the "Holy One of Israel."

Many civilizations too, know an inescapable, unyielding power standing above the gods. Fate is supreme; it cannot be evaded. The divine *pathos*, on the other hand, strives at overcoming destiny. Its dynamic character, which makes every decision provisional, conquers fate. In Greek theology, the highest power does not need man. Events are a monologue. But Jewish religion starts with the covenant: God *and* man. An apathetical, immobile conception of God could not possibly fit into prophetic religion.

The divine *pathos*, though it is rooted in His freedom, is not simply will. God as pure will is found in Islam. In the Koran, Allah is represented as a will removed from all considerations, working without any relation to actuality. Since everything is rigorously determined, the dialogue is again reduced from all considerations, working without any relation to actuality. Since everything is rigorously determined, the dialogue is again reduced to a monologue. Central is not the relation between Allah and man, but simply Allah himself. The prophets explicitly fought against the idea, widespread even in Palestine, that God was the Creator of the world but did not interfere with the course of nature and history. This essentially deistic notion has no place for any genuine connection between God and the world.

Source: Abraham Joshua Heschel, "The Divine Pathos,"
in *God in the Teachings of Conservative Judaism*,
ed. Seymour Siegel and Elliot Gertel
(New York: Rabbinical Assembly, 1985), 114–117.

The Hiding God

For us, contemporaries and survivors of history's most terrible horrors, it is impossible to mediate about the compassion of God without asking: Where is God?

Emblazoned over the gates of the world in which we live is the escutcheon of the demons. The mark of Cain on the face of man has come to overshadow the likeness of God. There has never been so much distress, agony and terror. It is often sinful for the sun to shine. At no time has the earth been so soaked with blood. Fellow-men have turned out to be evil spirits, monstrous and weird. Does not history look like a stage for the dance of might and evil—with man's wits too feeble to separate the two and God either directing the play or indifferent to it?

The major folly of this view seems to lie in its shifting the responsibility for man's plight from man to God, in accusing the Invisible though iniquity is ours. Rather than admit our own guilt, we seek, like Adam, to shift the blame upon someone else. For generations we have been investing life with ugliness and now we wonder why we do not succeed. God was thought of as a watchman hired to prevent us from using our loaded guns. Having failed us in this, He is now thought of as the ultimate Scapegoat.

We live in an age when most of us have ceased to be shocked by the increasing breakdown in moral inhibitions. The decay of conscience fills the air with a pungent smell. Good and evil, which were once as distinguishable as day and night, have become a blurred mist. But that mist is man-made. God is not silent. He has been silenced.

Instead of being taught to answer the direct commands of God with a conscience open to His will, men are fed on the sweetness of mythology, on promises of salvation and immortality as a dessert to the pleasant repast on earth. The faith believers cherish is second hand: it is a faith in the miracles of the past, an attachment to symbols and ceremonies. God is known from hearsay, a rumor fostered by dogmas, and even non-dogmatic thinkers offer hackneyed, solemn concepts without daring to cry out the startling vision of the sublime on the margin of which indecisions, doubts, are almost vile.

We have trifled with the name of God. We have taken ideals in vain, preached and eluded Him, praised and defied Him. Now we reap the fruits of failure. Through centuries His voice cried in the wilderness. How skillfully it was trapped and imprisoned in the templates! How thoroughly distorted! Now we behold how it gradually withdraws, abandoning one people after another, departing from their souls, despising their wisdom. The taste for goodness has all but gone from the earth.

We have witnessed in history how often a man, a group or a nation, lost from the sight of God, acts and succeeds, strives and achieves, but is given up by Him. They may stride from one victory to another and yet they are done with and abandoned, renounced and cast aside. They may possess all glory and might, but their life will be dismal. God has withdrawn from their life, even while they are heaping wickedness upon cruelty and malice upon evil. The dismissal of man, the abrogation of Providence, inaugurates eventual calamity.

They are left alone, neither molested by punishment nor assured by indication of help. The divine does not interfere with their actions nor intervene in their conscience. Having all in abundance save His blessing, they find their wealth a shell in which there is curse without mercy.

Man was the first to hide himself from God [Genesis 3:8], after having eaten of the forbidden fruit, and is still hiding [Job 13:20–24]. The will of God is to be here, manifest and near; but when the doors of this world are slammed on Him, His truth betrayed, His will defied, He withdraws, leaving man to himself. God did not depart of His own volition; He was expelled. *God is in exile.*

More grave than Adam's eating the forbidden fruit was his hiding from God after he had eaten it. "Where art thou?" Where is man? is the first question that occurs in the Bible. It is man's alibi that is our problem. It is man who hides, who flees, who has an alibi. God is less rare than we think; when we long for Him, His distance crumbles away.

The prophets do not speak of the *hidden God* but of the *hiding God*. His hiding is a function not His essence, an act not a permanent state. It is when the people forsake Him, breaking the Covenant which He has made with them, that He forsakes them and hides His face from them [Deut. 31:16-17]. God who is obscure. It is man who conceals Him. His hiding from us is not in His essence: "Verily Thou art a God that hidest Thyself, O God of Israel, the Saviour!" (Isaiah 45:15). A hiding God, not a hidden God. He is waiting to be disclosed, to be admitted into our lives.

The direct effect of His hiding is the hardening of the conscience: man hears but does not understand, seeks but does not perceive—his heart fat, his ears heavy [Isaiah 6]. Our task is to open our souls to Him, to let Him again enter our deeds. We have been taught the grammar of contact with God; we have been taught by the Baal Shem that His remoteness is an illusion capable of being dispelled by our faith. There are many doors through which we have to pass in order to enter the palace, and none of them is locked.

As the hiding of man is known to God and seen through, so is God's hiding seen through. In sensing the fact of His hiding we have disclosed Him. Life is a hiding place for God. We are never asunder from Him who is in need of us. Nations roam and rave—but all this is only ruffling the deep, unnoticed and uncherished stillness.

Source: Abraham Joshua Heschel, *Man Is Not Alone*
(New York: Noonday Press, Farrar, Straus and Giroux, 1997), 151–153.

· 5 ·

ROLAND B. GITTELSOHN

1910–1995

*R*oland B. Gittelsohn was the rabbi of Temple Israel in Boston
from 1953 to his retirement in 1977. Born in Cleveland, Ohio, he
graduated from Western Reserve University and Hebrew Union
College (Cincinnati), from which he received his rabbinic ordination
in 1936. Prior to Boston, he served as the spiritual leader of Central
Synagogue of Nassau County in Rockville Centre, New York, from
1936 to 1953.

Though a pacifist, Gittelsohn served as a chaplain in the navy during World War II, because he believed that it was necessary to fight
Hitler in an "obligatory war." He was awarded three ribbons for the
campaign in Iwo Jima and delivered there his most-quoted sermon at
the Fifth Division Cemetery on the day of its dedication. Years later, he
was one of the first to preach against the Vietnam War. A past president
of the Massachusetts Board of Rabbis (MBR), the Central Conference of
American Rabbis (CCAR), and the Association of Reform Zionists of
America (ARZA), he was also a member of President Truman's
Commission on Civil Rights. He died in 1995 in Boston at the age of
eighty-five.

Gittelsohn was one of the most vocal proponents of religious naturalism. He recognized that it is impossible to prove the existence of
God, and therefore he admitted that the acceptance of the Divine is a
matter of faith. Yet, the observable order and the intelligence in nature

point to the reality of God. In many of his writings, Gittelsohn, who was influenced by his early studies in science, defined God as the Power that animates the universe, or as "the Energizing Force which has been slowly working its way through evolution toward fulfillment of a plan" (Wings of the Morning, p. 166), even though many details of this ultimate plan have not been projected in advance or discovered by humanity. He also maintained that God created the cosmos over endless time "out of Himself." However, against many theists who argued that God is supernatural, he maintained that God functions not outside of the cosmos but within the universe, much as the yeast within the dough. Unlike Spinoza, who argued that God and the universe are one and the same, Gittelsohn believed that God is the Creative Power that is responsible for nature and the energy that sustains all existence.

For Gittelsohn, the universe is ruled by both natural (e.g., the law of gravity) and spiritual laws (e.g., the need for every child for love), though many of these laws still remain beyond our understanding. In order to attain security in life, one needs to live in accordance with the patterns that are part of the makeup of the universe. Because God functions through established patterns, Gittelsohn remarked, God's power is not unlimited, and therefore, God cannot create miracles. This realization, however, does not diminish God, for miracles bespeak of a universe ruled with caprice, and not through regularity and order observable in nature.

Gittelsohn did not conceive of God as a "person." Nor did he believe that God is a "personal God," with all human characteristics attributed to the divinity. Rather, he asserted that God affects our lives on a personal level through the natural and spiritual laws governing the universe. We experience God through our observation of nature, through our conscience, or through our love for others. Our world, he believed, is not perfect, but we are endowed with free will to make it better.

God as Power, Not Person

Not all modern religious Jews interpret God in exactly the same way. Some may harbor ideas which more closely resemble my grandfather's

thinking than mine; some may have changed the older religious conclusions even more than I have. For all, however, God is:

1. The Spiritual Power which created and sustains nature.
2. The Energizing Force which has been slowly working its way
   through evolution toward fulfillment of a plan. Not every detail
   of the plan has been projected in advance. There are certain
   major trends or directions inherent within the process itself.
   Exactly how these trends are implemented depends on environ-
   mental circumstances and on the degree of cooperation given by
   man as God's partner.
3. The Moral Power which impels and governs the operation of
   Moral Natural Law. We see a portion of this Power within ourselves in the form of conscience.

There is also a fourth possible interpretation of God. We can think
of Him as a Power within the universe, manifesting itself in the three
ways listed above, and we can also conceive Him as a Goal. We are not
the first to do so. The Talmud contains an interesting comment on the
statement in Deuteronomy (13:5), "After the Lord your God shall you
walk."

> Is it possible for a man to walk after the שכינה (*Shechinah*), God's
> Presence, of which it is written, "The Lord thy God is a devouring
> fire." But the meaning is to follow the attributes of the Holy One,
> blessed be He: as He clothed the naked, so should you clothe the
> naked; as He visited the sick, so should you visit the sick, as He
> comforted mourners, so should you comfort those who mourn; as
> He buried the dead, so should you bury the dead. [BT *Sotah* 14a]

God, in short, can be considered as a combination of all our ethical
goals. At one and the same time He can be the Moral Power impelling
us to improve and the Ethical Goal toward which our improvement is
aimed. He can be thought of as pushing us upward from where we are
and simultaneously pulling us toward Himself. In this sense, the more
ethical our behavior becomes, the more closely we can be said to
resemble the image of God in which we were created. An ancient
rabbi must have had something like this in mind when he said: "The

Holy One, blessed be He, the Lord who is called righteous and upright, has not created man in His own image save in the sense that man be as righteous and upright as He Himself."

Perhaps this will be clearer if we think of such separate ethical ideals as peace, humility, honesty, justice, mercy, righteousness, and truth. Let us do two things with this list:

1. Try to think of each ideal magnified to the point of perfection. Imagine what *perfect peace* would be like as a goal for which to strive—or *perfect truth* or *perfect justice*.
2. Think of these ideals, each magnified to perfection, put together in one great Master Ideal which becomes the goal of all our living. The word God can be used in modern Jewish religion to refer to this goal. God, thought of in this way, becomes a vision of perfection, an ethical pattern for human beings to follow.

We must guard against confusion. It is frequently and thoughtlessly said that God is love. To say that is to articulate but a tiny fragment of the truth being expressed here. God is not love; He is the Source of love. God is not justice or truth; He is the Source of justice and truth. Even when we suggest that God symbolizes all these values and many more, magnified to perfection and combined into a Master Ideal, we have barely begun to encompass the full meaning of God. For if these combined and magnified virtues were only products of the human mind, then it would be true that man created God. We can rightfully associate God with our goal of perfection only because it is He who enables us to think of moral perfection and aspire to approximate it. God is that reality in the universe which impels man to reach out for love, justice, and truth; which makes it possible for them to be realized; which conserves and sustains them in the same sense that He conserves and sustains the law of gravity.

Someone has suggested that the notion of God as the ethical goal of our lives may be seen in one of the Hebrew words our ancestors frequently used for God אל *(AYL)*. The identical consonants with a change of vowel make the word אל *(EL)*, meaning "to" or "toward." God may be thought of, then, as the goal of ethical perfection *toward which* we should strive.

Will anyone ever be able to reach this goal? . . .

Our Jewish answer to this question differs [from the Christian view]. We do not believe that any human being ever has or ever can reach the goal of ethical perfection, because we look upon it as a moving goal. As our ethical evolution progresses, our ideas and ideals of perfection likewise are improved. The closer we get to our goal of perfection, the more we are able to envision an even higher and loftier goal for the future.

In other words, our moving Master Ideal is much like the horizon. If, standing on a high tower, we looked toward the horizon and arranged for someone, standing where the horizon seemed to be, to mark that spot with a flag, and then started out to walk toward that spot, we would never reach the horizon. We would, to be sure, reach the spot where the horizon had been, but from our new perspective the horizon would still seem to be far off in the forward distance. As we move, the horizon moves with us. As we move forward ethically, our ethical horizon or goal also moves with us, so that, for modern Jews, God as the combination of all our highest ideals will always be a challenge, urging us to continual improvement. A non-Jewish writer, Barbara Spofford Morgan, wrote very much in the spirit of this Jewish point of view when she commented: ". . . those who set their hearts on what they cannot reach are the ones who carry civilization forward."

It has been suggested by some thinkers that our modern interpretations of God differ so greatly from older concepts that perhaps we need a new word for them. Those who have reached this conclusion suggest that we retain the word *God* for what it meant in the past and seek a different word for the Power and Goal this book has described. To suggest this is to forget that we are not the first to read new meanings into the word *God*. This process of reinterpretation has been going on throughout Jewish history. To adopt a new word each time a new interpretation appears would result in total confusion. The word *God* has always been used with reference to whatever men believed to be the cause of everything, the Ultimate Reality behind all other realities, the coordinating and directing Force responsible for the universe, to which each of us must finally hold himself responsible. God can still mean exactly that, even though we may differ widely in our understanding of what that Reality actually is.

We cannot insist on our interpretation as the only one, because no one really knows the nature of God. No one can *prove* that God exists. Eight centuries ago Maimonides proclaimed that we can ascribe only negative attributes to God; we can assert what He is not, without knowing what He is. The most for which we can hope is to discover evidence in the Universe and in our own lives which is best explained by faith in God. We must then try to live consistently with our understanding of God, while holding ourselves open to new experiences and new evidence which will perhaps change our interpretations and convictions in the future.

God is not the only kind of significant human experience which is beyond proof. It is also impossible to prove that one musical composition or artistic masterpiece is superior to another. It is impossible to prove friendship or love. Yet these are obviously among the most vital realities in life. We apply as much reason and experience to them as possible, then proceed to live by them in terms of what we called . . . rational faith.

We cannot prove that we have souls. Yet our observations of others and the most vital feelings within ourselves tell us that we are more than just physical mechanisms, that the most important part of us is more than material. We call that part of us our souls. Reason and emotion combine to assure us also that there is something spiritual at the very core of the universe. We may call the Soul of the universe God.

Source: Roland B. Gittelsohn, Wings of the Morning
(New York: UAHC Press, 1969), 166–170.

A Naturalist View

I am a religious naturalist—my correct identification today—because I believe that religious naturalism has at the very least been adumbrated within traditional Judaism.

I'm delighted to share this platform with my colleagues and friends, not merely for the personal pleasure it gives me, but also, and more importantly, because it demonstrates that Judaism, historic Judaism if you please, is broad and comprehensive enough to encompass the wider spectrum of theological alternatives we are presenting from this platform this morning. If we accomplish little else in the course of this symposium, let it at least become immediately apparent to every person present that there is indeed room enough within our Jewish tradition for a comfortable variety of theological views, so that no member of the CCAR or UAHC need ever feel that he has been cramped or forced to comply with a very narrow kind of theological view which is uncongenial to himself.

Having said that, let me proceed at once to establish, if I possibly can within my own personal limitations and the limitations of time, just what it is that the religious naturalist within Judaism believes (a) about God and (b) about prayer. And wherein the theological emphases of the religious naturalist may differ from the other legitimate religious postures represented on this platform, the religious naturalist asserts essentially that God is to be found within nature, not acting upon nature from outside itself. Now this involves, to be sure, a much deeper, broader understanding of nature than was formerly held. Men once thought of nature as being only physical; on that premise it then became necessary for religionists to assume the existence of a spiritual entity outside nature to account for that which in human experience is manifestly transphysical or extraphysical.

From the position of the religious naturalist it is possible to think of nature itself as encompassing both the physical and the spiritual. Science has helped us achieve this newer understanding by its propensity to see existence as unified and whole. One of the deepest insights of modern science is that the old boundary lines have been breached. My good friend, Dr. George Russell Harrison, dean of the School of Science at MIT, has expressed it this way: "The more closely one examines the border line between living and unliving matter, the more is one forced to conclude that there is no boundary that is definite, no place where a breath of life comes sharply to inform matter."

To which I would add: As it is with the organic and the inorganic—namely, that they partake one of the other with no sharp line of division—so is it with matter and energy, so is it with the physical and the spiritual. They are aspects of each other; where one happened to precede the other in time, the ultimate eventuality was potentially present from the inception. What glorious overtones modern science has thus added to the ancient watchword of our Jewish faith! As God is one, so the universe is one, life is one, man is one! That which is spiritual in man—his soul—has evolved out of his protozoan beginnings no less than his spine, his hands, or his brain. And such evolutionary development was possible precisely because there was soul within the universe from its beginning. God, to the naturalist, is the Soul of the universe. God is the creative, spiritual Seed of the universe—the Energy, the Power, the Force, the Direction, the Trust—out of which the universe has expanded, by which the universe is sustained, in which the universe and mind find their meaning.

I must insist, with all the emphasis of which I am physically and intellectually capable—the religious naturalist neither denies God nor diminishes Him. He simply enlarges his concept of nature enough to include God. It is not belittling God to talk of Him as a Life Force or as the creative, indefinable Soul of the universe. It is not subjecting God to subhuman form. To the contrary, it is precisely the person who insists on talking about God within a human vocabulary and in terms of human analogy who is belittling God.

Do I believe in a personal God? I must answer in a characteristically Jewish manner with a counterquestion. What do you mean by a personal God? If you mean by these words a God who can possibly be conceived in terms analogous to human personality, no, I do not believe in a personal God. But if you mean a God who is the most intense personal reality of my life, functioning personally in everything I think and feel and do, then God is indeed personal for me. I say that God cannot be encompassed within the terms of personality, not because He is *less* than personality but because He is ineffably and incomprehensively *more* than personality. I refuse to imprison God, as it were, within my lexicon of human psychology and human understanding.

I can understand why my ancestors had to do that, with their less sophisticated understanding of the abstract processes of reality. Our ancestors needed a transcendent view of God because they had so limited an estimate of the universe. A cozy, self-contained little universe —consisting of earth, sun, moon and a sprinkling of stars—that's too small a thing to encompass the Divine. But are we not ready to recognize that ours is an incomparably different kind of universe? Where our fathers knew only of one sun, we are aware of millions. Where they believed the light which emanated from the sun reached them almost instantaneously, we know that it takes eight billion years for light to travel from one end of the universe to the other—assuming, indeed, that the universe has ends. We know that if our earth were reduced in scale to the size of the period punctuating this sentence—which means to say, to a dimension of one-fiftieth of an inch—the sun would be, on that scale, nineteen-and-a-half feet away, the next nearest star would be removed from us by one thousand and five miles, the galaxy farthest known at this moment would be eighty-one billion, eight hundred thirty million miles away. All on a scale in which the earth is represented in diameter by one-fiftieth of an inch!

Is it really an affront to God to suggest that perhaps today heaven and the heaven of heavens can contain Him? God is transcendent to humanity, yes. He is transcendent to our galaxy, yes. But I am not so sure that it is any longer necessary to think of Him as being transcendent to the entire universe of nature. Here, then, in essential summary, is the first part of what I have to say. Here is what the Jewish religious naturalist believes about God.

How does prayer fit into such a concept? Well, let me give you four alternative statements, four ways of saying pretty much the same thing in attempting to express my understanding of prayer. Prayer is my constant effort to reinforce my relationship with the Soul of the universe, thereby to emphasize and realize my spiritual potential. Prayer is a reminder of who I am, of what I can become, and of my proper relationship to the rest of the universe, both physical and spiritual. Prayer is an inventory of the spiritual resources which nature has invested in me and a survey of how I can exploit those resources to their fullest. Prayer is a recapitulation of the spiritual laws of the universe and an encouragement to conform to those laws in my conduct.

The difference between prayer and ordinary meditation or introspection is that prayer must include a constant recognition of my relationship to something both outside and within myself, namely, to the Spiritual Core of Reality. The spiritual reserves within me are an aspect of a great spiritual reservoir outside me, even as the oxygen within my lungs at any moment is a part of the great reservoir of oxygen which constitutes the earth's atmosphere.

What, then, is the special emphasis of prayer to the Jewish religious naturalist? First, a negative emphasis. The religious naturalist vigorously, emphatically rejects the following statement made by another of our colleagues: "A religion based on prayer must picture God as a person." The religious naturalist denies that you must picture God as a person in order to pray. The religious naturalist insists, moreover, that prayer is not supposed to change God or His universe; it's rather supposed to change the person who is praying. It's supposed to help him conform to the nature of the universe, not beg the universe or its Creator to conform to his will. Prayer is supposed to help me do God's will, not cajole God into performing my will.

This is really not so radical an idea in Judaism as some may first suspect. God said to Moses at the shore of the Sea of Reeds when Moses turned to Him in desperation: "Why do you cry out to me? Tell the Israelites to go forward!" The Midrash, moreover, expands the terse comment reported in the Torah. It pictures God as saying: "Moses, there is a time for a long prayer and a time for a short prayer; the Egyptians are coming close—this is the time for a short prayer." The Midrash also asserts that the Sea didn't part until after the Israelites had entered it up to their noses. God would not respond to their prayers until after they had responded themselves! In Mishnah Berachot the rabbis tell us that a man standing on a hill, watching smoke rise from his town, should not pray "May the fire not be in my house." The fire is burning already; such a prayer can have no possible effect. The same passage insists that if a man's wife is pregnant, he must not pray that the child be either a boy or a girl, because the sex of the child has already been determined.

Does prayer accomplish anything for the religious naturalist? If it is a valid prayer, of course it does! But its effect is on me, not on God. What does *ozen sho-ma-at*—a listening ear—mean to the religious naturalist? I can answer best in terms of an analogy: As I sat before my typewriter, preparing my notes, I became aware of the fact that I was surrounded by shelves of books. All around me was intellectual power, the accumulated wisdom of many centuries. But the books on my shelves did not offer to intercede on my behalf. They did not jump off the shelf and open themselves to the right place and help me, whether I used them or ignored them. They were there as a spiritual resource for me to activate and energize if I so chose. Similarly, God is a Spiritual Power in the universe and in myself. He operates the same way, whether I pray or not. In the life of a tree it makes no difference whether the tree is aware of God's existence; in my life it makes an immense difference, for prayer is my way to activate and utilize a Power which otherwise remains dormant.

I will conclude with the words of Dr. N. J. Berrill, a distinguished Canadian zoologist who, though not a Jew and not speaking within the lexicon of religion, has nevertheless eloquently summarized the position of religious naturalism: "We need no faith in supernatural forces. We need only to recognize that our knowledge of the universe . . . shows that it is orderly, moral and beautiful, that it is akin to intelligence, that love and hope belong in it as fully as light itself, and that the power and will of the human mind is but a symptom of reality; that we, when we are most human, most rational, most aware of love and beauty, reflect and represent the spirit of the universe." (*Man's Emerging Mind*, p. 286, Dodd, Mead and Company.)

Source: Roland B. Gittelsohn, *The Theological Foundations of Prayer: A Reform Jewish Perspective.* Papers Presented at the UAHC 48th Biennial, ed. Rabbi Jack Bemporad (New York: UAHC Press, 1967), 43–52.

No Miracles Today

On a mountainside in New Hampshire is a tablet commemorating a landslide some years ago which wiped out an entire family. Visiting tourists are told that the family had constructed a shelter some yards from their home, anticipating that if a landslide should ever start, they would all run to the shelter and be saved. One night they heard rumblings which unmistakably announced the realization of their fears. Together they rushed out into the darkness to reach their place of safety. There were only a few yards to be traveled, but tons of earth came down upon them in an instant, and all were killed in the space between shelter and house. The next morning neighbors who had survived discovered that a huge boulder directly above their house had so divided the falling earth and rocks that the house itself hadn't even been touched. Had they remained there, they would have been saved. Rushing out for certain protection, all of them had been killed!

Obviously this tragedy can't be [easily] explained. . . . It would be a little farfetched, to say the least, to claim that the instant death of an entire family just seemed to be a tragedy, but was actually for their good. Likewise, the landslide couldn't very well be blamed either on their own or someone else's wrong-doing. The only explanation we can give is that somehow, by operation of the laws of nature, the wind and rain and soil erosion had created a condition whereby the earth and rocks began to fall down the mountainside. Once that had started, the force of gravity kept the slide falling and everything except the one spot which happened to be protected by the boulder was covered. Now then, if God were what primitive and ancient men supposed Him to be—an all-powerful supreme being who could do anything He wanted to do—then it would be quite proper and fair to blame the landslide and the resultant deaths on God.

But if God is the force or power which is responsible for the laws of nature and which must itself operate according to those rules, if God doesn't possess the power to work miracles, then we cannot intelligently expect Him to have saved this family. Furthermore, we must ask ourselves: What kind of world would this be if God *could* interrupt the laws of nature whenever He felt like it or whenever someone asked Him to in prayer? We can't have it both ways, you know. We can't rely on the benefits of a world which always operates by law, yet at the same time complain about its dangers.

If this were the kind of world in which God could at will make rocks fall upward or sideward instead of downward, then it would also be the kind of world in which other innocent people would be killed or in which we could never count on when or where the sun would shine or how long our earth could exist without colliding with some other planet. It shouldn't be hard to see that, tragic as life can sometimes be now, it would be filled with far more heartache and sorrow if nature's laws did not operate as they do. So another explanation for certain kinds of suffering is that it is the price we must pay for living in a universe on which we can always depend because it is operated by God.

Source: Roland B. Gittelsohn, *Little Lower than the Angels* (New York: UAHC Press, 1955), 288–290.

EMIL L. FACKENHEIM

1916–2003

A descendant of a long line of rabbis on his mother's side, Emil
L. Fackenheim was born in Halle, Germany, in 1916. His father was a
liberal Jew and a prominent lawyer. The middle of three brothers, Emil
attended the Liberal Seminary of Berlin (the Hochschule für die
Wissenschaft des Judentums) from 1935 to 1938 and was ordained in
1939. Among his teachers was the revered Rabbi Leo Baeck.

After Kristallnacht on November 10, 1938, Fackenheim returned to
Halle. It was there that the Gestapo found him and sent him to
Sachsenhausen, a concentration camp, where he stayed until February
of 1939. Fortunate to get a visa to England, Fackenheim left the same
year and went to the University of Aberdeen in Scotland. Thereafter,
having been accepted at the University of Toronto, he left for Canada,
where he also became the rabbi of Temple Anshe Sholom in Hamilton,
Ontario, from 1943 to 1948. In 1948, he became a member of the faculty of the University of Toronto and taught philosophy for thirty-six
years. When he retired in 1984, he made aliyah to Israel, became a fellow at the Institute for Contemporary Jewry at the Hebrew University,
and taught at the Jerusalem campus of Hebrew Union College–Jewish
Institute of Religion. He died in Jerusalem in September of 2003 at the
age of eighty-seven.

For Fackenheim, Jewish theology attempts to provide a coherent
account of the Jewish faith based on the assumption that God is a

supernatural God who has entered history. Faith is a personal decision and a positive answer that an individual can give to questions of ultimate significance. That is why Fackenheim spoke of it as a "leap in the dark." In the same way, God is a given. No rational explanation can exist to prove or disprove the existence of God. The belief in God, Fackenheim argued, is an "absolute existential a priori" about the Creator and Redeemer. In Jewish thought, he added, this God is a "present God," and not just a hypothesis.

Fackenheim maintained that God is not a distant God but a personal God who is infinite yet shows intimacy. However, our minds cannot comprehend this paradox of the "intimacy of the infinite." In order to understand our existential issues, we must turn to the allegorical language of the midrashic texts and speak of God "as it were."

Influenced by the philosophy of history of Georg Hegel (1770–1831), who taught that there is a historical process (he called it "Geist" or "Spirit") leading from one stage to the next until it reaches a stable structure at the end, Fackenheim identified certain key events in the history of the Jewish people, for example, the Exodus, the Revelation at Sinai, and the Crusades, that have created new moral demands. In fact, he identified God with the process that enfolds through the periods of history, requiring that we have authentic responses to each of these developments. For Fackenheim, the Holocaust is one of those "epoch-making" occurrences in the chain of Jewish continuity.

A survivor of Nazism, Fackenheim delved into the nature of evil in the universe with considerable sensitivity to those who perished during the war. In declaring the Holocaust a unique historical event in Jewish history, he argued that the commanding voice of Auschwitz calls us to become Zionists, to commit ourselves to total resistance to evil through acts of tikkun olam, to try to reestablish the trust that has been destroyed among the nations, and ultimately to remain faithful to Judaism by not giving Hitler a posthumous victory—what he calls the 614th commandment.

We do not know, says Fackenheim, where God was during the Shoah. It is possible, he argued, that just as God is infinite, so is God's pain. Because God loved the world so much, "He hid the infinity of His pain" lest the universe be destroyed once and for all. In this post-Holocaust period, Fackenheim stressed, our job is to revitalize our faith and bring a sense of humanity to our society.

Decision of Faith

The decision of faith differs from other decisions as radically as these do from objective detachment. Decision stems from the insight that existence is inescapable. The decision of faith stems from the insight that God is inescapable. Man surrenders his neutrality in the realization that he cannot be neutral; he surrenders authority over his existence in the realization that he cannot be his own authority. In the state of existential decision, he knows that he cannot refute God; in the decision of faith, he knows that he cannot reject or escape Him. He knows that whatever he decides, he is under the authority of God: Nebuchadnezzar does the will of God as fully as do Moses or David. Indeed, the very agony in which man tries to reject God, testifies to Him. And in rebellion, man harms not God, but himself.

We must understand clearly the specific nature of the decision of faith. A modern writer properly warns:

> If we believe in . . . a . . . God not because He is the truth, but assume His truth only because we believe in Him, then there are as many gods and as many truths and values as there are beliefs. [Dostoyevsky, quoted by E. Frank, *Philosophical Understanding & Religious Faith* (NY, 1965), 38]

If the decision of faith is on the same level as other possible decisions, man makes God's sovereignty or even His existence depend on his belief in, or acceptance of, Him. This is the final heresy. The distinctive nature of the decision of faith is that it is at the same time no decision at all, because in accepting God's sovereignty man realizes that he accepts that to which he is subject regardless of his decision.

We are here at the crucial point in man's religious situation. *Before* he makes the decision of faith, he is free not to make it. He may thereby lose all hope of ultimate integration; he may live a life of self-contradiction; he may arrive at self-destruction: all the same, he is free not to accept the "yoke of the Kingdom of Heaven." *After* the decision of faith, there is no freedom to reject God; there is merely freedom to rebel against Him. But in rebellion as well as in submission, man now testifies to God. Even the non-believer testifies to Him, through his tragic ignorance.

Here, then, we have the fundamental tension in the religious life: the decision of faith in which man expresses the irrelevance of all his deciding to the sovereignty of God is, nevertheless, the greatest of all decisions. Total submission to God is not only the ultimate in humility; it is also the extreme in self-confidence: "Everything is in the hands of Heaven except the fear of Heaven" [BT *B'rachot* 33b]. If God exists, He is the *absolute existential a priori;* yet man dares to leap from a position in which he is free not to accept Him to total acceptance of His sovereignty. Whence this momentous audacity?

Man finds the grounds for both his humility and his self-confidence in himself. He is in a state of dependence; yet he transcends it in that he knows it. It is because he knows of his sin that he cannot escape his obligation. Sin would not be sin if man could not know of it. Knowing it, he must face the responsibility to combat it. What is man's ultimate attitude to be? If humility leads him to surrender his obligation, he escapes from what he knows to be his responsibility. If awareness of his responsibility leads him to battle his weakness entirely by himself, he becomes involved in sinful pride.

From this contradictory situation the decision of faith derives both its audacity and its humility, which become an ineffable unity. Realizing the audacity implied in the decision of faith, man knows that to let his humility destroy this audacity is to escape from his responsibility. If there is a God, He does not wipe out man's responsibility; He makes it inescapable. He is each man's own personal God—"near," not "far."

But, all the same, man could not venture the decision of faith were it not for the fact that this daring is at the same time no daring at all, and that therefore man's supreme self-confidence is at the same time his supreme humility. For if there is a God, man's total dependence on Him includes both his dependence and his transcendence, both his acceptance and his rejection of Him. Man's faith, his own *decision,* is then at the same time *given.* Revelation, which becomes revelation only through man's decision to accept it as such, is then at the same time absolutely given, because God's sovereignty includes man's decision. For if there is a God, He is the sovereign of each man's personal destiny—"near," not "far."

The decision of faith, then, is the only decision which man can make without qualification. To accept the yoke of the Kingdom of Heaven is the only ultimate integration man can realize, because here it is not he alone who realizes it. But this ultimate integration does not imply an infallible security. On the contrary, because it transcends all evidence, proofs, and refutations, faith is the greatest of all risks. Even the ancients, who felt so secure in their faith, sensed this. "Even though He slay me, yet will I trust in Him," are the words of Job. The Mishnah says: "'Thou shalt love the Lord thy God with . . . all thy soul' (Deut. 6:5),—that is to say, even if He takes thy soul from thee" [BT *B'rachot* 9:5].

Modern man knows that the risk is vastly greater even than this. For he understands what the ancients in their faith were not always conscious of: the position of man before the decision of faith. In a paradoxical paraphrase of the passage of the Mishnah, modern man might tell himself: "'Thou shalt love the Lord thy God with . . . all thy soul'—that is to say: thou shalt love absolutely Him of whom thou hast certainty only by reason of thy love. And thou shalt rejoice in this thy unique opportunity for absolute love."

Source: Emil L. Fackenheim, *Quest for Past and Future: Essays in Jewish Theology* (Bloomington, Ind.: Indiana University Press, 1968), 45–48.

God's Existence

The biblical and rabbinic tradition is pervaded by the conviction that it is impossible to doubt or deny the existence of God.

The modern mind will at once attribute this conviction to philosophical naiveté and the inability to deal critically with evidence. But this notion hardly goes beyond the surface. It is true, of course, that the evidence presented for divine revelation is not examined as critically as it might be. Nature is too simply taken as evidence of a God who guides it. History is too naively assumed to prove divine retribution. The certainty stemming from personal experience is not subjected to adequate criticism. But, this kind of naive acceptance of evidence is only incidental to the certainty of the existence of God. For it is realized that the evidence frequently fails. Nature harbors evil as well as good. Human nature appears afflicted with shortcomings such as cannot be attributed to man's own fault. History, above all, shows conditions which impel a Jeremiah to contend: "Wherefore doth the way of the wicked prosper? Wherefore are all they secure that deal very treacherously?" (Jer. 12:1), and a rabbi must admit: "It is not in our power to explain either the prosperity of the wicked or the afflictions of the righteous" [*Pirkei Avot* 4:19]. "Times of wrath" occur, when "all people cry and weep, but their voice is not heard, even though they decree fast-days, roll themselves in dust, cover themselves with sackcloth and shed tears" [Tos. Derech Eretz, Perek Haminim, 31]. And often man finds no evidence in his heart of the presence of God.

But while the evidence can become doubtful, God cannot. If nature reveals evil, then God "form[s] light and create[s] darkness, make[s] peace and create[s] evil" (Isa. 45:7). The fact that men cannot see divine purpose evidenced in history merely proves that: "My thoughts are not your thoughts, neither are My ways your ways" (Isa. 55:8). If inner experience is dead, it is because God "hides His face" (Ps. 13:2; 44:35; 69:18), "stands off" (Ps. 10:1), "forgets" (Ps. 13:2), "forsakes" (Ps. 22:2), or "sleeps" (Ps. 44:24); but the failure of inner evidence never suggests that God does not exist. Even the great skeptic of the Bible, Kohelet, who regards life as a whole as vanity, concludes from this conviction: "This is the end of the matter, all having been heard: fear God, and keep His commandments; for this is the whole man" (Eccl. 12:13). No objective evidence to the contrary, and no feeling of being deserted, can affect the certainty of God. As Job puts it: "Though He slay me, yet will I trust in Him" (Job 13:15).

We cannot fairly dismiss this absolute and fact-defying certainty of God as the mental habit of a religious civilization. How then can we understand it? We shall be totally unable to do so unless we rid ourselves of the modern prejudice that all religious life is an evolution of religious *feelings* or *ideas*. In accordance with this prejudice, man forms notions of God with the assistance of external and internal evidence, and the more he becomes conscious of this activity of his, the more thoroughly does he arrive at a state of objective detachment in which he judges the merits of the God-idea, and weighs the evidence for the existence of God. However, when in Jewish tradition God's existence is nowhere doubted nor made dependent on evidence, this is not because man is here at too primitive a level to have reached the stage of objective and critical detachment; it is because of a profound certainty that such a detachment is impossible. *God's existence is man's existential a priori.*

*Whither shall I go from Thy spirit? Or whither shall I flee from
   Thy presence?
If I ascend up into heaven, Thou art there;
If I make my bed in the netherworld, behold, Thou art there.
If I take the wings of the morning,
And dwell in the uttermost parts of the sea;
Even there would Thy hand lead me,
And Thy right hand would hold me (Ps. 139:7–10).*

This is not a rather primitive and unscientific statement of a universal God-idea. From a God-idea one could "flee" at least to the extent of
viewing it in an attitude of objective detachment. The God of the Bible
is not an ultimate object; He is *the* Subject, each man's living, personal
God. Any attempt to subject God's existence to critical judgment is,
therefore, held to be insolence, because it means to judge the Judge. To
deny His existence is more than insolence: it is "folly" (Ps. 14:1; 53:2),
since it is the rejection by man of his own "light and salvation" (Ps. 27:1);
it is rebellion, since it is the attempt to replace God's authority by man's
(Ps. 10:4; also Ezek. 28:9). The denial of God is self-destruction or rebellion; it is never merely an erroneous objective statement. In his ultimate
relation to Reality, man must be *participant*; he cannot remain *spectator.*

Attempts to describe the nature of this God in biblical and rabbinic
tradition must be understood as part of this fundamental situation.
The avowed task here is not to describe consistently and adequately an
infinite God as He is in Himself, a task that could be undertaken only
by an objective spectator. The task is to describe the living relation
between this infinite God and finite man, and to do so as an inevitable
participant.

God is infinite and yet directly related to each finite person. This
is the inexplicable, yet indubitable, basic fact about God. He is
"enthroned on high and looketh down low" (Ps. 113:5-6). He is both
"far and near":

God is far, for is He not in the heaven of heavens? And yet He is
near, . . . for a man enters a synagogue, and stands behind a pillar,
and prays in a whisper, and God hears his prayer, and so it is with
all His creatures. He is as near to His creatures as the ear to the
mouth. [JT *B'rachot* ix e, 13a line 7]

The direct relation between the infinite God and the finite human person is by its very nature paradoxical. If this relation were one-sided, it would destroy itself; for then the infinite God would devour the finite person's freedom and his very identity. It is a mutual relation. "Everything is in the hands of Heaven except the fear of Heaven" [BT B'rachot 33b], is the word of a rabbi to whom human freedom is real yet limited by Divine Presence. But if this relation is a mutual one, then paradoxically the free actions and reactions of finite men make a difference to the infinite God. Biblical and rabbinic tradition express the reality of this paradoxical relation in a well-nigh infinite variety of metaphors. These metaphors, which are mostly anthropomorphisms, cannot be regarded as "impure" philosophical notions; they are *symbolic* terms designed to describe a relation which cannot be grasped in any terms other than symbolic. Occasionally the rabbis are fully conscious of this, especially when in their stress on human responsibility they even make the omnipotent God dependent on impotent man.

> *Ye are My witnesses, saith the Lord, and I am God* (Isa. 43:12). That is, when ye are My witnesses, I am God, and when ye are not My witnesses, I am, as it were, not God. [Midrash Psalms on Ps. 123:1]
> When the Israelites do God's will, they add to the power of God on high. When the Israelites do not do God's will, they, as it were, weaken the great power of God. [Lamentations Rabbah I, 33 on Lam. 1:6]

The paradox in these statements is fully intended, and the term *"as it were"* has the full rank of a technical term in rabbinic theology, indicating the symbolic character of the statement it qualifies.

Source: Emil L. Fackenheim, *Quest for Past and Future: Essays in Jewish Theology* (Bloomington, Ind.: Indiana University Press, 1968) 36–39.

Nature of God

The Nature of God Is Unknowable

The Bible teaches us that God is infinite and invisible, and therefore forbids the making of any likeness of God. No synagogue or temple contains His picture. However, we cannot help thinking about God and forming mental images of Him. But we must always remember that these images are made by us and are therefore only human creations. Nothing we can possibly imagine can resemble God, who made us. It is impossible for us to picture God as He must be.

But because we are human, we always think of God in human terms. Because of our human limitations, our thought about God must always be anthropomorphic—that is, it must endow God with human characteristics He doesn't really have. Even when we think of God as a super-person we are still thinking of Him in human terms.

It is not enough to imagine God as a man. And it is not even enough to imagine Him as a super-man.

Can we then imagine Him as an impersonal force or substance which fills the whole universe? This is an attractive idea to scientifically minded people, because they are familiar with the forces of electricity, magnetism and gravity.

But there is something terribly inadequate about the idea of an impersonal God. If God is an impersonal force, how can we pray to Him? How can we say to Him, *Baruch Ata Adonai*, Praised be Thou, O Lord? And this is the beginning of nearly every Jewish blessing that we address to God.

Judaism is based on the relation between man and an understanding, loving, answering God. In every Jewish prayer God is addressed as "You" or "Thou," or referred to as "He." But you cannot use these "personal pronouns" for an impersonal force or substance. You may have gotten angry at a chair you knocked against and said, "You stupid chair!" as though the chair knocked against you. But you didn't really think the chair was stupid—or intelligent. And you knew that it couldn't listen to you—that it wasn't really a "you." After you calm down, you always feel a little silly for having talked that way to an inanimate object.

Prayer can only have meaning, then, if addressed to a God who is more than a force or substance. When we say "You" or "Thou" to God, we must be sure He understands and responds, or at least is able to understand and respond. Otherwise, prayer would be the same as talking to yourself. We may not know how God responds to our prayers, but that is not so terribly important. The most important thing in prayer is that God does or at least can respond to us. To pray to a force that cannot hear is no better than to worship idols or to speak to wood and stone.

We Talk to God and God Hears Us

Religion is the belief in a living connection between man and God. It is the way of life of men who feel the presence of God and communicate with Him through prayer. Prayer is a kind of intimate conversation or talking, and we can only talk meaningfully to other persons. So a religion based on prayer must picture God as a person. So again we find ourselves thinking of God as a person. And in a way, this is better.

God surely resembles a human person far more closely than He does an impersonal force. Such forces may be so vast as to have us wholly at their mercy. Still, there is a sense in which the weakest and humblest human person is superior to all the cosmic forces taken together. He can know truth, do good, feel beauty and religious awe, while they can do nothing of the kind. For he has a mind and they are mindless. But can we think of God as mindless? If we do, we think of God as less perfect even than we are! But He must surely exceed us infinitely in perfection.

So if we must choose between picturing God as an impersonal force or as a person, it is better to picture Him as a person. That picture too is inadequate, of course, for God is infinite, but is the best picture we can form.

Source: Emil L. Fackenheim, *Paths to Jewish Belief* (New York: Behrman House, 1961), 53–55.

The Great Problem of Evil

But if God made the world and everything in it, He must have made evil too. And this is our great problem.

In this chapter we are not going to solve the problem of evil. What we will see is whether the presence of evil rules out the goodness and the omnipotence of God.

Some religions try to hide from this terrible question by denying the existence of evil. But evil will not let itself be denied. We can always find it.

There is not a single human being who has not experienced evil at first hand; wherever we turn, we can find it. Who has never been sick? And who does not know a friend or relative who died? Even if we could imagine a person who had never spent an unhappy hour all his life, he would eventually have to die.

Besides these physical evils, we are all familiar with moral evil, which is still worse. Antisemitism and racial and religious hatreds are moral evils. And whenever we think of men like Hitler, we know how terrible moral evil can be.

Atheists and agnostics may suffer from evil and fight against it as much as anyone. But at least they have no difficulty in explaining it. For them, it is a natural part of the universe, since the universe, as they see it, was formed by chance and is without purpose. So they say, "Why shouldn't it be evil as well as good?"

But the theist faces the opposite problem, the big problem. If the universe is created by a good and all-powerful God, why does He create evil, or at least permit evil to exist? This is what the Book of Job is concerned with, and what the prophet Jeremiah meant when he cried out, "Wherefore doth the way of the wicked prosper?"

It seems natural to believe that a good God could create only a good world. Therefore many thoughtful people decided that God's power was limited because He had not made the world completely good. This idea explains evil—but it takes away from God that power that makes Him truly God. If he is powerless to avoid evil, then we cannot look to Him for help and comfort when evil befalls us. But it is just then that we need God most.

We need Him to give us the assurance that even in the midst of evil we are not forsaken by Him, that we are not the victims of blind chance.

If we tried to sum up, in a single word, the secret of Jewish strength through the ages, that word would be the Hebrew word *Davkah*—"nevertheless." In times of greatest tragedy the Jew adhered, "nevertheless," most stubbornly to his faith. But how could he have done so unless he had believed that God was both all-powerful and good—that God was in control of the evil things that happen to us as well as of the good?

Is Evil Always Bad?

We know we won't be able to solve the problem of evil in this book. After all, it has remained unsolved for thousands of years. But we hope to be able to make the problem a little clearer and perhaps come a little nearer to a solution.

In the first place, we must ask if what seems to be evil is always really evil.

Take the example of pain. Nobody denies that a toothache is an evil thing. But if our teeth didn't hurt when cavities formed, we wouldn't know when to go to the dentist, and the sickness might spread. In a toothache, as in most other physical aches, the pain seems to be a signal that something is wrong. And if we pay attention to the signal, we can restore ourselves to health. The signal hurts, but it has to hurt to make us take notice. Ultimately, this kind of pain is good.

But this leads us to another question: Why does God let us get sick? No matter how many brilliant discoveries medicine makes, sickness is always with us. And even if one day the doctors learn how to cure all diseases, they will never prevent old age and death. Everything that is born must one day die. Therefore our ultimate question is, Why does God allow death?

Is Death Really Evil?

Try to imagine a world in which no living thing ever dies. Plants and animals and people would keep coming into the world, but no one would ever leave. Soon the earth would be terribly crowded. The world would be as packed as the New York subway during rush hour.

There wouldn't be enough food to go around, and all our time would be spent in the search for something to eat. When we found it, we would have to fight to keep it. All the other people and animals would be trying to get it, too.

Of course, you can try to imagine a better world in which there would be enough food, drink and shelter for everyone. There would be no fighting, and we would all be friends. But no matter how big you made such a world, if living things multiplied endlessly, the day would come when the struggle for food and elbowroom would start all over again. Only a world that kept growing with the population could keep from getting crowded, and such a world is almost impossible to imagine.

You might then try to imagine a world without either birth or death. Then all creatures could live together in peace, harmony and plenty. But the catch is that life as we know it means being born and growing and dying. What makes living organisms different from inorganic matter is that they develop and mature.

This life, as we know it, finds beauty, purpose and adventure only by growing. And without growth and change there would be eternal boredom, which is closer to death than to life.

Coming back to the problem of evil, we can say that some apparent evils are a kind of detour to good. Physical pain is often a warning which helps us steer clear of sickness, and even death appears to be a necessary part of the world as we know it. True, we could imagine a world wholly without evil, and this would be entirely different from the one in which we live. In fact, the Bible does just this when forming the picture of the garden of Eden, in which there was neither pain nor death. But the Bible also tells us that we are no longer in the garden of Eden, and that the world is still under divine providence. Thus it believes that the physical evils of our world sometimes serve a good purpose which may be clear to mortal man.

And so our Jewish heritage tells us that we must first abolish physical evil whenever we can. When we cannot destroy it, we must fight it to the best of our ability. Second, if we can neither abolish nor control a particular evil, we should look for a hidden good in it. And finally, if we cannot imagine what good end some apparent evils serve, we must always remember that God works in ways we cannot fully understand.

How Bad Are Moral Evils?

So far we have only talked about physical evils, such as pain, disease and death. These are natural enemies of man that he always fights against. But now we must deal with the moral evils which man himself creates. These evils—including cruelty, oppression, hatred and prejudice—are terribly familiar to all of us. There can be no necessity for man to perpetrate these evils, yet man always has.

Moral evil is a much harder problem to solve than physical evil. We have seen that pain, and even death, may be necessary parts of life. But what good purpose can possibly be served by envy, cruelty, injustice, oppression, and callousness?

There is absolutely no good purpose that we can ever find in a moral evil. When we call it a moral evil we mean just that. We mean that in the sight of God it is wrong, that it is against God's will and against His laws which He laid down for men so that they could live together in peace.

If a man dies, that is a physical evil, and we can learn to accept it. But if a man deliberately kills another man for greed or envy, this is moral evil. It never has a good purpose and it is always wrong. It can never be a means to a hidden good. Moral evil is something that men do that is contrary to the will of God.

Why does an all-powerful and good God allow this?

We can't possibly believe that God *wants* us to do evil. The Torah specifically bids us do good rather than evil, and the prophets look forward to a messianic future when moral evil will have ceased. So moral evil can't be a means to a hidden good brought about by God.

Why God Permits Moral Evil

According to the Bible story, when God first made Adam and Eve, they were innocent, and guilty of no evil. Then why did God permit mankind to fall into such terrible ways when they left the Garden of Eden? Since then, men have done much harm to one another. Soon it may even be possible for men to destroy the entire earth, and we know that it is not inconceivable that they might actually do it.

The Book of Genesis *(Chapters 3 and 4)* states the position of Judaism: Man, not God, is responsible for moral evil. God created man, but He endowed him with a free will. This free will was one of God's greatest gifts to man, and God meant him to make good use of it. But God would not force man to be good. If He did, then man's will would not be free. So when Adam first chose evil instead of good, it was his action, not God's—and when man today continues to choose evil, it is still his action and not God's.

There is nothing here that contradicts the idea of divine omnipotence. God is able to prevent man from choosing evil, but He does not do this. Thus, man can create evil because God permits him to do so for a higher good. That higher good, according to Judaism, is human freedom.

Let us compare God to a teacher and mankind to His pupils. As you have probably observed, there are two basic methods of teaching. The first method is the way we are all taught our ABC's. The teacher makes us say the same things over and over again, until we remember them. This is a good method for teaching simple facts and dates. But it doesn't work when we are trying to master a difficult subject. Then a good teacher must use the second method, which is to make the pupil think for himself.

The first method is efficient and, if the teacher knows his subject, the pupil's answers are always right. But though he knows everything, he may understand nothing. His knowledge is like that of a calculating machine, and his mind is not free.

If the teacher wants to cultivate a free mind, he must use the second method. He must let the pupil find things out for himself. This method too is efficient, and it produces pupils who think for themselves. Of course, if you think for yourself, there is the danger you may often come up with the wrong answers, as Adam did.

This is a dilemma which your parents had to face, particularly when you were very young. Your parents wanted to protect you from errors and dangers that they understood but which you may not have known about. And, on the other hand, they wanted you to grow up self-reliant, and able to make your own decisions, including your own mistakes. Many of the things you learned, you learned by experience, and you will learn many other things in the same way. So part of the problem of being a parent is to find the right blend of freedom and authority in bringing up a child who is protected, but not over-protected; free, but not without discipline; yet able to make his own decisions.

When God created man, He faced the same problem. He could have willed man to be good. But he permitted man to do moral evil, because only in this way could He give man his noblest gift, the human freedom of choice. Man can be a criminal, but he can also be a saint.

You must not think for a moment that we have now solved the problem of evil. We have explained why evil exists, but we cannot accept it. For we must never forget that the evils of human history often assume monstrous proportions. And when we think of such things as concentration camps or slavery or atomic bombs, we cannot help wondering if it might not have been better, after all, had man been a dumb animal without free will. But then we remember the good and the great goodness that man can achieve. And we know that with all our courage we must fight against evil.

Why Must the Innocent Suffer?

We have explained why there is physical evil, and why God allows moral evil. But what is most difficult to understand—most difficult of all—is that the evil done by the wicked is too often suffered by the innocent. How can a just and merciful God permit innocent people to become the victims of murderers, tyrants and persecutors? How can He permit innocent children to die in a war?

This question, which is the real heart of the whole problem of evil, has tormented religious people from the times of Job and Jeremiah till today. Often this kind of evil is so terrible that we cannot imagine any kind of purpose behind it, human or divine. Why has God so often allowed some men to enslave others, depriving them of their God-given freedom? What reason can be found for mass slaughter of innocent people?

Questions such as these nobody can ever answer, and the Book of Job teaches us that it is wrong even to try. We can sympathize with the suffering of the innocent; but we can never understand it.

But the Book of Job also teaches us that, though men don't know and can't know the purpose of this kind of evil, it may yet have a purpose—known only to God. Job himself is the greatest example of all times of this saving trust. He was a good man who suffered the worst misfortunes a man can suffer, and neither he nor anyone else knew why. Yet Job said: "Even though He slay me yet will I trust in Him" *(Chapter 13, verse 15)*. It was this belief, it was this faith, it was this trust in the goodness of God, that allowed Job to survive.

Source: Emil L. Fackenheim, *Paths to Jewish Belief*
(New York: Behrman House, 1961), 62–71.

God in the Age of Auschwitz

"When ye are not My witnesses, I am, as it were not God." At Auschwitz Jews were not His witnesses—not because of infidelity but because they were murdered. The memory of those is holy who witnessed to Him even then, and this to their dying moment. But that memory may not be piously exploited, as a means of forgetting that few could be witnesses, that most were not witnesses but victims. Elie Wiesel writes about three Auschwitz prisoners about to be hanged for some trifling offense, with the rest of the camp forced to watch what was a regular ceremony. There was one unusual fact about this particular ceremonial murder: One of the three was a child. Just prior to the hanging Wiesel heard someone behind him ask, "Where is God? Where is He now?" As they tipped the chairs over and the three were strangled, he heard a voice within himself answer, "Where is He? Here He is—He is hanging on this gallows." Wiesel never says that God is dying: As a Jew he could not say it, and during a walk on New York's Fifth Avenue he once told me that He could not respect a God lacking power. The God that hangs with that boy on the Auschwitz gallows, however, does lack power. He lacks it absolutely, and this because He persists in His intimacy with His people. Is the price paid for that intimacy, then and there, not a *total* loss of the infinity? We have cited Roy Eckhardt as saying that the whole purpose of the program was to reduce Israel to excrement. That program included the God of Israel.

"When I praise God He is lovely; when I do not praise God He is, as it were, lovely in Himself." At Auschwitz many did praise God to the end. But again pious exploitation is illicit. Again it is forbidden to forget those who failed to give praise because they were not yet able to speak, or because they could speak no more—the babies thrown into the flames, and the *Muselmaenner* already dead in spirit before they dropped to the ground. Did God remain "lovely in Himself" at Auschwitz? But He could remain so only if He failed to hear the screams of the children, and the no less terrible silence of the *Muselmaenner.* Such a God might preserve His infinity, but would He not have lost every trace of His intimacy?

"The intimacy of the infinite": Jewish faith has held fast to this principle ever since the Creator of heaven and earth became the God also of Abraham. It has held fast to it against every temptation and through every vicissitude. Has the Holocaust, at long last, destroyed it? Has it fragmented the God of Israel, into an intimacy of absolute impotence, and an infinity of absolute indifference?

We do not know what the murdered millions thought of this question: Their thoughts were murdered with them. We do not even know the thoughts of those who tried to communicate them to us: Doubtless many put them on paper, but most of the papers were lost or destroyed.

Among the few that survived is a collection of Shabbat and festival discourses given between 1939 and 1942 by Rabbi Kalonymos Shapiro in the Warsaw Ghetto. The mere fact that he put them to paper *after* having delivered them, and not before, is proof that they were meant to be not lecture notes but a document for posterity. But there is further proof: Having carefully recorded and dated them, the rabbi buried his notes, together with a letter addressed to someone who, he hoped, would find them. The work, published as *Esh Kodesh* ("The Fire of Holiness") in Israel in 1960, is the last great document of Polish Hasidism.

Even in his earlier discourses the rabbi has little recourse to the conventional wisdom that once more Jews are punished for their sins: Unlike some among the pious today, he knew that the disaster was too vast. But until the summer of 1942 he still tried to cling to the view that vast but meaningless catastrophes had befallen the Jewish people before, that they had always survived them and always would. An entry dated November 27, 1942, however, reads as follows:

> Only until the end of 1942 was it the case that such sufferings were experienced before. However, as for the monstrous torments, the terrible and freakish deaths which the malevolent murderers invented against us, the house of Israel, from that time on—according to my knowledge of rabbinic literature and Jewish history in general, there has never been anything like them. May God have mercy and deliver us from their hands in the twinkling of an eye.

More than forty years later, when all is known, what Rabbi Shapiro said in 1942 is still widely denied. Though the worst was unknown to him then, the rabbi did not shrink from the terrible truth.

In a discourse delivered on March 14, 1942, Rabbi Shapiro expounds a Talmudic passage that tries to reconcile two biblical passages. In the first (Jer. 13:17) God weeps in secret because His flock is carried away captive, while the second reads as follows: "Honor and

majesty are before Him; strength and gladness are in His place"
(I Chron. 16:27). How can both be in His place, asks the Talmud,
weeping and gladness? One is in the outer chamber, the other is in the
inner, is the reply. But which is where? On this the Talmudic text is
ambiguous, and conventional piety would lead one to assume that
earthly sorrow, if reaching the place of God at all, reaches only the
outer chamber, that in the inner all sorrow is transcended by gladness. Rashi reverses the imagery; I do not know why but am aston-
ished. Rabbi Shapiro seizes on Rashi and goes beyond him. There is
gladness in the outer chamber: God hides. Does He hide in wrath
against, or punishment of, His people? God forbid that He should do
so at such a time! Does He hide for reasons unknown? God forbid
that He should, in this of all times, be a *deus absconditus!* Then why
does He hide? He hides His weeping in the inner chamber, for *just as
God is infinite so His pain is infinite, and this, were it to touch the world,
would destroy it.* Is it still possible for a Jew to break through to the
divine hiddenness, so as to share His pain? Rabbi Shapiro does not
seem sure.

In Israel today what once was a children's song has become akin to
a hymn: *am yisrael chai,* "the Jewish people lives." How is it possible to
sing this song-become-hymn, to sing it joyfully? How is it possible to
go on to the next line, *od avinu chai,* "our Father still lives"? *It is possible and actual because, even then, the bond between the divine intimacy and
the divine infinity was not completely broken; because God so loved the world
that He hid the infinity of His pain from it lest it be destroyed; and because
Rabbi Shapiro so loved God as to seek to penetrate to the inner chamber, so as
to share in the divine pain, even at the risk that in the sharing he would be
destroyed.*

Source: Emil L. Fackenheim, *What Is Judaism?*
(Syracuse, N.Y.: Syracuse University Press, 1999), 288–291.

· 7 ·

EUGENE B. BOROWITZ

b. 1924

Considered the "dean" of the American Jewish philosophers of our time, Eugene B. Borowitz was born in New York City in 1924. He is a product of both Lithuanian rationalism and Hungarian Chasidism, and all his life he has tried to bridge the gap between traditionalism and modernity, intellectualism and the demands of the heart. After his graduation from Ohio State University in 1942, where he studied philosophy, he entered the Hebrew Union College and was ordained as rabbi in 1948. He received his first doctorate (D.H.L.) from the same institution in 1952 and his second one in 1958 from the Teachers College at Columbia University (Ed.D.). He then served congregations in St. Louis, Missouri, and Port Washington, New York, and was a navy chaplain during the Korean War. In 1957 he became the National Director of Education for Reform Judaism at the Union of American Hebrew Congregations in New York City, where he edited its books and prepared curricula and educational material. In 1962 he became a member of the faculty of the Hebrew Union College–Jewish Institute of Religion, New York campus, where he presently is Sigmund L. Falk Distinguished Professor of Education and Jewish Religious Thought. He has received numerous honors, including from Lafayette and Graetz Colleges as well as Colgate University. The National Foundation for Jewish Culture has bestowed upon him its medal for Jewish Cultural Achievement for his scholarship in Jewish thought.

Borowitz also served as the president of the American Theological Society.

A prolific writer and a lecturer, Borowitz has authored numerous articles and essays and addressed many audiences, both academic and informal, throughout his career. The former editor of Sh'ma: A Journal of Jewish Responsibility, a magazine he founded in 1970 and edited for twenty-three years, Borowitz is known for his many books on modern Jewish thought. In 1997 a Festschrift entitled Jewish Spiritual Journeys (Behrman House) was published on the occasion of his seventieth birthday, edited by Lawrence A. Hoffman and Arnold J. Wolf.

In the 1950s, a group of rabbis, mostly non-Orthodox, established a theological movement that stressed the centrality of Israel's covenant with God. The intention of this group, which included Steven S. Schwarzchild and Arnold J. Wolf, was to try to formulate a theology that responded to the needs of the time without abandoning the rich Jewish tradition that stood behind them. They started with the assumption that the revelatory event at Mount Sinai, no matter how interpreted and understood, was fundamental to the identity of a contemporary Jew who had encountered a demanding God with certain requirements for all time. Eugene Borowitz was one of these Jewish intellectuals, and it was he who in 1961 coined the term "covenant theology" to identify the new quest.

For Borowitz, a Jewish understanding of God cannot be separated from our views of Torah and Israel. It is through our particularistic perspective that we understand and respond to the universal demands of God. Arguing for a dialectic approach, Borowitz maintains that for a modern Jew, the Torah that emerges from the relationship between God and Israel has to be more individualistic and pluralistic than Orthodoxy would permit, more particularistic than the rationalists would advocate, more theocentric than the humanists are willing to accept, and more ethnic than the personalist thinkers would allow.

Borowitz holds that reason has its limitations and cannot lead us to God. Just as people are more than rational beings, so is religion more than an intellectual exercise. Everything serious therefore has to start with an element of faith that our sense of values comes from a transcendental source that commands us, and that this source is God. This

God, being the ground of our values, is more than immanent, for an immanent God cannot command. Therefore, he adds, we must accept that God, who is a personal God endowed with intelligence, emotion, and will, is not an impersonal process or energy. When we respond to God, we do so not out of our own individual perspectives, but out of a sense of covenant that binds all Jews together. Therefore, when we confront the question of autonomy that is so central in our modern thinking, we cannot give priority to our needs without ignoring the ties to the covenant that have made us who we are. It is this balancing act that continues to be the greatest challenge of our time.

A Holistic Context

A simplistic distinction between philosophy and theology lauds the former for beginning without assumptions and asserting only what reason requires, hence yielding new truth. It belittles theology as proceeding from faith, containing its content in advance and using reason not to generate truth but to bolster its preconceptions. I would agree that systematic religious thought often exhibits a certain circularity so that its major conclusions echo its grounding premises. How could it be otherwise? When one seeks to probe the most fundamental issues of reality—as theology seeks to do—the results ought to tell us about what is utterly primary and, therefore, should remind us of the premises on which the work proceeded. Today, we see such methodological circularity not only in theology but in most other intellectual disciplines. The methods we employ for our investigations turn out to be decisive for our findings, which is one reason we argue so much over proper methodology. And, in theology as elsewhere, if too much dissonance arises between the results of our studies and the preliminary intuitions or other knowledge we brought to them, we will consider revising our method of procedure, even to the point of a Kuhnian "paradigm shift."

The generative vision I bring to this work is holistic, a vision of a Judaism in which God and the Jewish people stand in an ongoing relationship structured by Torah as record and mandate, and the background of whose practice is God's relationship with all humankind. I believe our tradition centrally transmitted this understanding to me though I have reinterpreted it in ways particularly appropriate to our time. From my postmodern perspective, universalism can be legitimated only from a particular base. . . . So I proceed more from my Judaism toward the culture than did the modernists, who thought society had the surer truth. Working this way, we cannot proceed with the doctrine of God alone—for it is universal—nor the doctrine of Israel alone—how will we transcend the particular?—nor from the doctrine of Torah alone—who authorizes and who lives it? We must intimately correlate God, Israel, and Torah, rendering our Jewish theology holistic.

Here, as elsewhere, holism means the field effect of each element— each major Jewish belief—on each other element and their combination with each other to constitute a patterned entity. Two formal considerations flow from this. First, only the interaction between beliefs, not some alleged discrete content of each of them, gives each notion its special character in a given belief structure. Second, the pattern of the relationships between the beliefs—that is, which are primary, which secondary, which held in dialectical tension—gives the theology or religion its distinctive spiritual cast. Let us explore these methodological guidelines before applying them. Since gaining greater understanding of our God supplies the foundation for all that follows, I use that topic as an example of the effects of employing a holistic approach to specific theological motifs.

Source: Eugene B. Borowitz, *Renewing the Covenant*
(Philadelphia: Jewish Publication Society, 1991), 55–56.

God: The Ground of Our Values

As against all secular interpretations of being a Jew, commitment to the Covenant insists that a relationship to God is primary to the life of the Jewish people and the individual Jew. The first concern of our apologetics, then, needs to be the recapture of the living reality of God in individual Jewish lives and thus in the Jewish community. The major target in this regard is the crypto-agnosticism with which most Jews have evaded this issue for a generation or more. In the face of contemporary nihilism, I am convinced, the old hope of serious values without commitment to God is increasingly untenable. The second concern of our apologetics is to help the individual Jew identify personally with the people of Israel. That is somewhat easier in our present time of high regard for ethnic difference and the search for one's own folk roots. Yet the primary model most people use in their thinking remains the Cartesian one of the detached self seeking truth without preconceptions or commitments. This has particular appeal to Jews since it immediately releases them from Jewish attachment in accord with the social pressures on any minority to assimilate to the majority.

Moreover, if there is no universalism then Jews lose whatever right they have to be part of general society. It thus becomes important to argue that all selfhood, though possessing universal dignity, is historically and particularly situated. Because of its uncommon worth, if for no more theological reason, Jews should will to make the fact of their being born into the Covenant the basis of their existence.

This construction of our situation as Jews overcomes what I take to be the fundamental difficulty with previous theories. Those which were God-centered were reductive of our peoplehood. Yet those which made the Jewish people central so reduced the role of God in our folk life that they effectively secularized us. Furthermore, if peoplehood is the primary factor in Jewish existence what remains of the autonomous self? When the Covenant relationship is the basis of our understanding of Judaism, self, God and people are all intimately and immediately bound up with one another. This does not settle how in any instance the self will respond to God or to the Jewish people, relationship being too fluid for that; yet Covenant sets up a constraining dialectic in place of liberal Jewish anarchy, universalism or secularism.

Covenant Theology: God—and Evil

As to God, a new humility emerges. Persons have relationships which are deeply significant for their lives without fully or nearly understanding those with whom they have such relationships. As against rationalist models, *concepts* of God (clear intellectual envisagements of God) are of subsidiary interest—if not positively discouraged. Making concepts primary tends to make thinking a substitute for relating and implies a thinking humanity is God's equal. In a relationship thought is not abandoned but it must not dominate. It serves as a critic of faith and as explicator of its consequent responsibilities. This is the safeguard against superstition and cultism. At the same time there is openness to many forms of envisaging God. That is, any concept of God which makes relationship possible (or is appropriate to living in Covenant) is acceptable here. This seems closer to the traditional model of *aggadic* thinking than liberal theologies have been as a result of their emphasis on an idea-of-God as the essence of Judaism. And it provides for continuing intellectual growth in our understanding of God, a characteristic of all of Jewish history, particularly in our time.

Specifically, I do not see that thinking in terms of Covenant prohibits after-the-fact explanations of the God with whom one stands in relation, as an impersonal principle, or a process which has certain person-like characteristics (e.g., the conservation of values.) For myself, however, the most appropriate model of thinking about the God with whom I stand in relation is a personal one. That is not to make a detached, metaphysical observation concerning the nature of God but only to say that, when I try to think about God, this is the best basis I have found for drawing an analogy to the God with whom I stand in Covenant. Persons being the most complex things in creation, I find this an intellectually reasonable procedure. Further, my experience of being involved with God being a personal one, this envisagement seems appropriate. Some additional explication of what it means to say that God is person-like might, I think, be given.

The notion of relationship provides an approach to living with the problem of evil and, specifically, the Holocaust. Relationships exist not only when there is immediate confirmation of them but also in its absence. To trust means that the relationship is considered still real though no evidence for it is immediately available. One also believes such confirmation will yet be forthcoming. The practice of Judaism, the life of Torah, is an effort to build a strong relationship with God. Within the context of such closeness, Jews have largely been able to live with the evils in the world.

There are special reasons why it has been difficult to continue this approach in modern times, most notably the loss of our belief in personal survival after death. The Holocaust raised our problems in this regard to an unprecedented level of tension, for some to the point of breaking the relationship with God. It remains stupefyingly inexplicable. Yet, perhaps to our surprise, it has not destroyed the Covenant. For most Jews the ties with the people of Israel are far stronger than anything we had anticipated. The absence of God during the Holocaust cannot be absolutized. It should not be used to deny that God has since been present in our lives as individuals and in that of the people of Israel (notably during the victory—rather than the new-Holocaust—of the Six-Day War of 1967).

The perception of a transcendent demand upon us to preserve the people of Israel, the affirmation of a transcendent ground of value in the face of contemporary nihilism, have led some minority of Jews to a restoration of our relationship with the other partner in the Covenant, God. The absence of God and the hurt we have felt are not intellectually explained. Yet it is possible, despite them, to continue the relationship. For the intellectually determined the most satisfactory way of dealing with this issue is to say that God's power is limited. For those to whom this raises more problems than it solves, there is acceptance without understanding. Both positions are compatible with relating to God in Covenant. I find myself constantly tempted to the former though mostly affirming the latter, a dialectic I find appropriate to affirming the Covenant.

Covenant Theology: The People of Israel

As to the people of Israel, a full-scale ethnicity is presumed here, with the understanding that this ethnicity has itself been transformed by the Covenant relationship. In the transition which the Jews have been undergoing since their entrance into modernity, our social situation has tended to lead us into accepting either religious or secular definitions of the Jews. A sense of the Covenant relationship discloses that such interpretations are reductionist of the multiple layers of Jewish existence. With Covenant primarily a social relationship, primary attention must be given to the effort to live it in social form. The people of Israel having its historic-religious roots in the Land of Israel, the creation there of a Jewish society faithful to the Covenant becomes the primary manifestation of fulfilling Jewish existence.

The Jewish society on the Land of Israel, however, is always subject to the special judgment implied in the unique task it has undertaken, building the Covenant-centered society. While it is theoretically conceivable that such a Jewish society might exist without the political apparatus of a state, in our time statehood is the indispensable instrument of social viability in the Land of Israel. The State of Israel, then, as state, is a means to the fulfillment of the Covenant and not its end. Therefore criticism of it from the vantage of the Covenant purposes of the Jewish people may be considered a Jewish duty.

At the same time, since Jews can fulfill the Covenant relationship anywhere, it becomes possible to validate Diaspora existence. Jewish life there, however, will be judged not only in terms of its faithfulness to God but in terms of its creation of the sense of community so fundamental to the Covenant.

Covenant Theology: Torah—Duty as Personal Responsibility

As to Torah, our sense of Jewish duty emerges from standing in relationship to God as part of the people of Israel. Various theories of revelation might be appropriate to accepting relationship as basic to our existence. For me, the personalist teaching of God's presence as commanding permits me to retain my autonomy while setting me in an individual bond with the people of Israel. I find it especially harmonious with Judaism seen as existence in relationship and my experience trying to live it. However, it should be understood, as against strictly antinomian interpretations of such revelation, that I take the Jewish self not to be atomistic, unattached and individual when standing in relationship with God, but as one of the Jewish people. Hence, responding to the Divine presence cannot only be a matter of what is commanded to me personally at this moment (or what was commanded to the people of Israel at some other time) but what is commanded to me as one whose individuality is not to be separated from my being one of the historic Jewish people.

I therefore come to God with a cultivated consciousness of my people's past and its recorded sense of what God demanded of it. But this apperception is not determinative for me. The immediate experience of relationship with God is. I respond to God autonomously. Yet I do so out of a situation, Covenant, in which Jews have been over the ages and which many other Jews now share. While my time and place, while my individuality introduce certain new factors in the determination of what my duties must now be, I am very much like other Jews of the past and today. Hence, what my reactions to God will be are likely to be very much like theirs. Such responses must also include my consciousness of being one of the people of Israel today. Perhaps, in a heuristic spirit, the Kantian corollary may be displaced to give us some guidance: respond to God with such a sense of your duty that you could will that anyone of the Covenant people, being in such a situation, would respond with a similar sense of duty.

This approach does not restore Jewish law to us or the sense of disciplined action connected with law. I do not see how we can do that theoretically or practically. Law and autonomy are incompatible as long as we are not in the Days of the Messiah. We modern Jews therefore stand in a post-*halachic* situation. That is one of the keystones of our liberalism. Yet it is important to overcome the anarchy which autonomous individualism can easily lead to in so pluralistic a time as ours. (Since our Covenant relationship to God is as a people, it implies some common way of Jewish living.)

The older liberal approach of containing autonomy only within the moral law will no longer do. Intellectually it is not clear that every rational person necessarily must be obligated to the sort of ethical responsibility Kant and his followers took for granted. Jewishly it is clear that limiting autonomy by ethics necessarily makes all the rest of Jewish observance instrumental and therefore unessential. Practically this results in an enforcement of the societal pressures to live as universalists and ignore Jewish particularity. If particularity is of greater concern to us today theologically, the old ethics-ritual split must be rejected as conflicting with our intuition of our present Jewish duty. When action is determined by living in the Covenant relationship, no radical distinction can be made between the source of our ethical duties and our more directly "spiritual" ones. They all come from one relationship and therefore cannot be played off hierarchically one against the other. Yet within this I would suggest that something of the old insight of the liberals as to the primary significance of ethics remains. Our sense of how we must respond *to other human beings* comes rather directly from the personal quality of the relationship between us and God, thereby highlighting the personhood of all people and our responsibility to them. Our sense of what we wish to express *to God* directly comes mainly from who we are and what we as a community feel we want to do in response to God's reality. The former is more closely related to our sense of God, the latter to our response to God—though each involves the other aspect. They are not two disparate realms of commandment but points on a spectrum of relational response.

Obligation Without External Discipline—and Hope

I do not see that law can arise from such a sense of commandment. Yet it is quite conceivable that something like Jewish "law" might yet surface in our community. One referent of the decision-making process by the individual is the community. We could reach a time when a sufficient number of Jews trying to live in Covenant would do things in sufficiently similar a way that their custom could become significant for them and for other Jews to take into account in determining their Jewish duty. In some stable American-Jewish situation, one might then create, on a Covenantally autonomous basis, a communally influential pattern of living. This would be less than law but it would be more than folkways for the primary response would be to God. The creation of such patterns would be the modern substitute for *halachah* and it is thus possible to suggest that we live in a pre-*"halachic"* time, in this Covenantal sense of the term.

The goal for the individual Jew and the Jewish community remains what it has always been, to create lives of such everyday sanctity and societies of such holiness that God's kingdom will become fact among us. Restoring personalism to Judaism makes personal piety again possible, even mandatory. Ethics can no longer displace God's presence in our lives. Our recent tradition had so little confidence in human power that it waited with virtual resignation for God to bring the Messiah. The liberals had such unbounded confidence in human power that they as good as dispensed with God in trusting to themselves and in humankind's progressive enlightenment to bring the Messianic Age. A sense of Covenant makes messianism a partnership between God and the people of Israel. It requires patience on our part as well as continued religious action; yet it gives us courage despite our failures and hope despite an infinite task which laughs at our successes, for God too is bringing the Messiah.

Source: Eugene B. Borowitz, *Choices in Modern Jewish Thought* (New York: Behrman House, 1983), 282–289. (See also *CCAR Yearbook*, 1977, 160–170.)

On Evil

The Instrumental Explanation of Evil

Jewish teachers have gone on to argue that much evil that cannot be explained as our just punishment can be understood as God's means of refining our character. Go back in memory to what you consider the most important lessons of your life. Are they generally associated with your triumphs or with your bitter disappointments? For most of us, suffering has been the greatest teacher—we grew as we overcame a difficult family situation, a troubled love, a business reversal, a physical ailment, a soul-searing insight into our deep-seated frailty. Through such suffering, people often develop what is richest in their humanity.

Evil may be said to have another good use. It sets off and distinguishes what is good. Sickness points up the glory of health. Death reminds us to appreciate life and therefore utilize our time for worthy ends.

That is a somewhat harsh doctrine, so many talmudic teachers noted that God sends the cures along with the diseases. The rabbis' favorite therapy was God's gift of the Torah. If we devoted ourselves to it, they argued, we could overcome our Evil Urge. As the Yiddish proverb puts it, God smites us with one hand but blesses us with the other. In this kind of explanation, though the evil remains, it is justified by the good it eventually creates.

Alas, not every evil has beneficial consequences. Have you not seen people broken by tragedy and those around them never recover from what took place? Death often takes a loved one with such a wrench that we cannot then help ourselves or anyone else. Suffering seems as likely to diminish as to enrich us. A powerful God could surely find less hurtful ways of instructing us. Certainly we cannot explain the Holocaust in this fashion. True, it taught us never again to underestimate the human capacity to do evil or to dream that democracy and culture could alone bring the Messiah. God surely could have taught us that at far less a price than the Holocaust.

Can Evil Be Properly Compensated For?

When the argument about the usefulness of evil leaves many cases unexplained some thinkers then argue that God makes up for the evil by later sending us some great good. Thus it has been argued that the Holocaust, not the many years of Zionist effort, made it possible to establish the State of Israel. The greatest suffering the Jewish people has ever endured was followed by the greatest accomplishment in 2,000 years.

This effort to justify the Holocaust has been indignantly rejected by thinkers such as Elie Wiesel and Emil Fackenheim. Could anything make up for what Hitler did to us? Had someone said, "You may have a Jewish state if you will sacrifice 6,000,000 of your people in foul butchery," we would have spurned so vile and debased an offer. To suggest that a God with all power would need a Holocaust to create a state for us seems ridiculous. The Bible says God has twice made possible a Jewish state without anything approaching such tragedy. The extraordinary accomplishments of the State of Israel and the greater glories we hope it will yet achieve cannot begin to wipe out the enormity of the Holocaust.

The traditional version of this compensation argument was that the sufferings of this world are made up to us after death in the rewards of the life of the world-to-come. . . . If we firmly believed that God would reward us personally in our afterlife for the injustices of this world, I think that most of us would accept with little murmuring the troubles that confront us. That was the attitude of most Jews until relatively recent times. Evil disturbs us so greatly these days because most of us find it difficult, if not impossible, to believe in life-after-death. With no other existence to look forward to, suffering is a terrible experience in the only life we shall have. Could we overcome our disbelief, there are surely some cases, most notably the Holocaust, where the suffering was foul to the point of being irremediable. Even if we could accept the idea of this world as a vestibule to eternal, utter blissfulness, a God who is good should not create so evil a world as ours can be.

The Radical Modern Answer, a "Limited" God

Our consideration of God's goodness has given us no fully satisfying answer. That leaves only one further area in which to find a solution to our problem, the premise of God's complete power.

Some Jewish thinkers believe we must break with the Bible's faith in God in one respect. Their seemingly revolutionary proposal is that God is not omnipotent. Though God is good, there is real evil in the world because, for all the power God has, God is not strong enough to overcome it. God may be the greatest thing that is but even God is not perfect. God is limited in power.

Henry Slonimsky took a dynamic approach to God's finitude. He argued that we should think of God, like the best things we know, as growing. God will be "complete" and evil will disappear only in the Days of the Messiah. Then as Zechariah said, "The Lord shall be one and His name shall be one." (13:9) For Slonimsky, Mordecai Kaplan, and other thinkers who argue that God is limited (or finite), our responsibility for human destiny has now been greatly enhanced. Not God but humankind is the major agent that will bring the Messianic Age. Indeed our moral action becomes the means by which God achieves perfection, that is, victory in the world.

We can find hints of such a solution to the problem of evil in the classic Jewish sources. The Bible's strong appreciation of human freedom implies a limitation on God's omnipotence. The Talmud and Midrash often describe God as weeping over the destruction God brought on Israel, as if God did not have the power to do otherwise. One rabbi can picture God giving this self-description, "Woe to the king who in his youth succeeded but in his old age failed." (Lam. R., Intro. 24) Other rabbis suggest that human sin or virtue, as it were, detracts from or adds to the divine power.

The Jewish philosophers, from Saadya Gaon on (he wrote about 920 C.E.), also limited God by saying that God could not do the illogical. That has consequences for the problem of evil. Logically to have a world requires having matter. Things made of matter are necessarily perishable. God, despite having the power to do everything that logically can be done, could not create a world without decay and death. Thus, traditional thinkers acknowledge that there are limits even to what God can do. Today we should have even less timidity in fearing any diminution of the divine might for we know how much people can do to create the good. Affirming that God is good but acknowledging that God is not infinitely capable of effectuating goodness explains why there is real evil in the world.

If God's Power Is Limited, No Wonder There Are Nazis

I believe this theory is the only intellectually satisfying answer which has been given to the Holocaust. God "allowed" it because God didn't have the power to stop it. God was not strong enough yet to prevent this torment and we did not use our moral capacity to compensate for God's weakness.

The same may be said of other evils we face. God is doing all the good God now can do. We cannot blame our suffering on a God who, like ourselves, does not have all power. Psychologically we can easily understand that people in previous ages imputed to God the omnipotence they wished they had. This new theological position claims to be a more mature understanding of God. It calls us to give up our infantile fantasies of All-Powerfulness and replace these with the reality of human moral growth and cooperative effort.

Hans Jonas takes this approach when he describes god as the originating, ordering reality of our universe that now affects it only as an attracting moral goal. Harold Schulweis will make no claims about reality but suggests that we use the word God to describe what is most godly in human beings and thus is affirmed as worthy of our devotion. In these and other versions, most notably Harold Kushner's statement, many modern Jews have found the concept of a limited God deeply satisfying as they have faced life and history.

For all my appreciation of its intellectual sophistication and its Jewish roots, I do not finally find the doctrine of a limited God acceptable. I keep wondering who is in control of the evils over which God does not have power. I am so taken with the Jewish notion of the oneness of God that I do not see the universe as having more than one orderer—and that means I do not envision the awesome power of evil as excepted from the one cosmic order which God rules.

I also question whether a limited, so to speak, a weak God is worthy of worship and daily trust. Can such a God grow strong enough, as our tradition puts it, to bring the Days of the Messiah? After the Holocaust particularly, I find it difficult to trust human goodness sufficiently to say that we will supply what God lacks. A limited God plus falliable human beings hardly seem worthy of my deep-seated Jewish faith that goodness will triumph in history and God's Kingdom will one day be established upon earth.

There is, however, much in this new theory for Jews like me to admire. It does not evade the harsh reality of evil. It does not mitigate the goodness of God. And it calls upon us to utilize our moral powers to the fullest. I find this position far more realistic and admirable than sensational announcements that, after the Holocaust, Jews can no longer believe in God at all. But for all its attractiveness, I find this theory creates more religious problems than it solves.

The Surprising Death of the Old Agnosticism

Paradoxically enough, instead of driving us to atheism, the discussion of the Holocaust in the 1970s has prodded Jews to faith. Most Jews would have dispensed with God after the Holocaust if they thought such disbelief would leave their commitment to personal value and social quality undiminished. Until recently, we took it for granted that one need not believe in God to be dedicated to human betterment. One could count on people's innate goodness, particularly as channeled by modern education, popular culture, and a society concerned with human welfare, to produce high character. Most liberal Jews could afford to be agnostic because we were certain of the spiritual quality of Western civilization. We could welcome the death-of-God because we had a substitute source of value.

Gradually it has dawned on us that our old optimism about human nature and culture is no longer warranted. What has died for us is not the God of Jewish tradition. We hadn't believed in that God for some time. Rather we have lost our faith in our old real "God," humankind. The Holocaust and the subsequent social traumas we now associate with our disillusionment smashed our idol. Reason was applied to mass murder; esthetics lightened the off-duty hours of murder camp guards; European humanism could accommodate itself to nazism; and the best of the democrats knew what was happening and kept quiet. Since the mid-1960s we have increasingly lost our faith in the moral purity of America. No institution in our society, no branch of our government, no human relationship we trusted in has shown itself free of the possibility of corruption if it has not already demonstrated it. And we ourselves have turned out to be the biggest question mark of all. Is there anything left to be disillusioned about? Our world seems empty.

Then shall we say that the Holocaust merely reflects reality? That it demonstrates that there is no meaning to the universe? With no values inherent in it, naturally some people will arise from time to time to exemplify its ultimate nothingness.

Such theorizing "explains" the Holocaust but does so with a horrifying consequence. It says that it is quite natural to be a Nazi, that, in a neutral universe, one has as much right to be a Nazi as to be a Jew! That goes too far in disbelief for many of us. We may believe little, but we believe more than that the world is empty of values. The Holocaust has taught us we have at least this faith: we must never obliterate the utter qualitative distinction between the killers and the killed.

Denying the Void, Reaffirming the One

I am convinced that as some Jews gained this consciousness a new spiritual self-awareness arose in the Jewish soul. It is one thing to say that I believe nothing—but, of course, I take it for granted that all reasonable, sophisticated people can be counted on to be humane. It is quite another thing to run into people who, because they believe there are no ultimate standards of human decency, feel they may do as they please. Today no-faith quickly leads to no-limits. Compared to such a nihilistic stance our previous affirmation that we believed nothing was an exaggeration. We may not believe much but we do not, most of us, believe nothing. In affirming a cosmic standard of difference between Nazis and Jews—and the everyday commitment to righteousness which is its corollary—we respond to a reality that far transcends us or our culture, both of which it brings into judgment and calls to responsibility. On some such inner path as this, many in our time have found their way, tentatively but strongly, to what our ancestors called God. Ironically, the Holocaust, which led us to protest against God, has by its exemplification of absolute evil brought us back to a perception of the primacy of absolute good.

That leaves us in a most difficult situation, the familiar one of Jewish tradition. The evil is real and God is good. If there is ultimate unity in the universe then it must mean, somehow, that God is the embracing power of all that is, including the evil. "I form the light and create the darkness. I make peace and create evil. I am *Adonai* who does all these things." (Isaiah 45:7) We are back where we began, with three beliefs which separately seem compelling but which will not fit together logically.

What Holds a Paradoxical Faith Together?

Most Jews in the past have held that faith although it was not logical. Despite their pride in thinking for themselves and their high appreciation of intellect, they did so, I would guess, out of piety. They trusted God even though they did not understand God. Perhaps we may say that when life and logic pushed them to the limit they trusted their intuition of God more than they trusted their reasoning about God.

This piety was reflected in their way of life. The commandments encouraged them to be aware of what the good God was doing for them in everything that happened to them. Each portion of Good, each unusual sight, each event, from seeking a king to excreting one's bodily wastes, was an occasion for blessing God. Jewish life overflowed the acknowledgments of God's beneficence.

When one lives with such a pervasive sense of God's gifts, the evils we endure generally appear few and small compared to all we have been given. To almost all of us, God has been overwhelmingly good and generous. Because of that perspective, most Jews have been able to say with the pious Job, "Shall we then take all the good God gives us and not accept some evil?" (2:10)

Even during the Holocaust, Eliezer Berkovits reminds us, the believers often retained their faith in God. The dramatic proclamations of God dying in the Holocaust were made mainly not by people who were in the death camps but, much later, by those who had been safe, miles away. We should not be surprised at such unbelief as occurred, Berkovits contends, for it is the common modern condition. What should evoke our religious admiration to the point of awe, he insists, is the faith that did not waver even in Auschwitz. In such lives the sacred manifested itself in hell. We owe these saints the benefit of such belief as we can muster. In faith, not in disbelief, we perpetuate their spirit.

Many modern Jews find they cannot easily respond to life in a spirit of awe and gratitude, particularly when they think of those whose lives are filled with unmerited suffering. Others recognize that God's goodness to us and our responding duty to do the good we can must ground everything else we know and do. Thus, like generations of Jews before them, they first affirm God's goodness and then try to overcome or accept evil.

How shall we conclude this chapter when we cannot end the discussion? I turn to a message which was found after the Holocaust on a cellar wall in Cologne: "I believe in the sun even when it is not shining. I believe in love even when I do not feel it. I believe in God even when He is silent."

Source: Eugene B. Borowitz, Liberal Judaism
(New York: UAHC Press, 1984), 200–207.

On Prayer

In June 1953, two months before I was to be discharged from the Navy, an event occurred which had a substantial impact on my life of prayer. Being stationed not too far from Wilmington, Delaware, I had agreed to cover for Rabbi Herbert Drooz—an older friend from student days—while he was at that year's CCAR meeting. One day I received a call from the congregation asking me to conduct a funeral. On my way there my car was broadsided by an uninsured ne'er-do-well, the brakes of whose borrowed car had failed at a stop sign. The next day, after slipping in the wading pool where our baby was frolicking, I discovered that my urine was the color of *Kiddush* wine. I felt fine otherwise, but the Navy doctors insisted on hospitalization and various unpleasant tests, and, though the color of my urine cleared, they refused for complicated medical reasons to release me. They treated my immediate problem, an apparent tear in the kidney wall, with an injunction to drink as much water as I could. Of the odd ramifications of that series of events all that is relevant here is what it taught me about my body and prayer.

One day in the hospital after the umpteenth trip to "the head," it occurred to me that the Rabbis had a blessing after a visit to the toilet. Of course, as a properly modern sophisticate I had learned to pooh-pooh such backward, uncouth elements of traditional Jewish practice. (How barbaric it seemed to me a few years earlier, at Steve Schwarzschild's mother's funeral, that the mourners and others actually threw a shoveful of dirt on her coffin—a practice I have since often tenderly participated in.) Now I needed to do something about my primal sense of thankfulness every time my kidneys and bladder worked well. So overcoming my smugness, I first studied and then began to recite the *asher yatzar* prayer. "We call you 'Blessed,' *Adonai* our God, ruler of the universe, who fashioned human beings wisely and created in them many orifices and hollows, all the while knowing most clearly that if one of them should gape or seal, it would be impossible to stand before You. You are 'Blessed,' *Adonai*, curer of people, worker of wonders." That articulated just what I wanted to say; no, it said more than I would have thought to say and said it better.

I gained three things from that experience. First, I began to appreciate the aura of a life punctuated with *berakhot*. That started me learning how to respond to various situations with blessings, traditional ones or ones I make up to fit an occasion. To this day I have not been able to implement that insight fully, though I still work at it fitfully. Second, I learned to appreciate the Rabbis as spiritual guides. Though I had already completed my first doctorate, I, like many a Reform Jew, felt quite superior to the rabbinic tradition and many of its quaint ideas about how to serve God. But while I had thought I could transcend my body, the Rabbis, despite their smelly privies, knew the excretory system was too important a part of being human to be barred from our relationship with God. From then on, I began to trust them and their "way" more and to approach their behests as spiritual disciplines which might enrich my impoverished inner life.

The third consequence deserves special attention because it was so unexpected that it remains something of a continuing surprise to me. I have come to recite many prayers during the day but I do so quietly, to myself. I do not find my old friends and neighbors, though respectful of my practice, comfortable when I do so on anything but formal occasions. Of all the prayers I say, none surfaces more constantly in my consciousness than the *asher yatzar*. It is, I suppose, my closest equivalent to a *mantra*. Perhaps that may be attributed to the innumerable times I have said it (a sum increased as the years have passed with their predictable prostate problems and the diuretic I take for mild hypertension). It took on fresh urgency a decade or so ago when one of my coronary arteries closed down. Whatever the external impetus, I see that comparatively lengthy blessing as a demanding, ongoing spiritual exercise in accepting my contingency—my mortality, to be blunt. It speaks to me of life's fragility, of its utter dependence on countless teeny apertures not closing up or gaping wide. To a physically vigorous, intellectually adventurous, act-oriented, busybody like me, that is a daunting message. More, the prayer says that this dependency is perfectly clear to God. And I, thankful that this arrangement still works for me now call God "Blessed" or "Praiseworthy" or whatever one makes of that overloaded symbolic package, *"Barukh."* I do not bridle that the closing words praise God as "healing all flesh" for I do not see that as a nonsensical denial that some illnesses are chronic, others destructive, and many fatal, but as a celebration of the curative role of excretion. There is something quite "wondrous" about this work, as the final words of the *berakhah* put it and so I, leaving the toilet, sanctify this otherwise profane moment through words the Rabbis taught me. Surely it took a rare combination of realism suffused with spiritual genius to direct us to love God afresh each time our organs have produced our urine or feces, and I am its grateful beneficiary.

The lessons of this *berakhah* have had a de-Copernican effect on my soul and my theologizing. Modernity put humans at the center of the universe so we are shocked, even outraged, when it does not conform to our desires. But each *berakhah* teaches that the world is ordered more as God would have it than as I would. Whatever else the classic metaphors for God—"Creator" and "Ruler"—imply, they convey the primal Jewish intuition that God (whether limited or infinite) is the most basic reality in the universe. I may be very significant but the world is God's, not mine. It is humbling that, having devoted myself to reestablishing God's reality in non-Orthodox Judaism, I only came to understand this in "my flesh," as the Psalmist says, by praying the blessing for going to the toilet.

Knowing the world is more God's than mine, I have come to realize that "Anything can happen to anybody at any time," and I have made that scary sense of contingency a part of my piety. Though I still regularly get nauseous when confronting another tragedy, I try to face it determined to do what I can to overcome it and, when that is unlikely, with something like the classic Jewish mood of acceptance. Paradoxically, not evading what may transpire has intensified my appreciation of the present and all the goodness God continually showers on me.

Let me extend this theme a bit. Understanding the universe as God-centered and not me-centered has helped me also appreciate God's greatness. There is something awesome about this world and every revelation of the subatomic or the astrophysical realm only heightens my appreciation of the mystery. We need to remember that the Awesome One behind this cosmos is the One before Whom we stand in prayer. So the first act of prayer is to put aside our private agendas and "set God before us." That, I take it, is the reason for the lavish praise of God at the start of our services. The Rabbis, knowing most people then, as now, come to services preoccupied with themselves, have tried to help us transcend it. Knowing we could never praise God's greatness sufficiently (so the *Nishmat kol chai*), rabbinic realism limits what we say and modern Judaisms have tended to be even more concise.

A paradox accompanies this awareness of transcendence for it is just I, excretory animal that I am, who know this. More, the Present One, the Fundament of all being, is involved with me personally. How incredible it is that nothings such as me may often easily be intimate with God, no less. That special closeness gives humans unalienable honor, dignity, challenge—and in this extraordinary "far-near" experience, Jewish prayer came to be and flourished.

I have introduced these not uncommon themes of Jewish piety to explain two additional aspects of my prayer life. I have not been able seriously to argue with God. That has often been suggested in our day as a way of responding to intractable evil. It has some basis in Jewish tradition (though I think it a lot less prominent than do many of its protagonists). In this respect I share something of Abraham Heschel's piety, one which, because it begins with an acknowledgment of God's incomparable greatness, transforms what one finds one can say to God. This seems so miserably passive that I have tried to do what others suggested and indict God for some evil I should think God would find intolerable. I have not been able to carry it through for my strong sense of God's greatness arises to preempt that. I have also come before God and sought merely to ask some penetrating questions about a given outrage, yet I have been met only by implacable silence. None of this has ever made me feel rejected or spurned by God simply for coming to God and honestly trying to pour out my heart. I know God is great enough to pay attention to me in any momentary distress I bring to my prayer. Sometimes, coming to pray, I realize that what has been riling me is really too silly to pray about. (Is that one meaning of God answering before we ask?) But I also am confident that if a matter, even a small one, is important enough to me to bring to God—who else will fully listen and understand me?—then God, the incomparable Transcendent, "cares for" me enough to "want" me to do just that.

What part of these reflections was directly the outcome of my saying the *asher yatzar* blessing and how much I have come to connect with it over the years, I do not know. I have found that the nodes around which my spirituality have turned, like this *berakhah*, arise on their own and can decline in power in an equally incomprehensible way. Thus I would never have imagined that the *asher yatzar* blessing would have such resonance for me over all these years. Yet the *Birkhot Hashachar*, which for a long time powerfully suffused my getting up and dressed each morning, now has mostly lost its special magic. Therefore, despite all the benefit one gains from the discipline one's spiritual guide teaches, one must finally also discover and go on one's own soul-enlarging way.

I have made prayer a habitual but uncompulsive life discipline that has its own urgency. This involved me in one aspect of the famous clash between the contrasting Jewish prayer ideas *keva*—fixity—and *kavanah.* People generally think of it as a fight between spontaneity and rule. Identifying prayer with an uninhibited upsurge of the soul, they bridle at praying fixed prayers at fixed times, as Jewish tradition prescribes. But should the value of prayer be measured by human experience alone? If God is real, indeed the Ultimate Reality, then we ought to pay attention to God, regularly. And if our relationship to God is not merely a private creation but one that derives from and contributes to the Jewish people's ongoing Covenant with God, then our prayer life should largely be structured by the wisdom of corporate Jewish spirituality. Giving new weight to *keva* does not resolve the *keva-kavanah* problem but only restores *kavanah* to its place as the strived-for, difficult, prayer idea. Let me quickly add that I have rarely been at ease with the balance I have achieved.

But I have been theologizing when I mean to tell my story. As prayer became a regular part of my life I learned to do it better. The words and phrases began to flow more easily from page to eye to heart to mouth to God. I came to love the services and the wisdom behind them, at least as they refracted in shifting ways through my soul. I came to trust their language more and resist the difficult phrases less, though some passages have never opened up to me and I now doubt that they ever will. I also discovered a new talent. Though I was never a good memorizer, I gradually, almost naturally, became able to recite long passages of the liturgy by heart. That too made it easier for me to find the service an incomparable means of learning-expressing-renewing old Jewish pieties.

Source: Eugene B. Borowitz, in *Jewish Spiritual Journeys*, ed. Lawrence A. Hoffman and Arnold J. Wolf (New York: Behrman House, 1997), 182–187.

RICHARD L. RUBENSTEIN

b. 1924

Richard L. Rubenstein, president emeritus, distinguished professor of religion, and director of the Center for Holocaust and Genocide Studies at the University of Bridgeport, is a widely known historian of religion and theologian whose writings deal primarily with the impact of the Holocaust and the interplay between Judaism and Christianity. Rubinstein was born in New York City in 1924 to parents who were first-generation Americans of Eastern European background. He did not receive a formal Jewish education but was sent to an elite public school for high performers.

Even though Rubenstein did not grow up with a strong religious identity, he was interested in matters of the spirit and, at one point, even considered becoming a Unitarian minister. However, the evolving Nazi threat in Germany came to have a profound impact on him. He soon realized that he could not give up his Jewishness and therefore began to view Judaism purely as a religion, yet one devoid of Zionism. Having come into contact with Rabbi Nathan Perlman of Temple Emanuel in New York City, he applied and was accepted at the Hebrew Union College in Cincinnati but left in the spring of 1945. During this period he had also enrolled at the University of Cincinnati in 1942, from which he graduated with a B.A. in 1946. Later on, Rabbi Wolf Kelman, of the Jewish Theological Seminary, encouraged him to pursue his studies there, and he was ordained in

1952. He received his master's degree from Harvard Divinity School in 1955 and his Ph.D. in the history and philosophy of religion from Harvard University's Graduate School of Arts and Sciences in 1960. From 1958 to 1970, he served as director of the B'nai B'rith Hillel Foundation and adjunct professor of humanities at the University of Pittsburgh. In 1970, he moved to the Florida State University and remained there for more than twenty years as professor of religion. In 1977, Rubenstein was named "Distinguished Professor of the Year." From 1995 to 1999, he served as president of the University of Bridgeport.

It has been said that Rubenstein's book After Auschwitz *(1966; 1992) has initiated a major theological debate on the meaning of the Holocaust in modern times. In addition, he has published* Power Struggle *(1974), an autobiographical confession, where he discusses many aspects of his theological development.*

More than traditional text studies, it is the awareness of the Holocaust that had a decisive influence on Rubenstein's religious thinking. He came to realize that the most important issue for the modern Jew is to find an identity compatible with the reality of Jews living in a Christian world. World War II, according to Rubenstein, has shaped Jews as no other historical event in recent times.

Theologically, Rubenstein takes exception to the traditional view that Jews are the suffering servants of God. He rejects the old explanations about Jewish suffering—among others, that it is the result of our sins, that God is testing our loyalties, that Israel is a compensation for the losses during the Holocaust, or that we will receive our rewards in the world-to-come. He believes that no such God is worth worshiping. We are living, he notes, during the times of the "death of God." However, Rubenstein insists, God does not die. The ideology of the "death of God" is more of a cultural reaction than a theological stance. Rubenstein, in spite of those who wish to place him among the nihilists of the "God is dead" theology, is not an atheist. For him, the old Father-God of traditional monotheism may be dead, but God is still a reality. Following Paul Tillich, Rubenstein argues that God can be viewed as the ground of being, but also as the focus of ultimate concern. Like many other mystics, he too considers God as a being with no limit and no end. God is, in his view, "Holy Nothingness." God is so rich that

God is not "Nothing," but simply represents "superfluity of being"
(After Auschwitz, p. 298).

Justice at Auschwitz

Those of us who prefer to wait until the arrival of the glorious messianic future before taking it into account have yet to find a credible
alternative to the dilemma mentioned above: we can either affirm the
innocence of Israel or the justice of God but not both. If the innocence
of Israel at Auschwitz is affirmed, whatever God may be, He/She is
not distinctively and uniquely the sovereign Lord of covenant and
election. If one wishes to avoid any suggestion, however remote, that
at Auschwitz Israel was with justice the object of divine punishment,
one must reject any view of God to which such an idea can plausibly
be ascribed. Although not an atheist, I did assert that "we live in the
time of the death of God." The meaning of that statement is summarized in the following passage:

> No man can really say that God is dead. How can we know that?
> Nevertheless, I am compelled to say that we live in the time of the
> "death of God." *This is more a statement about man and his culture
> than about God.* The death of God is a cultural fact. . . . Buber felt
> this. He spoke of the eclipse of God. I can understand his reluc-
> tance to use the more explicitly Christian terminology. I am com-
> pelled to use it because of my conviction that the time which
> Nietzsche's madman said was too far off has come upon us. There
> is no way around Nietzsche. Had I lived in another time or anoth-
> er culture, I might have found some other vocabulary to express my
> meanings. . . . When I say we live in the time of the death of God,
> I mean that the thread uniting God and man, heaven and earth, has
> been broken. We stand in a cold, silent, unfeeling cosmos, unaided
> by any purposeful power beyond our own resources. After
> Auschwitz, what else can a Jew say about God? (Italics added.)
> [Rubenstein, *After Auschwitz*, 1st ed. (New York: Bobbs-Merrill,
> 1966), pp. 151–52.]

Today, I no longer regard the cosmos as "cold, silent, unfeeling." At
the very least, insofar as man is a part of the cosmos and is capable of

love as well as hate, the cosmos cannot be said to be entirely cold and silent. My earlier position can be seen as the expression of an assimilated Jew who had returned to Judaism because of the *Shoah*, devoted a quarter of a century to Jewish learning, committed himself to the defense of his people and its inherited religious traditions, and then found that he could no longer believe in the God of that tradition or in the crucial doctrines of covenant and election *without regarding Auschwitz as divine punishment*. Given both the loss of faith this entailed and the events of World War II which brought it about, my view of the divine-human relationship was, at the time, understandably bleak. Today, I would balance the elements of creation and love in the cosmos more evenly with those of destruction and hate than was possible in 1966. What has not changed is a view of God quite different from the biblical and rabbinic mainstream, as well as an unqualified rejection of the notion that the Jews are in any sense a people either chosen or rejected by God. On the contrary, Jews are a people like any other whose religion and culture were shaped so as to make it possible for them to cope with their very distinctive history and location among the peoples of the world. Put differently, I have consistently rejected the idea that the existence of the Jewish people has any superordinate significance whatsoever.

Rejection of the biblical God and the doctrine of the Chosen People was a step of extraordinary seriousness for a rabbi and Jewish theologian. These views understandably elicited the question whether anyone who accepted such views had any reason for remaining Jewish. For millennia the literature and the liturgy of normative Judaism have been saturated with the idea that God had chosen Israel and that the obligation to obey the laws and traditions of the Torah was divinely legitimated. Why, it was asked, should anyone keep the Sabbath, circumcise male offspring, marry within the Jewish community, or obey the dietary laws if the God of the Bible did not exist?

From one point of view there is considerable merit to these questions. From another there is none. Without a credible affirmation of the existence of the God of the prophets and the rabbis, Judaism becomes a matter of personal preference, a preference some may be tempted to abandon. Immediately after World War II the argument was advanced that racism prevents any escape from Jewish identity. In reality, intermarriage provides an escape route for the grandchildren, if not the children, of mixed marriages. Those who desire to abandon Jewish identity can begin the process even if they cannot complete it. Nevertheless, a knowledge of the negative consequences of unbelief does nothing to enhance the credibility of a belief system.

In the 1960s and 1970s, I responded to the question of whether Judaism can be maintained without traditional faith by arguing that the demise of theological legitimations did not entail an end to the psychological or sociological functions fulfilled by Judaism. Save for the case of conversion, entrance into Judaism is a matter of birth rather than choice. Even conversion to Christianity does not entirely cancel Jewish identity. There is an ethnic component to Jewish identity, intensified by recent historical experience, which persists long after the loss of faith. Every Jew says of the *Shoah*, "It happened to us." For non-Jews, the *Shoah* is something that happened to another people. Just as no Armenian can ever forget the Armenian genocide during World War I, Holocaust consciousness has become an ineradicable component of the Jewish psyche. Religion is more than a system of beliefs; it is also a system of shared rituals, customs, and historical memories by which members of a community cope with or celebrate the moments of crisis in their own lives and the life of their inherited community.

Religion is not so much dependent upon belief as upon practices related to the life cycle and a sense of shared historical experience. No matter how tenuous the faith of average Jews or Christians, they normally find their inherited tradition the most suitable vehicle for consecrating such events as the birth of a child or a marriage. In a crisis such as the death of a parent or child, the need to turn to the rituals of an inherited tradition is even more urgent.

Although in 1966 I had become convinced that there is a void where once God's presence had been experienced, it did not follow that Judaism had lost its meaning or power or that a theistic God of covenant and election is necessary for Jewish religious life, at least for the first and second post-Holocaust generations. Dietrich Bonhoeffer had written that our problem is how to speak of God in an age of no religion. I saw the problem as how to speak of religion in an age of the absence of God. Judaism can be understood as the way Jews share the decisive times and crises of life through the traditions of their inherited community. The need for that sharing is not diminished in the time of the death of God. If it is no longer possible to believe in the God who has the power to annul the tragedies of existence, the need religiously to share that existence remains. In place of the biblical image of God as transcending the world he has created, I came to believe that a view of God which gives priority to immanence may be more credible in our era. . . .

In mysticism and dialectic pantheism I found a view of God I could affirm after Auschwitz. Ironically, by virtue of His, or perhaps Its, all-encompassing nature, the God who is the Source and Ground of Being is as much a God-who-acts-in-history as the transcendent Creator God of the Bible, as any reader of Hegel would understand. What the dialectical-mystical interpretation excludes is the distinctive ascription of guilt to Israel and the category of divinely inflicted punishment to the Holocaust. *Creative destruction and even destruction transcending the categories of good and evil may be inherent in the life of Divinity, but not punitive destruction.*

The dialectical-mystical elements in my thinking have endured; the pagan element has proven less durable. In the aftermath of the *Shoah*, with the rebirth of an independent Jewish state for the first time since the Judeo-Roman Wars, there was a certain plausibility to the argument that a people that is at home lives a very different kind of life than a band of wandering strangers. During the whole period of their wanderings, the vast majority of the Jewish people prayed that they might be restored to the land of their origin. Wherever they dwelt in the Diaspora their lives and their safety were wholly dependent upon the tolerance of others. During the two thousand years of the Diaspora, Jewish history always had a goal, namely, return to the homeland. That goal was given expression in prayers originally written in the aftermath of the Judeo-Roman Wars and still recited three times daily in the traditional liturgy.

With his nineteenth-century Reform Jewish ideas about the "mission of Israel," Maybaum rejected the spirit of these prayers, arguing that the Diaspora was "progress" and an integral part of God's plan for humanity. By contrast, I identified the Diaspora as a form of communal alienation and further argued that the Holocaust had demonstrated how hazardous it is for any people to be utterly dependent for their security on a majority that regarded them as religiously and culturally alien, especially in times of acute political, social, or economic stress.

If Jewish history had as its goal return to the land of Israel, Jewish history appeared to have, at least in principle, come to an end when that goal was attained in 1948 with the establishment of the State of Israel. It may have made sense to worship a God of history while Jewish history was unfulfilled, that is, while Jews still envisioned the goal of their history as a return to Israel in the distant future. The Jewish situation changed radically when that goal appeared to have been attained. Not only did Jewish history seem to have come to an end, but after Auschwitz the God of History was no longer credible. In the biblical period, whenever the people had felt at home in the land, they turned to the earth gods of Canaan. Biblical monotheism had effectively defeated polytheism but not necessarily nature paganism. After Auschwitz and the return to Israel, the God of Nature, or more precisely the God who manifests Himself, so to speak, in and through nature was the God to whom the Jews would turn in place of the God of History, especially in Israel. This is consistent with the view that religion is essentially the way we share the crisis moments, that is, the turning points, of both the life cycle and the calendar. My rejection of the biblical God of History led me to a modified form of nature paganism.

Source: Richard L. Rubenstein, *After Auschwitz: History, Theology and Contemporary Judaism*, 2nd ed. (Baltimore: Johns Hopkins University Press, 1992), 171–175.

After the Death of Father-God

There is the problem of the God after the death of God. The focus of the synagogue upon the decisive events and seasons of life gives us a clue to the meaning of God in our times. At one level, it is certainly possible to understand God as the primal ground of being out of which we arise and to which we return. I believe such a God is inescapable in the time of the death of God. The God who is the ground of being is not the transcendent, theistic God of Jewish patriarchal monotheism. Though many still believe in that God, they do so ignoring the questions of God and human freedom and God and human evil. For those who face these issues, the Father-God is a dead God. Even the existentialist leap of faith cannot resurrect this dead God after Auschwitz.

Nevertheless, after the death of the Father-God, God remains the central reality against which all partial realities can be measured. I should like to suggest that God can be understood meaningfully not only as ground of being but also as the *focus of ultimate concern*. As such He is not the old theistic Father-God. Nor is He Reconstructionism's "power that makes for salvation in the world." He is the infinite measure against which we can see our own limited finite lives in proper perspective. Before God it is difficult for us to elevate the trivial to the central in our lives. The old Hebraic understanding of the meaning of idolatry is important for an understanding of the meaning of God as the focus of ultimate concern. Idolatry is the confusion of a limited aspect of things with the ground of the totality. This is not the occasion to catalogue the idolatries of our time. That task has been well done by others. If an awareness of God as the ground of being does nothing more than enable us to refrain from endowing a partial and limited concern with the dignity and status reserved for what is of ultimate concern, it will have served the most important of all tasks. The ancient Hebrews regarded idolatry as a special form of enslavement. Nothing in our contemporary idolatries makes them less enslaving than their archaic counterparts. God can truly make us free.

We live in a culture which tends to stress what we can do rather than what we can become. A few examples will suffice to illustrate the encouragements to idolatry and self-deception with which our culture abounds. We are forever encouraged to deny the passing of time in our overestimation of the importance of both being and looking young. One of our greatest needs is to acknowledge our temporality and mortality without illusion. By so doing, we are not defeated by time. We establish the precondition of our *human* mastery over it. As the focus of ultimate concern the timeless God reflects our seriousness before our human temporality.

Another decisive contemporary need is to learn how to dwell within our own bodies. That is not so easy as it may seem. Fewer capacities come harder to Americans than the capacity to dwell within their

own bodies with grace, dignity, and gratification. We become carica-
tures of our human potentialities when we fail to acquire this wisdom.
By coming to terms with the biological nature of the timetable of life,
we experience an enormous liberation yet develop the capacity for
equally great renunciations when necessary. In the presence of God as
the focus of ultimate concern, we need no deceptive myths of an
immortal soul. We are finite. He is eternal. We shall perish. He
remains ever the same. Before Him we confront our human nakedness
with truth and honesty. In this venture, our voyage of self-discovery is
enormously aided by Judaism's insistence through ritual and tradition
on our continuing awareness of where we are in the biological
timetable of life. The ancient Gnostics disparaged the God of the Jews
as the God of this world. They asserted that all of His commandments
were concerned with the conduct of life in this perishing cosmos.
They correctly understood Judaism in their hostility. Unlike
Gnoticism, Judaism refused to turn the regard of Jews away from the
only life they will ever know, the life of the flesh in this world. God as
the focus of ultimate concern challenges us to be the only persons we
realistically can be, our authentic, finite selves in all of the radical inse-
curity and potentiality the life of mortal man affords.

One cannot pray to such a God in the hope of achieving an I-Thou
relationship. Such a God is not a person over against man. If God is
the ground of being, He will not be found in the meeting of I and
Thou but in self-discovery. That self-discovery is not necessarily
introspective. The whole area of interpersonal relations is the matrix
in which meaningful and insightful self-discovery can occur. Nor can
the I-Thou relation between God and man be achieved through
prayer. This does not do away with worship. It sets worship in proper
perspective. Even Buber admits, in his discussion of the eclipse of
God, the contemporary failure of personal prayer. While prayer as
address and dialogue has ceased to be meaningful, the burden of this
paper has been to suggest some of the ways in which religious ritual
has retained its significance. Ritual is more important today than
prayer save as prayer is interwoven with ritual. Our prayers can no
longer be attempts at dialogue with a personal God. They become
aspirations shared in depth by the religious community. As aspiration
there is hardly a prayer in the liturgy of Judaism which has lost its

meaning or its power. Worship is the sharing of ultimate concern by the community before God, the focus of ultimate concern.

Paradoxically God as ground does everything and nothing. He does nothing in that He is not the motive or active power which brings us to personal self-discovery or to the community of shared experience. Yet He does everything because He shatters and makes transparent the patent unreality of every false and inauthentic standard. God, as the ultimate measure of human truth and human potentiality, calls upon each man to face both the limitations and the opportunities of his finite predicament without disguise, illusion or hope.

There remains the question of whether the religion of God as the source and ground of being, the God after the death of God, is truly a religion. Can there be a religion without a belief in a theistic, creator God? Pagan religions have never celebrated such a God. As I have suggested elsewhere, in the time of the death of God a mystical paganism which utilizes the historic forms of Jewish religion offers the most promising approach to religion in our times.

Judaism no longer insists on the affirmation of a special creed. It has long since ceased rejecting its communicants because of ritual neglect. This does not mean that Judaism had descended to the level of a tribal herd bound together by a primitive and externally enforced we-feeling. No religion can exist without a meaningful form of sacrifice. Though it is not always apparent, contemporary Judaism does have its form of sacrifice. It is just as meaningful and in some ways more demanding than the older forms. This form of sacrifice is peculiarly appropriate to our new understanding of the meaning of God and the power of symbols in contemporary Judaism. Our sacrifice is not philanthropy. Nor is it the renunciation of personal autonomy which some traditions demand. The sacrifice required of those who would participate in the community of ultimate concern is perhaps one of the most difficult in today's society. It is the sacrifice of that pride through which we see our individual roles, status, attainments, or sophistications as in any way more significant than that of any other human being with regard to the decisive events in the timetable of life. We share in the synagogue what we experience in common from birth to death. These events which we celebrate with the traditions of Judaism are the really decisive events. We can succeed in the world of affairs yet, humanly speaking, be wretched failures in the business of life if we fail to put a goodly measure of energy and attention on the decisive events. The traditions and ritual of the synagogue call upon us for this kind of concentration. That is why the sacrifice of pride in attainments which are not central to the business of life is so essential. I do not wish to disparage worldly attainment or professional competence; I want to suggest the wisdom of Judaism in insisting upon its essential emptiness when the business of life is ignored. Each of us before God as the focus of ultimate concern must regard the real challenges of his personal existence as essentially the same as those of any other human being. Whether we are intellectuals, merchants or laborers, we are born in the same way, need the same love, are capable of the same evil and will die the same death. Concentration on what is of genuine significance in the business of life is the contemporary form of the renunciation of idolatry.

The religious symbol and the God to whom the religious symbol points were never more meaningful than they are today. It is no accident that the twentieth century is characterized by theological excitement and renewal. Our myths and rituals have been stripped of their historic covering. No man can seriously pretend that the literal meanings given to our traditions before our time retain much authority today. Happily, in losing some of the old meanings we have also lost some of the old fears.

God stands before us no longer as the final censor but as the final reality before which and in terms of which all partial realities are to be measured.

The last paradox is that in the time of the death of God we have begun a voyage of discovery wherein we may, hopefully, find the true God.

Source: Richard L. Rubenstein, "The Symbols of Judaism and the Death of God," in *God in the Teachings of Conservative Judaism*, ed. Seymour Siegel and Elliot Gertel (New York: Rabbinical Assembly, 1985), 231–234.

God: Holy Nothingness

In place of a biblical image of a transcendent Creator God, an understanding of God which gives priority to the indwelling immanence of the Divine may be more credible in our era. Where God is thought of as predominantly immanent in the cosmos, the cosmos in all of its temporal and spatial multiplicity is understood as the manifestation of the single unified and unifying, self-unfolding, self-realizing Divine Source, Ground, Spirit, or Absolute. The names proliferate because we are attempting to speak of that which cannot be spoken of or even named, as mystics in every age have understood. Moreover, the cosmos itself is understood to be capable of vitality, feeling, thought, and reflection, at least in its human manifestation. As the Ground of Being and of all beings, Divinity can be understood as the ground of feeling, thought, and reflection. Human thought and feeling are thus expressions of divine thought and feeling, albeit in a dialectical form.

In the West emphasis on Divine immanence has been expressed in mysticism and nature paganism. If one finds the transcendent God of covenant and election lacking in credibility, some form of mysticism can become a meaningful religious path. Another alternative would be some form of Buddhist enlightenment. The Buddhist view reminds us that religion and theism are not necessarily identical.

To choose immanence, mysticism, nature paganism, or the quest for Buddhist enlightenment is to choose a synthesizing *system of continuity* over a dichotomizing *system of gaps*, such as faith in the radically transcendent Creator God of biblical religion, who bestows a covenant upon Israel for His own utterly inscrutable reasons. Deutero-Isaiah expressed the unbridgeable gap between God and humanity in biblical religion when, speaking on God's behalf, he declared: "For my thoughts are not your thoughts, neither are your ways my ways, saith the Lord. For as the heavens are higher than the earth, so are my ways higher than your ways, and my thoughts than your thoughts" (Isa. 55:8, 9). The inherent logic of the gap between the radically transcendent biblical God and humanity finally comes to full expression in Calvinism's doctrine of double predestination, which holds that, at the very first instant of creation, the sovereign, omnipotent Creator predestined all of humanity to either election or damnation and that no human institution, action, or petition can have the slightest effect on a person's eternal destiny. Cut off completely from any influence upon the Creator, men and women can only glorify from afar the one who may be the Author of their eternal damnation.

In philosophy and philosophical theology, choice of a system of continuity reflects a preference for Hegel over Kant, Buber, Kierkegaard, and Barth, who stress the infinite qualitative difference between God and humanity. Among the systems of continuity we find mystical and pantheistic traditions that affirm the ultimate, though not necessarily the immediate, unity of God, humanity, and the cosmos.

To understand the preference for a system of continuities over a system of gaps, it is helpful to recall Hegel's reformulation of Kant's distinction of *Verstand* (understanding) and *Vernunft* (Reason). Hegel defined the activity of *Verstand* as the analytic definition, organization, and fixation of seemingly discrete phenomena—the hard, concrete, matter-of-fact events and the existents of the empirical world. He characterized *Verstand* as "isolated reflection," insisting that it could only apprehend a partial, limited aspect of reality. *Verstand* can analyze discrete phenomena; it cannot understand the ultimate interconnectedness of all things. For Hegel, the finite, empirical existence apprehended by *Verstand* is not what it appears to be; it is actually the self-manifestation of the single, universal, infinite Ground and Source. Were this not so, reality would be divided into mutually repellent sectors that are incomprehensible to and incommunicable with each other. Beyond the empirical world of dichotomous oppositions and discrete, isolated entities, there is, according to Hegel, a unified totality that can be rationally and conceptually grasped. Thus, belief in the transcendent God of History, who relates to the empirical world as subject to object, is an expression of the partial and incomplete perspectives of *Verstand*. Although not false, the finite perspectives of *Verstand* are partial. They constitute developmental stages within the all-encompassing activity of speculative Reason or *Vernunft*, which is the Absolute or *Geist* for philosophy and Divinity for religious mysticism. It is, however, important to note that Hegel does not deny the reality of concrete entities. He holds that the Absolute exists only in and through its finite constituents: *"Ohne Welt ist Gott nicht Gott."* (Without the world God is not God.) [G. W. F. Hegel, *Begriff der Religion* (Leipzig: Felix Meiner, 1928), p. 148]

Stressing the indispensable nature of each and every finite entity and event in the world as an expression of the underlying Absolute, Hegel attempted to comprehend all of nature and history as expres-

sions of the self-positing, self-unfolding rational totality. Instead of
seeing God, man, and nature as separate and distinct, which would be
the perspective of *Verstand* without *Vernunft*, Hegel insisted upon the
"identity of identity and nonidentity" of phenomena. He sought to
demonstrate that humanity in its historical development and nature in
its evolution are expressions of the same ultimate Reality. I would add,
absent the unifying comprehension of *Vernunft*, *Verstand* is the mode
of comprehension appropriate to a system of gaps; *Vernunft* is the
mode appropriate to a system of continuities. Above all, *in a system of
continuities there are no mystifying leaps of faith.*

Among Hegel's successors, the Hegelian left denied the divinity of the
Absolute. However, in a theological reading of Hegel, the divinity of the
Absolute or *Geist* is affirmed. According to Hegel, religion can only anticipate the reconciliation and ultimate union in the Absolute of nature,
humanity, and Divinity in the *subjectivity of faith and feeling.* Like the guru,
Hegel regarded religion as the fence for the young tree yet to take deep
roots. For Hegel, philosophy alone can attain the reconciliation in its
comprehensiveness through the activity of *Vernunft*. Indeed, for Hegel
true philosophy is nothing less than the Absolute's fully rational, self-
transparent knowledge, so to speak, of Himself *in se ipsum.* Hegel's
thought expresses a perennial human aspiration, namely, humanity's
desire to understand its place in the order of things with lucidity and without self-deception or bad faith. That same aspiration can be seen in dialectical mysticism and Buddhism. For me, however, true self-knowledge
and the insights of dialectical mysticism attain the reconciliation.

Although deeply indebted to Hegel, I believe that his quest for a
system of continuity can best be achieved by turning to another name
for the Unnameable. I also believe there is a conception of God which
does not falsify or mystify reality, as a system of gaps must inevitably
do, and which remains meaningful after the death of the transcendent
God of History. It is a very old conception of God with deep roots in
both Western and oriental mysticism. In this conception, God is spoken of as the Holy Nothingness, *das Heilige Nichts,* and, in Kabbalah,
as the *En-Sof,* that which is without limit or end. God, thus designated, is regarded as the Ground and Source of all existence. To speak,
admittedly in adequate language, of God as the "Nothingness" is not
to suggest that God is a void; on the contrary, the Holy Nothingness

is a *plenum* so rich that all existence derives therefrom. God as the "Nothing" is not absence of being, but a superfluity of being.

Use of the term *Nothingness* to point to the divine reality rests in part on an ancient observation that all definition of finite phenomena involves negation. In order to know something, we must know what it is not. The infinite God, the Ground of all that is finite, cannot be defined, for there is nothing outside of God, so to speak. In no sense is God a definite thing or a being bearing any resemblance to the finite beings of the empirical world. *The infinite God is not a thing; the infinite God is no-thing.* At times, the mystics spoke of God in similar terms as the *Urgrund*, the primordial ground, the dark unnameable Abyss out of which the empirical world has come.

At first glance, these ideas may appear to be little more than word play. Nevertheless, thinkers in all of the major religious traditions express themselves in almost identical images when they attempt to communicate their conception of God. Those who believe that God is the Source or Ground of Being usually believe that discrete human identity is coterminous with the life of the physical organism. Death may be entrance into eternal life, the perfect life of God, and it may also end pain, craving, and suffering, but it involves the dissolution of individual identity. Thus, in speaking of God, we also formulate a judgment concerning the nature and limitations of human existence.

Perhaps the best available metaphor for the conception of God as the Holy Nothingness is that God is the ocean and we the waves. Each wave has its moment when it is identifiable as a somewhat separate entity. Nevertheless, no wave is entirely distinct from the ocean, which is its substantial ground. Furthermore, because the waves are surface manifestations of the ocean, our knowledge of the ocean is largely dependent upon the way the ocean manifests itself in the waves.

The waves are caught in contradictory tendencies. They are the resultants of forces that allow them their moment of separate existence. At the same time, they are wholly within the grasp of greater tendencies that merge them into the oceanic ground from which they are momentarily distinguished without ever really separating from it. Similarly, all living beings seek to maintain their individual identities, yet there is absolutely nothing in them which does not derive from their originating ground. This is especially evident in the most intimate of all human activities, sexual love. Nothing could be more private or personally involving. Nevertheless, at no time is the individual more in the grip of universal forces than in the act of love. Only to the extent that we are capable of letting these overwhelming forces flow through us of their own accord is the act of love complete and fulfilling. Only those who have the capacity to lose themselves totally in love can achieve this fulfillment.

The same reality is evident in the life cycle. Because our bodies are the most deeply personal aspects of our beings, identity begins as body identity and the earliest development of the ego is as body ego. Our fundamental projects are related to the care and nurture of our bodies. Yet, nothing is more universal and impersonal than the shape, demands, and sexual character of our bodies. We do not choose to be born; we do not choose our gender; we do not choose the course of our life from its beginnings in cellular existence through physical maturity, old age, and finally, death. We simply repeat, each in our own way, a destiny common to billions of other human beings. Admittedly, we possess a measure of freedom to work out our distinctive path in the world. Nevertheless, both the individual and the race are the consequence of vast, nonpersonal forces that transcend yet permeate their every activity and project.

Questions about the relation between discrete phenomena and universals are not new. In the Middle Ages there was an important controversy in the field of logic and metaphysics concerning the nature of universals. One group of thinkers, the nominalists, regarded the universal as the *name* given to a class of objects that resemble each other. Another, the realists, argued that the universal has an extra-mental *reality* of its own which is exemplified in each of its particulars. We call their system realism. The controversy has been one of the most abiding and complicated in the history of philosophy. Since the time of Luther, there has been a tendency, especially in countries strongly influenced by Protestantism, to regard individuals as real and universals as merely names, although Hegel obviously regarded the Absolute, the Universal *par excellence*, as the one and only true reality. The social and cultural expression of the triumph of nominalism is reflected in the growth of individualism and the stress on private rather than corporate experience. In the political order nominalism was paralleled by the rise of the middle class and its preference for free, unregulated competition and commerce.

Although realism has largely gone out of fashion, its insight into the extent to which our personal and social lives are pervaded by universal, nonpersonal forces suggests that the doctrine contains important insights. In addition to human biology, the interdependent character of the human world renders questionable the idea that individuals are the primary reality and universals but a name. Apart from the complex processes of production in a high-technology civilization, within the privacy of the home each family participates in the contemporary revival of corporate experience. Through the communications media, especially satellite TV, we share identical sensory experiences and even thought contents. When the war with Iraq commenced, even Secretary of Defense Dick Cheney and General Colin Powell admitted that they got much of their initial information from watching the same media source as the general public, CNN. Marshall McLuhan has suggested that one effect of the communications revolution has been to bring about the return of tribalized man, whose experiences are more corporate, sensuous, involving, and universal than those of the inner-directed, isolated individualist described by David Reisman in *The Lonely Crowd*. Like archaic men and women, their contemporary descendants tend largely to share common media images and thought with their peers. In the age of the global village, it is more apparent than ever that we are not isolated, private individuals, but exemplification of the all-embracing, universal totality we name as God.

Although we can press the metaphor of the ocean and the waves too far, it is very useful and very old. The Sumerians saw all things, even the gods, arising out of the divine oceanic substratum of existence, which they called Nammu. Nammu was the archaic sea goddess in Sumerian mythology. She was not the goddess of the sea, but the *goddess who is the sea*. Hegel used a similar metaphor at the conclusion of the *Phenomenology* when, after describing the full scope of human activity and passion in the course of history, he concluded that all of the apparent diversity of both natural existence and the drama of history was the self-positing expression of one underlying, ever-changing, and yet ever-constant divine Spirit or *Geist*. He adapted a line from the poet Schiller to summarize this paradox of divine unity and diversity:

nur
> *aus dem Kelche dieses Geisterreiches*
> *schäumt ihm seine Unendlichkeit.*

Only
> *The chalice of this realm of spirits*
> *Foams forth to God His own Infinitude.*
[Hegel, *Phäenomenolgie des Geistes*, p. 565
(*Phenomenology of Spirit*, trans. A. V. Miller, p. 493)]

When God is imaged as the Holy Nothingness, the divine Ground of Being is thought of as beyond all finite categories. It may be the source and precondition of the empirical world, but it is not identical with that world. There is an inescapable tension between God's essential unity and his process of self-manifestation in the multiplicity of the empirical world. Hegel caught something of the tension between God as ground, on the one hand, and the natural and historical world as epiphenomenal manifestation of the divine Reality, on the other. This is reflected in the preface to the *Phenomenology*:

> *Per se* the divine life is no doubt undisturbed identity and oneness with itself, which finds no serious obstacle in otherness and estrangement. . . . But this "per se" is abstract generality. . . . The truth is whole. The whole, however, is merely the essential nature reaching its completeness through the process of its own development. [G. W. F. Hegel, *The Phenomenology of Mind*, trans. J. B. Baillie (London: George Allen and Unwin, 1931), p. 81.]

> Spirit alone is reality. It is the inner being of the world, that which essentially is, and is *per se*; it assumes objective, determinate form and enters into relations with itself—it is externality (otherness) and exists for self; yet, in this determinateness, and in its otherness, it is still one with itself—it is self-contained and self-complete, in itself and for itself at once. [Ibid., p. 86.]

Hegel used a very complicated philosophical language to express the idea of the fundamental identity of God as unchanging unity and of the world as the divine means of expressing itself in diversity. I prefer the more graphic metaphor of the ocean and waves, but the fundamental conception underlying both images is much the same.

Hegel called the divine Ground *Geist* or Spirit; Paul Tillich used the term "Ground of Being." There is nothing original about my use of Holy Nothingness. All three designations reflect a preference for metaphors rooted in maternity rather than paternity. Words like "ground," "source," and "abyss" have maternal overtones. This is also true of the image of God as the oceanic substratum. In the symbolism of both religion and dreams, ocean often represents womb. In the evolution of the species, the womb is a surrogate ocean providing mammals with a replica of their original aquatic habitat through which they can reproduce in an encompassing fluid and recapitulate the evolution of the race in their own ontogenesis.

Terms like "ground" and "source" stand in contrast to the terms used for the biblical God of History. The biblical God is known as a supreme king, a father, a creator, a judge, a maker. When He creates the world, He does so as do males, producing something external to Himself. He remains essentially outside of and judges the creative processes He has initiated. As ground and source, God creates as does a mother, in and through her own very substance. As ground of being, God participates in all the joys and sorrows of the drama of creation, which is, at the same time, the deepest expression of the divine life. God's unchanging unitary life and that of the cosmos's ever-changing, dynamic multiplicity ultimately reflect a single unitary reality.

Source: Richard L. Rubenstein, *After Auschwitz: History, Theology and Contemporary Judaism*, 2nd ed. (Baltimore: Johns Hopkins University Press, 1992), 295–302.

· 9 ·

ZALMAN SCHACHTER-SHALOMI

b. 1924

The Jewish Renewal movement is grounded in the prophetic and mystical traditions of Judaism. One of its most significant figures is Rabbi Zalman Schachter-Shalomi (or, as he is known to most people, Reb Zalman). His hyphenated name is a result of his combining his original name Schachter (meaning "slaughterer") with the name Shalomi ("my peace") in an attempt to achieve spiritual balance. He was born in Poland in 1924 but raised in Vienna. His father, a Belzer Chasid, made sure that he had both a religious and secular education. At the age of sixteen, Schachter, fleeing from the advance of the Nazis, went to Belgium and spent some time in an internment camp in Vichy, France. Finally, he arrived in New York City in 1941 by way of West Africa and the West Indies. Once in the United States, Schachter enrolled in the Lubavitcher Yeshiva in Brooklyn and was ordained as rabbi in 1947. He served various congregations, and in the mid-1950s, feeling the need for a wider education, he entered Boston University, earning a master's degree in psychology of religion. He continued his studies at the Hebrew Union College, where he received his doctorate (D.H.L.) in 1956.

Reb Zalman's academic career began at the University of Manitoba, Canada, where he was professor of religion and head of the Department of Near Eastern and Judaic Studies. In 1975, he moved to Temple University in Philadelphia as professor of religion and Jewish mysticism and psychology of religion. In 1962 he founded B'nai Or Religious Fellowship, which in 1978 changed its name to P'nai Or, and later became ALEPH: Alliance for Jewish Renewal. Through this national organization, Schachter-Shalomi offered new programs in Judaism with the purpose of enhancing the inner life of its members. In the late 1960s, Reb Zalman was instrumental in the creation of Havurat Shalom in Boston, the first Chavurah in America. The Chavurah began as a study group but also focused on religious practices within a mutually supportive environment. In 1989, he founded the Spiritual Eldering Institute in Philadelphia. He is presently the chair of the Naropa Institute in Boulder, Colorado, and rabbinic chair of ALEPH.

In his younger years, Reb Zalman was very much influenced by Jewish mysticism as practiced and taught by the Lubavitcher movement. Following his teachers, Schachter-Shalomi too argued that it is possible to experience the Infinite right here and now, and that beneath the surface of the outside world one can discover the Divine. He has not deviated from this basic premise, even though he has gone on to develop an interest in the universality of the spiritual truths found in many other religions, engaging in study and dialogue with Catholic monks, Native American elders, Buddhist teachers, Sufi masters, and humanistic psychologists in an attempt to learn from them.

In his writings, Reb Zalman has argued that Judaism, like many other Western religions, is suffering from a lack of religious experiences. He therefore gives primacy to ritual over doctrine, the yearning for God over theological discourse. Religion, he notes, must be felt in the heart. For him, God is internalized in our souls and consciousness, and projected externally into the cosmos. No one knows what God is like. Each person needs to decide this matter on his or her own. This God is not the Old Man in the Sky or the Great Mother giving birth to the universe but is an immanent Presence that nourishes all of us and draws us to Him/Her. God's will is manifested through the natural laws of the universe. We can best approach God not through our intellect alone but through our emotions and experiences. Therefore instead of praying, Schachter-Shalomi maintains, we need to "daven," an art form of worship where we present ourselves with proper concentration and the totality of thoughts and feelings. In Reb Zalman's words, it is "living the liturgical life in the presence of God" (Paradigm Shift, p. 162).

Praying in God's Corner

"If you talk to God, you're religious; if He answers, you're psychotic." Such is the inconsistent view of the rationalist. In this wry sentence, the psychiatrist Thomas S. Szasz neatly sums up the ironic dilemma of trying to understand the *spiritual* by approaching it on the level of the intellect. Such an effort may provide philosophical entertainment, but it does not get you any closer to God, or help your conversation with Him. You can take so long analyzing your relationship to God that you never get around to the experience; you can spend too much time talking *about* Him and not enough talking *to* Him.

When approaching God, it is best to turn down your mental computer and switch over to your feelings, even if this makes you self-conscious or appear foolish in your own eyes. For talking to God, the intellect is not the best tool; God is not interested in your I.Q., nor is He impressed by your learning. The heartfelt prayers of an unlearned person are worth more than the perfunctory recitations of the scholar.

We meet God in time and space. In one sense, we enter His spatial aspect when we place ourselves in His presence. Abraham Joshua Heschel wrote: "We cannot make God visible to us, but we can make ourselves visible to Him."

A specific setting or atmosphere is not required when you want to place yourself in God's presence, but obviously some settings are more conducive to prayer than others. Watching a sunrise on a mountain top is usually a helpful place; a crowded subway car at rush hour is more difficult. It is a fact, though, that sometimes we fail to make contact in the most appropriate settings and succeed in those that would seem to be most dismal.

Still, we need all the help we can get. Generally speaking, there is a proper time and place for everything. This old saying is the underlying message of Ecclesiastes, and it is one of the great truths: the universe unfolds in an endless sequence of appropriate actions and reactions. In its broadest meaning, this concept deals with the workings of the physical universe of galaxies and solar systems, of electrons and neutrons. In a more finite, human sense, it suggests that something that is right for one time and place is wrong for another; that something difficult or impossible in one time or place may flow freely in another.

Most of us set aside special places at home for specific activities—a reading chair, a sewing corner, a hobby table. The reason is clear; a space intentionally planned for a specific activity will enhance the performance of that activity. Similarly, it helps to set aside a place to pray, a place to talk with God.

God's corner does not have to be elaborate; probably, the simpler it is, the better. It should, however, be a place in which you can totally relax and feel comfortable. God is already there: create an atmosphere to help you talk with Him. Light candles; candlelight is richer than electric light. Set your senses free of their ordinary, everyday fare. In this way, they will respond freshly rather than by habit. Some incense or other aromatic substance may help lead your senses away from the mundane and toward the spiritual. You also might want to have a pad of paper and a pencil handy, in the event that you want to jot down an insight.

When the physical space of God's corner is prepared, consider the element of time. When should you use that space and how frequently?

First of all, some form of regularity is important. Scheduled expectations have a way of fulfilling themselves. So it is a good idea to establish a regular timetable. Prayer times are best established by the rhythm of the day and our own internal rhythms. For the purposes of prayer, we want to be in touch with the *cyclical time* of a day's actual coming and going rather than with the *linear time* ticked away second by second on the clock.

Universal traditions, including the "traditions" of the animals, point to dawn and dusk as the most fitting times to reach out beyond ourselves. They are in-between times, rich and suggestive times when light and darkness blend together, when two contrary qualities coexist in the same time and space—the best times for prayer.

"He makes the day to pass and brings on the night." In our hearts we know the night will pass and day will come again. God is manifested in cyclical time, in the recurring flow of recreation. Words of praise and thanks then come easily to our consciousness: "Oh, ever living and existing God, may You always rule over us."

In the Jewish tradition, two periods of time are held to be especially good for sitting in God's presence. One is the period during which the sunlight fades away at dusk, and the other is the period between the rising of the morning star and the appearance of the first rays of the sun. At such times your whole being will respond, in agreement with the natural cycle.

After you have created an atmosphere and found a time, lie back on pillows or assume a position that allows your physical self to be as comfortable as possible. Focus on your body, using some of the techniques suggested in "The Teachings of the Body." Breathe deeply, in and out. Relax your muscles, one by one, until they are as tensionless as possible. Exhale with a sigh, as heartfelt as you can allow yourself, and begin to talk.

Don't worry if you have no words ready. The words will come. Most likely you will feel foolish saying words to the candles when there is no one in sight. Don't get caught up in this feeling. Dismiss it. It is appropriate to your relationship with other human beings but inappropriate with God. So begin to talk, and get the words out of your mouth in as pure a form as you can, without dressing them up, or editing, or hedging.

It might occur to you that you are only going through some empty motions, since God by His very nature knows everything. In His omnipotence, God already does know, but that is not the point. The value you get from talking to God is in the conscious, intentional act of presenting yourself—thoughts, feelings, and all. It is standing naked before God, opening your heart to Him, to Her, and saying with every cell and tissue and glimmer of awareness in your being, "HERE I AM! THIS IS ME. THIS IS HOW I AM."

It's natural to experience a buzz of digressions and self-consciousness. Bear with it. It might last a while, but it will pass. Then something else will happen.

From a deep place in your heart, an affirmation will rise that what you are doing now is the right thing to be doing. You will try to speak. Perhaps you'll say a word or two. Before you know it, you'll be crying.

Tears will stream down your face, not bitter tears of grief, not tears of anguish or rage, but tears from your heart, sweet tears. These tears are the prayers of your soul, prayers for which you have not yet found the right words.

Don't be frightened when you start to cry. It's all right. You've placed yourself in a highly charged situation. It is no small thing to consciously present yourself to God and bare your heart. Some people say it's like taking hold of a live wire. Others say it's like stepping off a cliff and not falling. Tears are a very common response. Most people who have had spiritual experiences in the presence of God are familiar with them.*

At first, when the soul is mute and untutored, you won't have the words to express the deep feelings that rise to your own awareness at the moment you want to present them to God. Nevertheless, you will try. You will speak falteringly, perhaps with great effort. But you will speak.

The words will begin to come; you'll hear them with your own ears. Let the flow continue. Keep the process going. Tell God what you feel in the most private part of your being. Keep aiming for the raw, unadorned truth.

You don't have to impress God; He is not impressible. There is no competition involved, nor any other game. You will say things to Him that you've never been able to say to anyone, including yourself. At times, your ears will hear words from your own mouth that will shock and pain you. But don't stop.

As the process of peeling away the layers of yourself continues, keep talking. Present the process to God, step by step. Say everything. Say whatever wells up, and as soon as you understand that there is another layer of truth beneath it, tell God. Say something like "God, I still have to give you a deeper truth of me." Then say the next layer as it rises up in you.

When you have gotten this far, you have accomplished much. The process is in motion. You are truly talking to God. Now it is His turn to talk to you.

---

*Tears are infinitely expressive. At an early period of his life, the Baal Shem Tov (called the Besht) worked as a *shochet*, one who slaughters animals in the manner prescribed by Jewish Law. The rule is to cause as little pain as possible, so the knife must be honed to perfection. When the Besht sharpened his knife, he wet the sharpening stone with his tears.

Every once in a while, pause, sit back, breathe deeply. Become passive and allow for a response. Invite a reply to form in your consciousness. If particularly strong thoughts occur to you at this moment, you may want to write them down.

Instead of or in addition to this passive approach, you might even offer your mouth as an instrument of divine reply. On this matter, the Baal Shem Tov once said, "When I weld my spirit to God, I let my mouth say what it will, for then all my words are bound to their root in Heaven." Perhaps you will say words or even phrases, or receive indications on the inner plane in silence. In whatever form they take, these words or indications are God's reply to you and your needs.

At this moment, you will probably experience a sweet feeling in your entire being. Relish it. Enjoy it. It is from God. It is a manifestation of God in you, and you deserve it.

You have just communicated with the cosmos, an act of the greatest moment because it is a conscious recognition of the living universe. Further, it is your intentional attempt to get in tune with the universe. The content of your message—whatever you are experiencing at the moment—is not what matters most. The key is the act itself, the recognition that the universe is alive and responsive in you and to you.

Talking to God once can be an electrifying experience. Talking to Him regularly will nourish your soul and change your life.

Source: Zalman Schachter-Shalomi, *The First Step*
(New York: Bantam Books, 1983), 87–92.

What Can One Say about God?

What can one say about God?

Shema Yisrael, Y-H-V-H is our God, YHVH is ONE!

The Hebrew for the Name of God is *Yud Heh Vav Heh* and is not pronounced, yet each one of the letters has meaning. And all these meanings for each letter, separate and then together, make for the simultaneity that is the most goddest God godding endlessly. So it is better not to look for God as a noun of something that exists but as that infinitely-inging, the never-ending process of being and not existing.

The aspect of God that we most often mean is that of the Creator whose work is perfect.

Heh! It is perfect.

God is the answer to the big "W"s, What, Who, Why, Where, When. God is a constant making, what made us be, whose designs we can only guess at, who must be underneath what is and makes it BE! That one is not apparent to our sight. But at special times we can see how together-fitting, how perfect it all is; even with what we think of as "flaws," irregularities. How come everything that gets cold shrinks and gets heavy, and water, when it freezes, expands! Figure what this world would be like if water, in freezing, shrank and sank to the bottom. There would be no life as we know it. So the perfection of the design points to a designer. This then is God the Creator, the *Bore Olam.* The more science finds out about how this universe began, the more closely it gets to what our religion teaches us and what our souls' intuition teach us, inside tuition.

Shema Yisrael, YHVH is our Creator, YHVH is ONE!

Vav, You are loved!

In our hearts we crave to hear one message—are we loved? Times occur when we know that there are no accidents in the world. God is a loving that is vaster than a parent's loving. This caring One who holds us in pleasure and in pain, who wills us to grow toward Her/Him-self. This is God, the *Ahavah Rabbah,* the great love.

That two bodies attract each other in space, the law of gravity is God, the loving, the flow in which people care for each other, the flow in which a cat licks her kittens clean, the flow in which if you ask a question "Why?" and there is another person caring enough to respond and to provide an answer. And the "Because" that makes sense because answering is a basic form of caring, which coming from God we call revelation. And when we pray and we feel we are attended to, that loving is God. So too is the wanting to make babies, and willingness to labor in giving birth, and the nursing that comes from close to the heart, that is the loving godding. The arms that wait to receive one old and worn, one fatally injured and dying, that too is that divine loving.

Shema Yisrael, YHVH cares for us, YHVH is ONE.

Heh, All is clear.

That we know anything at all is a wonder. That we know so much is overwhelming. That it all fits together is even more amazing. And that when we really know something well it also teases us to know what we don't yet know at all really. The clarity that makes sure that despite not knowing fully we know enough to do the right thing here and now, that also makes it clear that what we think is so, is really not so. That which is present to us in Torah and to other folks in the revelations addressed to them, that is God the TRUTH, the Source of all knowledge.

God is an awareness that spans from knowing psions and muons, quarks that live nanoseconds and are gone, and at the same time being the awareness that contains a solar year, one in which the sun turning once around the galaxy takes 360 million years. This awareness embraces all life and permeates each cell, each microbe and virus, beehives and anthills, rain forests and oceans. This awareness knows all, not by "thinking" them but by being them—us, and not being—at least 18,000 times each second. We are cells of Mother Earth's global brain and her knowing, and her knowing is the knowing of God, the *Melekh Ha'olam.*

Shema Yisrael, YHVH is Aware, YHVH is ONE.

Yud, I am holy.

Deeper in me than my own knowing, my "I-am awareness" and your knowing your "I-am awareness" there is something vaster, more precious than existence, than love, than knowledge. We call that "holy," sacred, a kind of God-special, enduring beyond what changes and enduring changes beyond our habits of enduring. That is sacred.

That I—am—that—I-am is
deeper than deep,
higher than high,
tinier than infinitesimal
and bigger than infinite,
older than ever
and younger than now,
beckoning and unapproachable,
judging with utter truth
and totally forgiving

longed for, adored, and dreaded
avoided and ultimately embraced
with the deepest surprise
"Hey, I am That!
You are that
and this is That too!"

 Shema Yisrael, YHVH is HOLY, YHVH is ONE!

 So this is why we cannot say the word YHVH. We can't do it with our mouth and mind, with our words and thoughts all at once.

 It is perfect—the last *Heh,* You are loved, the *Vav,* All is clear, the upper *Heh,* and I am holy, the *Yud,*
Shema Yisrael
Our Creator,
who is aware of us,
cares for us,
is holy,
YHVH is ONE!
YHVH your God is Truth!

    Source: Zalman Schachter-Shalomi, *Paradigm Shift: From the Jewish Renewal*
      Teachings of Reb Zalman Schachter-Shalomi, ed. Ellen Singer
      (Northvale, N.J.: Jason Aronson, 1993), 135–137.

When I Use the Word *God,* What Do I Mean?

> *Barukh Hu*
> *IT is perfect*
> *You are loved*
> *All is clear*
> *AND I AM HOLY*

In the recent, rationalistic past people talked about God as a Being. They used a noun and implied some substance, albeit omni-omni and infinite. In the tradition of the medieval theologians, they sought to define the word in some ways in which the questions about the existence and nature of God could be answered in a philosophically self-respecting way.

The arguments for the existence of God, teleological (somebody had to make the world, it shows planning), ontological (one could not conceive of a God unless there were one), helped give a person a good and decent God idea.

But, upon deeper reflection, one realized that all one had gotten was a regression stopper. The best way not to have to continue raising questions was to answer with God. Once the trump card "God" was played, one could not take another step behind the answer and raise a further question.

This recognition itself made it useless to engage in God talk. Not being under philosophical compulsion, we were also not under social compulsion. The power of the consensus of the pious had become weakened in the two world wars and the subsequent breakdown of the surface tension between Jews and the rest of the world.

On the ethnic home front they had said that there is God, Torah and Israel, but God was the great backdrop for Israel, and if you could not claim chosenness from a transcendental source, a *Bialik* and *Ahad Haam* could still claim it for us on the basis of our Torah.

Our contact with God came largely after a spell of some sort of atheism, a process of adolescent debunking, getting high on the *chutzpah* of our iconoclasm.

We did not need to become believers in God because of the big questions, nor did we have to—especially after the Holocaust—look for the God ideas of the past. We could have chucked it all. It still is fashionable to be, if not atheist, then Buddhist-agnostic.

But we had experiences. They were so close to madness that before our time few people talked to each other about them to compare notes. The climate of what is plausible in an ordered universe did not admit that an infinitesimal chemical substance should alter perceptions so that the worlds for which we had no words could manifest.

Or the sexual and the divine had been divorced so long from each other by that repressive consensus that the transcendence of the boundaries of the skin, the physical, erotic, as well as the mental and the psychic and the cosmic telepathy experienced could not fit into anything we had been taught in any serious way. Here and there some words used by the mystics seemed to echo with significance, but what came in a decisive way was that experience.

Still, as we had shared in the experiences, we also talked about them. It had been "far out," "too much." We had to talk about the way time had been observed as flowing and with it the sameness and the differences were organically connected. We described to each other how we had "gone through the changes." And we learned some basic mind-soul disciplines, and when we focused on the experiences, that had gone deeper, way deeper than the disciplines took us by our effort—and here the word *grace* seemed to fit well—we became aware that other words could better express our experience than those that we got in translating our tradition into the terms of the *Zeitgeist* just running out of steam.

We also saw that we came back to the same reality we had left, though with an altered perspective. The tension between the perfections experienced and the mess in which we lived and breathed served as an immense goal to reshape our reality maps and our reality. We simply had to improve the quality of life and learn to make harmony and peace on the planet.

Part of that process was making new words that expressed the dynamism. Not for the noun God do we look. What we had experienced was not a static ENTITY. So VERB and PROCESS are
words that are better. Infinitely—inging
what ever was do/act/pass/happen—ing.
And that infinite/inging was the most
pervade/ing, sustain/ing, creating/ing
love-ing, care/ing, feel/ing
understanding, image/ining, integrate/ing, conceptualize/ing
BE/ing
blowing our minds with identity beyond belief
shattering our concepts as inapplicable to that reality
rebirthing us as loved children of the universe who have every
right to be here and now and for all the devastation of that
living through it also gave us renewed life, vigor, energy, zest.

Godhead, Eyn Soff, Brahman were closer to the reality than Lord, Father, King, Judge.

The sense of Identity of that Being with all the roles assigned to HIM? HER also came through, yet because of the Be/ing behind the roles we saw them, names, metaphors, masks, Sephirot, Archetypes, the reality in the great conjunctive, the holy AND became the strongest paradigm of our theologies.

So the And between good and evil, Jew and Gentile, *Shabbos* and the week, holy and secular; this And, the infinitely *And/*ing ONE to serve that *Aleph* means to let oneself become aware of one's identity with the *Aleph*, to map reality in harmony with the *Aleph*, to be attuned to the compassion of the *Aleph*, to function in the flow of that *Aleph*.

So the *partzufim*, metaphor, and archetypes are the clothes *Aleph* wears.

When I speak of God's Name I mean all there is in that holy AND.
All nominative being, totally intransitive I AMming endlessly.
All times and spaces, everything dative integrating endlessly
All beings related by the gravity-Love-attracting each other
endlessly, holistically cognitively AND
All objects discretely unique existing excluding all others.
AND the name is all these four in the same HERE AND NOW
and when I become aware of what I just wrote
I, the servant in the accusative,
I, the child in the genitive
I, the conceptualizer of data
I am that I am
I experience *Barukh Hu uVarukh Shemo.*
AND I SERVE YOU
AND YOU CARE FOR ME
AND WE MAKE IT UP AS WE GO ALONG
AND THAT GOD IS *Aleph*
YUD AND *HEH* AND *VAV* AND *HEH* AND . . . THE AND

Source: Zalman Schachter-Shalomi, *Paradigm Shift: From the Jewish Renewal Teachings of Reb Zalman Schachter-Shalomi*, ed. Ellen Singer (Northvale, N.J.: Jason Aronson, 1993), 139–142.

HAROLD M. SCHULWEIS

b. 1925

Harold M. Schulweis, a highly respected Conservative rabbi of our time, is the spiritual leader of Valley Beth Shalom in Encino, California, where he has served since 1970. Born in New York City in 1925, he received his B.A. from Yeshiva University in 1945 and went on to study philosophy at New York University. He then attended the Jewish Theological Seminary in New York and received his rabbinic ordination in 1950. He pursued his studies at the Pacific School of Religion, in Berkeley, California, obtaining his doctorate in 1972.

A longtime supporter of the Reconstructionist Movement, Schulweis was influenced by the writings of Rabbi Mordecai M. Kaplan and became a member of the Board of Governors of the Reconstructionist Rabbinic College. He launched the Synagogue Havurah program in his congregation, which now has become a national project. Schulweis is also the chairman and founder of the Institute for the Righteous Acts (1962) and the founding chairman of the Jewish Foundation for the Righteous (1986).

Schulweis has spoken and written extensively on many Jewish topics. He has been the senior editor of Sh'ma, *and a contributing editor to* The Reconstructionist *and* Moment, *as well as* The Baltimore Jewish Times. *In addition, Schulweis taught at the City College of New York, the University of Judaism in Los Angeles, and the Hebrew Union College–Jewish Institute of Religion, Los Angeles campus. He is the recipient of many honors and awards, including the Israel Prime Minister's Medal in 1975.*

Schulweis raises the question of the appropriateness of viewing God as a person. He argues that once divinity is conceived as a person, God becomes open to investigation, judgment, and criticism. Yet, no amount of traditional explanations can satisfactorily tell us what the essence of God is, for, as most people readily acknowledge, this is beyond our human understanding. Therefore, Schulweis suggests, we need to go from "God the noun" to "God the verb"; in other words, from subject to predicate. He calls his approach "predicate theology," where God is identified with godliness, such as helping the poor, healing the sick, and clothing the naked. The question is not whether one believes that God is merciful or caring, but whether doing mercy and acting with care are godly acts. We can easily relate to the second, while we cannot fathom the first.

Schulweis sees a precedent for his thinking in the distinction between the two terms by which God is known in the traditional texts: Elohim and Adonai. The first represents the reality as it is, that is, God as the power behind amoral nature; whereas the second points to the ideal, to the possibility of transformation, the ground of moral goodness that enables us to repair the flaws of nature. In his view, Elohim and Adonai are one, embracing the oneness of reality; necessity and possibility go together. Even though the qualities of godliness are many, they all share the same purpose by being interdependent and by being subordinate to the ideal of "goodness."

From God to Godliness

God did not create theology. Men differ in temperament, in needs and wants and their theologies reflect those needs. This should not mean the denigration of theology, but it should introduce a necessary measure of theological modesty in our claims. I have argued the importance of the God-idea before many diverse groups, especially in college circles, and for many years. I have noted an interesting response to two different ways of formulating the God-idea. In one form I ask how many could subscribe to the belief that God is just, merciful and good;

that it is He who uplifts the fallen, heals the sick and loosens the fetters of the bound. The question is generally met with reluctance, at best with agnostic reserve and frequently with strong denial.

The other formulation asks how many would affirm that justice, mercy and goodness are godly; that uplifting the fallen, healing the sick and loosening the fetters of the bound are divine. Here the response is largely positive and most often enthusiastic. What is the meaning of these different reactions? Is it a response to style or to religious substance? Is it the aim of the theologian to prove the existence of the Subject God or to convince others of the reality of the divine predicates? Does my religious interest lie in persuading others that the divine Subject possesses certain qualities, or is it to identify, exhibit and name those qualities as themselves divine? Is the theological task to encourage faith in the Subject or to elicit faith in the Predicates of divinity? Which is more important religiously, morally and liturgically—to endorse faith in the "who" or in the "what" of divinity, fidelity to Elohim or to Elohut? And what difference does there appear to be in the minds of those who are willing to affirm (a) that that which heals the sick is godly while denying (b) that it is God who heals the sick?

The Grammar of Subject Theology

Theological statements are traditionally expressed in terms of subject-predicate relations. However God is portrayed, whether as Person, Being, Power or Process, one speaks of Him as a Subject to which there is attached a number of qualities. Here Orthodox, Reform, Conservative and Reconstructionist prayer books alike follow the same subject-predicate formula: "Blessed are Thou, O Lord our God who . . ." The very language of our theological and liturgical forms focuses attention upon the Subject who brings forth the bread from the earth, establishes peace in the heaven, reveals, rewards, punishes, judges and forgives. The language of Subject theology rivets our attention upon the divine Subject and frames the way we look for and at divinity.

The very grammar of our ordinary language is biased towards Subject theology. To say "God" is to use a concrete noun which insinuates the naming of some separate entity. George Berkeley long ago warned that it is only grammatical convention which makes us "apt to think every noun substantive stands for a distinctive idea that may be separated from all others: which hath occasioned infinite mistakes." Despite Berkeley's strictures against the ontologizing bewitchment of language, for most people, "God" is a concrete noun which suggests a corresponding substance, something or someone which underlies the predicates assigned to Him. The Subject is independent of the predicates as the noun is of its adjectives. Modern philosophers have noted that this grammatical prejudice played an analogous role in classical philosophy which favored substantives over verbs and prepositions. Bertrand Russell argues that such linguistic bias led to the erroneous notion that "every proposition can be regarded as attributing a property to a single thing, rather than as expressing a relation between two or more things." It is to avoid such theological limitations that Kaplan insists that God be considered as a functional, not a substantive noun, a correlative term which implies relationship, e.g., as teacher implies pupil and king implies subjects.

Yet, the inherited language of traditional theology and prayer reflects the dominance of the Subject. And it is the Subject, whether described through the categories of classic or modern metaphysics or the biblical notion of a divine Personality, which is regarded as alone unqualifiedly real, objective and independent, and worthy of worship.

The Depression of the Predicates

What happens to the predicates of divinity within the systems of traditional theology? They live under the shadow of the Subject and at its mercy. Characteristically, theologians have qualified them out of their independent and affirmative meaning. They may be analyzed away as negative qualities, puns (homonyms), equivocal or essentially incomprehensible. All that is known for sure is that God is, or that God is He who is, i.e., that God is Subject. But as to His character, His attributes, these must be accepted with a grain of salt. The caution over ascribing literal meaning to the predicates of divinity derives from a sensitivity to the change that in so doing we are projecting our own human values upon the Subject. Even the Biblical theologians, who will have nothing to do with the bloodless negative theology of the philosophers, tend to suppress the moral predicates of the living God. For they sense that to hold firmly to the moral connotation of the divine predicates, to cling to the positive and humanly comprehensible meaning of such attributes as goodness and justice and mercy is to risk playing havoc with the Subject.

Theodicies Defend the Subject

Most especially when confronting the gnawing problem of evil and the suffering of innocence, the traditional theologian feels compelled to mute the original moral meaning of the predicates. To defend the Subject, and that is the core concern of all theodicies, the moral predicates must be rendered inapplicable to the Subject. Reciprocal divine human convenant or not, moral *imitatio dei* or not, confronted by the patent immorality of events, the theologian grows aware that the danger to the Subject comes from the moral predicates within. For the Jobian outrage with which the theological defenders of God must deal is based upon earlier belief in the moral predicates of divinity. Reluctantly but invariably the theodicies of Subject theology feel compelled to raise the divine Subject beyond the reach of the moral predicates. The underlying strategy of traditional theodicies is to render the Subject invulnerable from the internal attack of the moral predicates. The warm and full-blooded intimacy with a personal moral God must be cooled. The moral attributes originally ascribed to the divine Subject are now discovered to be *qualitatively* other than the same moral attributes ascribed to human conduct. The meaning of God's goodness is not simply "more than" human goodness, it is "wholly other," apart from the connotation it possesses in the domain of human affairs. Over and again, relief is found in the assertion that the Subject's ways are not the ways of man, nor Its thoughts ours. It is a costly defense. For the denial of the human comprehensibility of the moral attributes of God is accompanied by the denial of human competence to make moral judgment. If "good and evil" in the eyes of God are construed as qualitatively different from that understood by man, then man's judgment and emulation of God's moral traits are invalidated.

Source: Harold M. Schulweis, "From God to Godliness," in *God in the Teachings of Conservative Judaism*, ed. Seymour Siegel and Elliot Gertel (New York: Rabbinical Assembly, 1985), 237–240. First published in *The Reconstructionist*, Feb. 1975.

The Image Within

To follow the rites of passage from birth to death is to trace the route of the self's spiritual career as it grows from one stage of life to another. From the covenant at birth to the first day at school, from the moral autonomy marked by the bar/bat mitzvah to the biblical counsel to marry and leave the parents and cleave to one's spouse, from the cutting of the fringes of the prayer shawl laid upon the body of the deceased at the funeral to prayers of remembrance at *Yizkor*, the journey of transitions and transformations of a life are brought to awareness, refining and deepening the sense of the sacred underlying all of them.

Each transition helps us come to terms with the dual wisdom of letting go and holding on. In every rite, some ties are loosened to free us for further attachments. As celebrants, we are like aerialists on a swinging trapeze, letting go of one ring to catch hold of another. Something old is loosened and something new is discovered in the transformations that are marked through the rites of passage. At my bar/bat mitzvah, I am no longer a child. I have assumed new responsibilities and obligations that I did not own before. At my wedding, I transform my syntax from "I" and "mine" to "we" and "ours." At my death, I am no longer obligated to perform mitzvot. I am dependent upon others for the continuity of my memory.

In each of the markers of the transition and transformation, what is constant? What is the unsevered cord that provides the continuity between one stage and another? The fixed referent that runs through all of the rites of passage is found in the root principle called in Hebrew *Tzelen Elohim*, the divine image. It is introduced in the biblical account of the creation of the human being and is elaborated in rabbinic thought: "And God created man in His image, in the image of God created He him; male and female created He them" (Genesis 1:27). The Image of God within is the root metaphor that captures the unique Jewish understanding of the human self, its inner life, and its profound relations with God and humanity. In the biblical account, the human being has a special status and responsibility. All other creatures God formed by God's word, except the human being, whom God created through God's own acts: "The Lord God formed Adam from the dust of the earth. He blew into his nostrils the breath of life, and man became a living being" (Genesis 2:7).

The *Tzelem Elohim* signifies both the uniqueness and universality of the human soul. While no man is a clone of another, all human beings, regardless of race or religion, are born imprinted with the Image of the Imageless God. The powers of the Image within are variously named: soul, spirit, breath, intellect, will, conscience. Every child enters the world stamped by the divine Image.

But the Image of God is not a sealed package. People were created with the capacity "to become" what the Image of God implies: the cultivation of the sacred potential within the depths of their rational and emotional moral being. The Image is an aspiration, a resemblance rather than an identity with God. The actualization of the Image is a never-ending process, coterminous with life itself, a work in progress from the first to the last breath of human life. The appreciation, cultivation, and refinement of the Image of God is the spiritual subtext of the rites of passage. The liturgy and ritual drama expressed in these rites commit and recommit us to this evolution.

Imitation of Godliness

In Judaism, the essential test for us as human beings is living our lives in a way that makes manifest the attributes of godliness. But as one rabbinic Sage asks, how is it possible for a fallible, mortal human being to fulfill the mandate to walk in God's way, seeing that God is described as "a devouring fire" (Deuteronomy 4:24). How can the finite soul emulate the mysterious essence of divinity?

It is not the face but the back of God that is imitated. It is not the penetration of the secrets of God's essence that is the goal, but the observed consequences of God's moral behavior that is the path to be sought. God informed Moses, "I will take away My hand and you shall see My back, but My face you shall not see" (Exodus 33:23). God is Imageless, but God's ways are discernible and emulatable.

God made for Adam and Eve coats of skin and clothed them. As God clothed the naked, so do thou. God visited Abraham when he was ailing at the oak of Mamre. As God visited the sick, do thou also. God comforted Isaac after the death of Abraham. As God comforted the bereaved, do thou also. God buried Moses in the valley. As God attended to the deceased, do thou also (Talmud, *Sotah* 14a).

God is verified, made true *(veri-facere)*, in our lives not by syllogistic argument or the declaration of dogmas, but by acting out the accessible attributes of divinity. The gift of *Imago Dei*, the Image of God, pulls us toward *imitatio Dei*, the lived imitation of God. Belief in God's reality and goodness is behaved.

The Image of God, shadowed in the human being, implies a special closeness with God, a unique human collegiality with the Divine. Acknowledging the gift of the Image, the human being is elevated as a partner with God in sustaining and transforming the self and its environment. The internalized Image bears testimony to the divine-human resemblance, a shared moral affinity. To become aware of the ideal Image of divinity within is to become conscious of human power and human responsibility. The prophet Isaiah acknowledges that divine-human kinship when he cites God's address to the people: "Ye are My witnesses saith the Lord" (Isaiah 43:10). The Rabbis translate God's claim conditionally, "If ye are My witnesses I am the Lord, and if ye are not My witnesses I am, as it were, not the Lord" (*Sifrei D'varim* 33:5). Herein lies a Jewish theology of human self-esteem, a self-respect gained not by self-aggrandizement but by the self's aspiration toward godliness. A theology of self in a community of shared values resides in the strands of each and every rite of passage.

The Jewish insistence on the interdependence of divinity and humanity encourages the creative involvement of the self in God's universe. Consider the passage in Genesis 2:5 wherein we are told that in the beginning there was no shrub or herb in the field because "God had not yet caused it to rain upon the earth and there was no human to till the soil." The connection between the falling rain from heaven and the human tilling of the earth symbolizes the significance of human-divine interdependence. The biblical verse describes the transaction between the given from above and the transformation from below. Where there is no action emanating from below, there is no action emanating from above. It is only when the human being prepares the earth beneath that a mist rises up from the earth, watering the face of the earth. So it is that partnership with God carries profound theological implications for the prayers and benedictions that surround the rites of passage. For example, focusing on the Image of God within us allows us to respond to conventional theological questions in another way. Does God hear our prayers? Does God answer our prayers? Does God act in history? Does God care? Belief in the divine Image within internalizes and reverses these questions. The questions now turn reflexive. Do I hear? Do I respond? Do I intervene? Do I care? Our questions about God are God's questions about us. Where the immanent Image is denied or ignored, the dialogue between divinity and humanity is broken off. As the late-nineteenth-century rabbi Elijah Benamozegh asserted, "When we seek God, it is God who seeks Himself in us" (*Israel and Humanity*, 1995).

The Image within binds heaven and earth. The whispered voice of the internal Image is not in the heavens above nor in the oceans beneath. It is close to you, in your mouth and in your heart that you may act on it (Deuteronomy 30:14). The passage to the eternal is internal.

Self-Awareness and the Significance of the Rites

To recover the sanctity of the rites of passage we need to become aware of the revolutionary implications that follow from the belief in the endowed Image of God. What we celebrate in every state of life is the divine potentiality inherent in us. In the first century C.E., Rabbi Akiva said, "Beloved is man, for he was created in the Image of God. But it was by a special love that it was made known to him that he was created in the Image of God" (Talmud, *Taanit* 11a, 11b). Self-awareness of the Image is central to the spiritual renaissance of the ritual life.

Despite the wretched record of humans' ability to deface the Image, despite the personal failure and tragedies of the self, the tradition clings to the possibilities, potentialities, and purposes of the Image. No notion of inherited sin can destroy the sacred character of the Image. A contemporary Orthodox thinker, J. B. Soloveitchik, refers to the "innermost core of the soul that remains something pure, precious and sacred in man's soul" (*On Repentance*, 1980). To acknowledge the Image within us is to affirm belief in the possibility of repentance, transformation, and renewal of the self. Consciousness of the divine Image within brings to the foreground awareness of what we may become and what the world may become. Soloveitchik asserts of the human being, "No one can help him. He is his own redeemer; he is his own messiah who has come to redeem him from the darkness of his exile to the light of his personal redemption" (ibid.). In the process of self-transformation, the human being assumes the role of co-creator. As interpreted in the tradition, God implanted in us an ideal Image with the capacity to renew ourselves and ascend to a higher level. The Image is the companion at every station of our development, a presence in every rite of passage.

Source: Harold M. Schulweis, *Finding Each Other in Judaism*
(New York: UAHC Press, 2001), 6–10.

On Miracles

Fundamentalists treat miracles literally. The outstretched hand of God, the rod of Moses, the turning of the water into blood, the rivers filled with frogs, the dust turned into gnats, the affliction of the Egyptian population with flies and the cattle with pests, the visitation upon people and beasts with boils, the covering of the earth with hail and locusts, darkness and the death of the firstborn—all these events are interpreted verbatim. Nonfundamentalists also revere the Bible, but they are uncomfortable with the implausibility of its miracle events. Miracles insult common sense. To give the text credibility, many nonfundamentalists merely replace literal scripture with literal science. In the course of making the miracle palatable for the scientific appetite, they spoil its religious sense.

In many modern rabbinic commentaries, the ten plagues visited upon Egypt are explained along scientific lines. The explanation recalls that between June and August the Nile turns a dull red because of the presence of vegetable matter; this is followed by the production of a slime that breeds frogs; when decomposed, frogs beget flies that in turn spread disease.

Such a "scientific" reading falls between the stools, missing the seat of our religious concerns. For if the biblical reports of the plagues turn out to be natural phenomena, in what sense are they miraculous? If a miracle is only a coincidence of natural events, it has nothing to do with divine design or purpose. At best, scientific explanations may show that the so-called miracle could have happened. But no scientific account of the plagues can support the religious claim that the alleged miracle was caused by divine intent. Not "how" and "what" but "who" and "what for" are demanded by those who question the truth of miracles. Are the plagues acts of God or accidents of nature? Is it serendipity or God's intervention that miracles demonstrate?

Belief in miracles implies faith in a hidden purpose working behind the curtain of history. Not science but theology is challenged to explain the divine design of miracles. If the miracles as narrated in the Bible are not literally the work of the hand of God, are we to conclude that their claim to be miraculous is false?

Getting Help from the Tradition

The post-biblical rabbinic tradition contains many suggestions for moderns who find themselves caught between the natural or supernatural interpretations of the meaning of miracles. Many of the traditional commentaries focus on the moral significance of the event called miraculous. The concern is less on how it happened than on its spiritual meaning. It is not whether the event can be explained as a natural occurrence or a supernatural intervention that determines its miraculous character but what the event signifies morally that determines its miraculous spiritual character. Many of the commentaries, for example, find in the episodes of the Egyptian plagues a moral drama of poetic justice.

The Nile River that Pharaoh worshiped as a god is turned into blood as a symbolic punishment for throwing the innocent male children into the river to drown. The land is filled with frogs because Heqt, the Egyptian frog goddess of fertility, assists women in labor. The pharaoh who is jealous of the fertility of Israel sees blessings of the goddess of fertility turn into ecological curses. Similarly, the darkness of the dungeons blots out the Egyptian sun god, Re. Symbolic explanations flow from the rabbinic moral conviction that, "Whatever measure a man metes out shall be measured to him again." In short, the attention to the plagues focuses on their moral symmetry, not their supernatural cause.

The attempt to naturalize miracles proves as counterproductive as the effort to translate the metaphors of the psalmist into scientific terms. "The sea saw it and fled, the Jordan turned back in its courses, the mountains skipped like rams, the hills like young sheep" (Psalm 114). It is not the disruption of the natural order of the world that evokes the psalmist's wonder but the trust in the power of morality in history to triumph over nature. Mature faith is trust in the spiritual purpose that transforms life.

Faith without miracle is perceived in the tradition as superior to faith that depends on miracle. "Dearer to God is the proselyte who has come of his own accord than all the crowds of Israelites who stood before Mt. Sinai. For had the Israelites not witnessed the thunders, lightnings, quaking of the mountain and sounding trumpets they would not have accepted the Torah. But the proselyte who saw not one of these things came to surrender himself to the Holy One and took the yoke of heaven upon him" (Tanchuma on Genesis 12).

Moralizing Miracles

Moderns have much to learn from the classic rabbinic interpretation of the miraculous. In the Book of Numbers, the people of Israel are punished for their transgression of speaking against God. God sends serpents to poison them. Moses prays for the people's life and is answered by God: "Make thee a fiery serpent and set it upon a pole and it shall come to pass that everyone that is bitten, when he sees it shall live. Then Moses made a serpent of brass and sat it upon a pole and it came to pass that if a serpent had bitten any man, when he looked unto the serpent of brass, he lived" (Numbers 21:4–9).

On the face of it, this biblical account contains obvious marks of a supernatural miracle. The miracle came as a divine response to Moses' prayer and amazingly saved those poisoned by the serpents. Yet the sages of the tradition do not acknowledge such a straightforward literal interpretation. They ask rhetorically, "Do brazen snakes kill or bring to life?" Instead they read the biblical story as a spiritual lesson designed to teach that "When the Israelites directed their thoughts on high and kept loyal to God they were healed, otherwise they pined away" (Talmud Rosh Hashanah 3:8). What happened to the brazen serpent that Moses made in the desert according to God's instructions? We read further in the Bible that the figure of the serpent was turned into an icon of idolatrous worship and that much later it was broken into pieces by the righteous King Hezekiah. For this dismemberment the king was praised, for he did what was right in the sight of the Lord (II Kings 18:4).

This rabbinic refusal to accept literally a biblical account of an alleged miraculous event is not unique. The rabbis deal with a similar episode recorded in Exodus 17:11 in much the same way. There we are told that Israel prevailed in its battles with the Amalekites only when Moses' hand was raised, but was defeated when Moses let his hand down. Instead of reveling in this biblical account of a miracle, the rabbis protest: "But could the hands of Moses promote or hinder the battle? That cannot be." Why can't it be? It is rejected because the story as it stands smacks of magical thinking. The rabbis explain the biblical miraculous event allegorically. Whenever the people retained their belief in God, were loyal to His word, and turned their faces toward the heavens, they were victorious; but when their faith flagged, they were defeated. In this manner, a supernatural account is transposed into a spiritual value.

Divine intervention does not disrupt nature. Therefore, the rabbinic tradition could assert that biblical miraculous agencies such as the manna, Moses' rod, and Noah's rainbow were created before they occurred in history. They were created on the eve of the First Sabbath of creation in the twilight (Ethics of the Fathers 5:6). We honor God's creation of an orderly and intelligible nature. The sages preferred seeing in the apparent aberrations of nature what the philosopher Harry Wolfson calls "a preestablished disharmony." Divine wisdom and goodness lie not in rupturing God's reign of universal law but in the reliability of the steady order of the world. Faith is not dependent on miracles. Miracles depend on faith. And faith, far from blind, sees life's deeper truths.

The Miracle Worker

The Jewish reluctance to interpret miracles literally has an impressive history. Both the biblical and rabbinic traditions are concerned that miracle working not infiltrate the faith, for that would threaten human autonomy and responsibility. The Bible itself is wary of the charismatic's sleight of hand. "If there arise among you a prophet or a dreamer of dreams and gives you a sign or a wonder, and the sign or the wonder comes to pass whereof he spoke to you saying 'Let us go after other gods which you have not known and let us serve them,' you shall not heed the words of the prophet or the dreamer of dreams, for the Lord God is testing you to see whether you love the Lord God with all your heart and soul" (Deuteronomy 13:1–3). Not the medium but the message is to be heeded. Not the charisma of the personality but the character of the content of prophecy must be validated. The success of miracles and wonders is irrelevant to the truth and meaning of the message.

In the Exodus epoch, Moses' rod is the medium for miraculous events in Egypt and before the Red Sea. But some of the classic commentaries of the tradition demythologize the rod. According to one rabbinic commentary, since the Egyptians were convinced that it was the rod that produced the plagues and divided the sea, God said to Moses: "Cast away thy rod so that they do not say, were it not for the rod he would not have been able to divide the sea" (Midrash Exodus Rabbah 21:9). The rod itself has no intrinsic power. Indeed, when Moses later strikes the rod against the rock to force it to bring forth water in the desert, it is deemed a blasphemous act, though here too, the rod produced a miraculous event. Because of his abuse of the rod, Moses is denied entrance into the promised land. It is not the rod but the nature of purpose to which it is put to use that entitles an event to be raised to the status of the miraculous. Miracles to be worthy of the name must serve a higher purpose.

Miracles and Medicine

There were and are true believers who look askance at human natural invention on the grounds that such initiative supplants the miraculous works of divine intervention. The history of religion records many controversies in which the pious even sought to ban the use of medicine because such human activity was deemed to be an arrogant replacement for faith in God. If God afflicts us with illness, He and no other can and should cure the ailment. To circumvent God's will by human ingenuity denies God's exclusive sovereignty. For such people, true faith is gazing upon the desert icons of the bronze serpent. Only absence of belief in the miracle turns people to medicine and physicians for help.

Maimonides characterized this attitude as a perversion of piety. "If someone suffers from hunger and turns to bread and, by consuming it, heals himself from his great suffering, shall we say that he had abandoned trust in God? Just as I thank God when I eat for His having provided something to satisfy my hunger and to give me life and sustain me, thus should I thank Him for having provided that which heals my sickness when I use it" (*Commentary of the Mishnah Pesachim* 4:10). To depend on miracles is to belittle our divinely given intelligence as well as our moral responsibility.

Miracles and Wisdom

Faith in miracles is no mark of piety when it is introduced at the cost of disrespecting human intelligence and of mocking the reality principle. A key discussion in the Talmud centers around the claim made by some sages that people who are engaged in fulfilling a religious precept are never harmed. That assertion is challenged by other rabbis, who cite the contrary case of a son who dutifully obeyed his father who asked him to fetch some eggs from the nest in a tree. The son climbed a ladder, and, following the biblical precept, chased away the mother bird to spare her the anguish of seeing her eggs taken. About to return to his father with the eggs in hand, the son fell from the ladder and was killed. Where, the rabbis asked, was the promised protection for the son?

The severity of the question is bolstered by two scriptural verses in which longevity is promised to those who honor their fathers and mothers, and long life is assured those who dismiss the mother bird before taking the eggs from the nest (Deuteronomy 5:16; 22:6). In our case, the son was neither guarded from harm nor rewarded for his piety. Does God not keep His word? Rabbi Eleazar rose to explain the apparent contradiction. The son had chosen to stand on a rickety ladder, so his fall was likely. "One must never stand in a place of danger expecting a miracle to protect the faithful" (Talmud Kiddushin 39b). Faith is no protection against carelessness. Rabbi Eleazar goes on to note that the prophet Samuel, who trusted in God, would not go to King Saul initially though the Lord commanded him to do so. Samuel's reason for not obeying God is approved of because where injury is likely, one must not rely on miracles. "And Samuel said, how can I go? If Saul hear it, he will kill me" (I Samuel 16:2). Trust in God does not call for disregard of reality. Prudent judgment is an essential aspect of faith.

How to Teach Miracles Today

On occasion, the philosopher Abraham Joshua Heschel would open his evening lectures with an announcement that he had just experienced a miracle. He went on to explain to the puzzled audience that he had observed the setting of the sun. For Heschel, the miraculous is discovered through the faithful eye. It is not to be looked for in the strange events in nature but in the ordinariness of our existence. "To pray," he wrote, "is to take notice of the wonder, to regain a sense of the mystery that animates all beings, the Divine margin in all attainments."

How can the idea of the miraculous be meaningful to us today? We may be guided by the biblical Hebrew term for miracle, *nes*, which means "sign." Its Hebrew synonyms, *oth* and *mofeth*, in the Bible are translated as "signal, standard, ensign." In the Septuagint, the Greek translation of the Bible, *semeion* (which means "sign"), is used to translate *nes*. A miracle is an event that signifies something of "sign-ificance," something that makes an important difference in my life or in the life of my community. A miracle is an intimation of an experience of transcending meaning. The sign-miracle does not refer to something beyond or contrary to logic or nature. It refers to events and experiences that take notice of the extraordinary in the ordinary, the wonder in the everyday, the marvel in the routine.

Sign-miracles do not violate reason or nature. They are natural moments in our lives that we recognize as transforming. For many, the birth of a child is such an event. When a child is born, husband and wife are transformed into parents. They are no longer only inheritors but become transmitters of values. The natural biological account of birth does not compromise the spiritual significance. What is significant is the meaning of this newborn for the family, for humanity, for the world. With masterful irony, Maimonides described the bias of those who are blind to the "miracle" of the natural. He noted the absurdity of those who cannot see the greatness and goodness of God in the natural events and oppose scientific explanations as if they denigrated God's wisdom. Maimonides observed that if you explain to some pious sages that it is God who sends a fiery angel to enter the womb of a woman and forms the fetus there, they would accept it as a religious account of God's power and wisdom. They would marvel at the miracle that the "angel" is a body formed of burning fire whose size is equal to a third part of the whole world. But they would be repelled by the explanation that God "has placed in the sperm a formative force shaping the limbs and giving them their configuration." They would foolishly shirk from the idea that this natural force is what is meant by the "angel" (*Guide to the Perplexed*, Part II, Chapter 6).

The tradition refers to ordinary events that prove to be significant moments in our lives as "hidden miracles." Hidden miracles are all around us. A major prayer recited thrice daily is worded to acknowledge thankfully "Thy wonders and Thy miracles which are daily with us evening, morn, and noon." The signs of transcendence are discovered within the ordinary course of living. To see the divine in the natural and the rational, in the application of human intelligence and goodness, is a major insight of the Jewish tradition. The exercise of human talent, energy, and dedication and the course of nature glorifies God.

Rabbi Baruch of Mezbizh was asked why, in a popular prayer, God is called "creator of remedies, awesome in praises, doing wonders." Why should remedies stand next to wonders and even precede them? He answered: "God does not want to be praised as the Lord of supernatural miracles. And so, here, through the mention of remedies, nature is introduced and put first. But the truth is that everything is a miracle and a wonder."

Preparing for the Signs of the Miraculous

How can we sensitize ourselves and our children to the signals of divinity in the normal course of nature? How are sign-miracles experienced morning, noon, and night, as the prayer book states?

I cut my hand. The wound hurts and bleeds. I wash my hands, cleanse the wound, apply an antiseptic and bandage. Days pass and beneath the bandage a scab is formed. What can I learn from this prosaic event? I can pay attention to the natural healing process in my body aided by the intelligent application of medicines. Normal "miraculous" events are transactions between that over which we have little control and that over which we have a measure of control. It marks a partnership between the given and the transformed. Left unattended, the cut might have become infected. The washing, the medicine, and the bandaging are essential parts of the healing. Still, the scab cannot be said to have been formed by my will or wisdom. Healing exhibits a collaboration between potentiality and actualization, between the conscious and unconscious powers. Healing points to the human as well as to that which is beyond human powers. Curing is a cooperative venture between self and other. Who, having undergone surgery, is blind to the "sign" of healing?

The philosopher Mordecai M. Kaplan used the ordinary phenomenon of children's growth as illustrative of this-worldly "signs." Children enter the class at the beginning of the term. Their height is recorded. At the end of the term the children's height is remeasured. The children have grown. What accounts for their growth? Clearly it relies on the human care of the self, proper nutrition, exercise, sleep. The human contribution is necessary, but not sufficient. There is something beyond that accounts for the normal mystery of human growth. The collaboration of human and nonhuman energies is a factor that enters the miracle of growth. Height may be largely under genetic control, but someone whose chromosomes permit him to be six feet tall may never attain that height because of malnourishment.

Sign-miracles are results of human and nonhuman interaction. They entail the appropriate cooperation of the will, intelligence, and care, which themselves are manifestations of the divine and the potentialities given for us to transform.

The Miracles of Wine and Bread

The kinds of observations I have cited imply alternative theological approaches to the perception of miracles. They help overcome the commonly held notion that the measure of the miraculous is in the violation, not the regularity, of natural law and the rules of logic. They help us see that we have something to do with the performance of miracles. This approach remains a point of great contention. Conventional theology is apprehensive of the human dimension in the religious explanation of miracles—indeed, in the understanding of anything that is religious. Though an antihumanist bias predominates in the teaching of popular theology, it is far from the whole of Jewish tradition. We need to pay attention to those traditional insights that do not excommunicate the human from the realm of the divine. The theistic humanism within the religious tradition has a critical bearing on how we play our role in ethics, ritual, prayer, and the miraculous. As the petitioner has a vital part in the fulfillment of prayer, so the person of faith plays an important role in perceiving and implementing the normal miracles in our daily lives.

Theological humor is as rare as it is revealing. One anecdote tells of a man stranded on the rooftop of his home, surrounded by floodwaters. He prays to God to be saved. A rowboat with rescuers comes by and offers him safety. He turns them away, confident that God will save him. A helicopter flies overhead and lowers its rope ladder. The pilot urges him to climb the ladder. He turns the pilot away, resolute in his faith that God will save him. The waters rise, and in disappointment the imperiled man protests to his maker: "I am a believing man and have always proclaimed my trust in you. Why have you, Lord, forsaken me?" The echo of the heavenly voice responds: "But my son, I sent you the men in the rowboat and you dismissed them. I sent you the pilot and you refused his help. Why have you forsaken Me?"

Faith is a way of seeing and a way of responding to what we see. The idea of the miraculous that excludes human action and reaction to events, like that of prayer that excludes the worshiper from the petitions, overlooks the divine presence within nature and humanity. A classic rabbinic colloquy expresses insight into the interactive human-divine relationship that bears upon the notion of everyday "sign"-miracles. Rabbi Akiba is challenged by the pagan Tineus Rufus: "Whose deeds are greater, those of God or of man?" Akiba replies, "Greater are the deeds of man." The pagan is surprised by Akiba's humanistic response. To provide evidence for his assertion, Rabbi Akiba brings forth sheaves of wheat and loaves of cakes. Akiba asks, "Which are superior?" Unarguably the loaves of cakes excel (Midrash Tanchuma Tazriah 19:5).

Akiba's demonstration was not to raise man at God's expense but to point out the wrongheadedness of Tineus Rufus's split thinking. The latter presented Akiba with an either/or alternative. Either God or man, either the deeds of God or the deeds of man, are superior. This blinds Rufus to the cooperative relationship between God and man. Akiba's sheaves of wheat represent the givenness of God through the seed, water, soil, and sun, which men did not create. The cakes, on the other hand, represent the human transformation of that which is potential into actuality. The traditional *motzi* benediction is not made over the sheaves of wheat but over the baked bread. Akiba calls attention to the daily sign-miracles. Breaking bread is as miraculous as dividing the sea. Similarly, the kiddush benediction is not made over grapes but over the wine that is brought to controlled perfection by human hands. Wine, not grapes, represents the fullest expression of the holy, the transaction between the godly human and nonhuman nature.

Source: Harold M. Schulweis, *For Those Who Can't Believe* (New York: Harper Collins, 1994), 47–61.

Predicate Theodicy

Summing up his ministry the minister confessed that he had spent the first half of his career informing his flock that God is a loving God and that for the remainder of his career he spent his energies explaining why He isn't. In their interpretations of the universe and of the nature of God, theologies raise unreal expectations and foreshadow their theodicies. The mind-set of traditional theology cultivates the expectations of the believer and, with the failure of their realization, conditions him to ask certain kinds of questions and to accept as valid only certain kinds of answers. The believer confronted by a serious illness, for example, may be expected to pray to God who heals. The liturgical form reflects a linear causal relationship between the subject and the patient. Should the patient recover, all praise is due to Him who saves.

Should he fail to recover, theological explanation must refer to the subject as well. However the competence of the attending physicians and the strength of the patient may be involved in the outcome, the believer considers them secondary factors. They are regarded as ancillary agents of the primary cause of sickness and health, the singular divine subject. The subject may govern the affairs of the world obliquely, use the auxiliary elements and agents according to His inscrutable design. In the last analysis, behind the screen of natural conditions, it is the Subject of History and Nature who presides, whether by "luring" or by direct intervention or by granting permission.

The very framing of the question, "Why did it happen?" "Why did he have to suffer?", presupposes a number of unarticulated notions which rule out of order certain "obvious" answers. Scientific answers which explain "how" it happened and "what happened" are not satisfactory. They may be appropriate in the realm of impersonal events, e.g., "Why did the metal expand?" but such explanations appear frivolous and demeaning in answer to the question, "Why was my child blinded?" To cite a medical report, to refer to congenital factors or those of contagion or accident, will be grudgingly acknowledged only to be followed by "why" questions of another order. "Why did it happen to *my* child? Why did it happen *now*? Why did it happen to *me*?" The questions are limitless. They seek only those answers which share the tacit assumptions of the question. Such "why" questions demand "who" answers. The "why" questions grow out of a mode of thinking which understands the personal events of the universe as results of the will of personal purposive agents. "Why" means "for what purpose or cause or reason was this done to me and mine?"

To resolve the patent discrepancy between the moral promise on the one hand, and the suffering of the innocents and the prosperity of the unrighteous on the other, the defenders of God exercise their mind-reading of the inscrutable subject. Though His will be unknowable, somehow the theologian knows that it is willed for our good. Though His moral predicates are not ours, somehow the theologian knows that they are good and good for us. Though our afflictions make us weep, somehow they flow from His permission and are thus at bottom good for us, if not now then posthumously. The affliction is real enough, and the real agent cannot be a power other than God.

Therefore, the affliction must be deserved. Only the brazen are unable to find some inadequacy in self or in related selves which would justify such chastisement. The very denial of culpability is testimony of their guilt. The believers will eschew hubris and submit to religious masochism. They may find consolation in setting the burden of grief upon the shoulders of the subject. For better to live safe in His redeeming mystery than to live in the presence of unspeakable atrocities over which persons have no control.

The haunting question "why me?" cannot be answered on its own terms. Entailed in the "why" is an unstated set of presuppositions about the character of the world and of God. It rises out of a theological atmosphere of occult powers exercised upon the world. "Why?" means "what for?" It calls for deciphering the hidden motives of a supramoral and suprapersonal Ego. The manner in which the problem of evil is formulated is unanswerable not because it is intrinsically so complex but because it begs the question. To answer the question according to the demands of the questioner is to submit to the assumptions under dispute. For answers which deny those presuppositions, there is no recourse but to redirect the question.

The tragic character of an event does not imply the presence of a purposive agent lurking behind it. It does not automatically indicate that there is a "who" which directs such occurrences and whose intent it is our theological task to uncover. If events of this order have "meaning" it does not imply that some suprahuman energy deliberately planned their occurrence in order to judge us. Meanings are wrested out of chaos and absurdity. What endows them with sanctity is not their purported origin in the mysterious will of a divine subject, but the character of the interpretation through which we shape constructive response out of destructive event. That a spark of meaning may be salvaged from the darkness does not explain or justify the cause of the catastrophe. Contrary to popular assumption, it is not natural to ask "why" in the sense of "what for" before the presence of every tragedy which befalls humanity. That response to tragedy is theologically conditioned. A predicate-oriented theological view would not give rise to that kind of question, nor would it expect an answer in terms of a supernatural teleology. "Why" need not be construed as soliciting theoretical or empirical information but may be heard as a terrifying cry of distress. "Why" in this instance is equivalent to "woe." To this out-cry the proper response is not a scientific or theological explanation but a compassionate arm around the other's shoulders. What is asked for is no analysis of causes, only the presence of a supportive other, an ear which listens without judgment. For those who find consolation in the promise of a world controlled by an unfathomable Agent and of an ultimate reward, nothing can or should be said. For those, however, who feel that such strategies insult their common moral sense and observation, and like Job refuse to accept the presupposition of an accusatory theodicy, another way must be found. For it is not God who fails them but the way that God has been conceptualized. For them the contradictions between the moral ideal and the reality need not result in apostasy. With reflection and candor, the conflicts may yield different discoveries about the nature of God and the world.

From Whence Ungodliness?

To return to our opening discussion of the prayer for the sick, the inversionary principle interprets differently the disturbing events and the healing process. Sickness, suffering, and death are unequivocally real and evil. Persons may overcome the severity of their blows, may even grow stronger in coping with them. But such courageous respons-es do not justify their presence. The heroism of the sightless manifests qualities we may rightly call godly; it does not legitimate the loss of sight and make it good. "Woe unto them who say of evil it is good, and of good it is evil; that change darkness into light and light into dark-ness; that change bitter into sweet and sweet into bitter" [Isaiah 5:20].

Whence this ungodliness? For subject theology the roots of all events are traced vertically above, originating in the will and wisdom of a hypostatized subject. Its logic personifies good and generates angels and is not less likely to personify evil and generate demons. Fearing the heresy of dualism, all events below are said to originate from one source above, from the One who "forms light and creates darkness, makes peace and creates evil" (Isaiah 45). Such absorption in one governing subject threatens to blur moral distinctions.

In predicate thinking, the vertical line is bent horizontal. Evils are real and are of many sorts. The predicates of evil are experienced as real, as are the predicates of good. Neither set of predicates requires a subject, divine or demonic, to explain their origin and power. Evils are not the work of a malevolent suprapersonal will, but acts and events which threaten human growth, equilibrium, and fulfillment. Their causes may be unknown, but their mystery is not due to their origin in some occult satanic agency. They are not sent down or up from a demonic realm designed to hurt or punish innocence. Evils are of all kinds and are all subject to analysis and investigation, social, economic, political, physiological, medical. However awful their consequences, they originate from the natural soil in which we live and must be coped with accordingly. Allowed to be mystified, radicalized, and reified, evils are transmuted into a suprapersonal demonic threat before which human beings can do nothing but wring their hands or wait upon a suprapersonal benevolent force to counter the enemy. Understood as natural aberrations of natural forces, the variety of their forms may be dealt with, some actively resisted, some accepted, some sublimated, each according to its own nature.

A powerfully suggestive myth on the nature and forms of evil is recorded in the Talmud, which tells of the capture of the Evil Tempter. The captors sought to kill it but were warned that with its destruction, the entire world would fall apart. They imprisoned it nonetheless. Three days later they looked throughout the land for a fresh egg and could not find one, for when the sexual drive is extirpated, no eggs are available; where the libido is destroyed, civilization is ended. Those who held the Evil Tempter captive were themselves held fast in the vise of a dilemma. If they killed the Tempter, the world would be unable to endure; if they let it loose, evil would be free to roam the land. The captors begged for half-mercy, asking that the Tempter should live but not tempt. To this request the divine echo responded, "They do not grant halves in heaven." The myth reminds man that evil is often mixed with good, and that some forms of evil possess energies which when properly sublimated can serve for good. Without justifying evil, the myth speaks to the ambivalence and naturalness of evil as well as to the ways it can and cannot be confronted.

Source: Harold M. Schulweis, *Evil and the Morality of God*
(Cincinnati: Hebrew Union College Press, 1983), 133–137.

· 11 ·

ALVIN J. REINES

b. 1926

Alvin J. Reines, professor of Jewish philosophy at the Hebrew Union College–Jewish Institute of Religion, Cincinnati campus, was born in 1926 in Patterson, New York. His family included many prominent Orthodox rabbis who were committed to Zionism, such as Yitzchak Yaakov Reines, the founder of the Mizrachi movement. His own parents, however, were classical Reform Jews. After graduating from Yeshiva University, Reines enrolled in New York University to study law. However, soon afterward he left law school and entered the Hebrew Union College–Jewish Institute of Religion, from which he was ordained in 1952. From there he went to Harvard University and received his Ph.D. in 1958 as a student of Harry A. Wolfson. During his studies there, he specialized in medieval philosophy with a concentration on Maimonides and Abravanel. He was particularly influenced by the thinking of the prophet Amos, as well as the author of the Book of Ecclesiastes. In the modern period, it was Buber, but also contemporary empirical philosophy and scientific cosmology, that had an impact on his theological approach.

In 1970, a group of his students established the Institute of Creative Judaism. The purpose of this organization was to develop educational and liturgical material consistent with the Jewish polydox community. He continues to serve as the chairman of the board to this day.

Reines's significant contribution to Jewish theology is the idea of polydoxy (literally, "many beliefs"). This form of religion affirms the ultimate right of every individual to religious autonomy. Even Judaism, he says, incorporates various types of religion, some more polydoxic than others. For example, he argues that Orthodox Judaism is not compatible with the idea of polydoxy because it affirms a belief in verbal divine revelation of Torah, which is binding and authoritative, and consequently does not allow for deviation based on individual choices in matters of theology and religious practices. On the other hand, Reform Judaism, the movement to which he belongs, is compatible with polydoxy, because it rejects divine verbal revelation and instead postulates human authorship of sacred texts. In so doing, both Reform Judaism and polydoxy enable autonomous individuals to choose freely from among many religious alternatives.

Reines argues that, inasmuch as human beings have limited powers (e.g., we know that we will die one day; our understanding is circumscribed by our physical and emotional shortcomings), how we respond to the conflict of our finitude becomes our religion. This response is often related to the idea of God, a word that has various meanings in our language. Within a polydoxic framework, theology, which deals with the meaning of the word "God," needs to be based on objective evidence and empirical verifiability by individuals.

According to Reines, God is "the enduring possibility of being," which can be verifiable through sense-data (he calls them "sensa," plural of "sensum," referring to data that appear in an immediate awareness to one of the five senses) as well as self-data (he calls them "selfa," plural of "selfum," referring to the evidence relating to one's intramental life). Sensa and selfa, he notes, are actual entities and can be called "being."

Reines calls this view "hylotheism" (from Greek hyle, meaning "matter"), that is, "matter is God," where the word "matter" is understood as potentiality and possibility (as in Aristotelian philosophy), and not in the medieval sense of body. For Reines, God is not the "ground of being," but "the enduring possibility" of being. In hylotheism, God is viewed as always a possibility, always becoming, never an actuality, simply because to be actual is to be limited.

The consequence of this point of view is that God cannot exist without the universe, as God has no meaning without being. Furthermore, this God is a finite God where the possibility of future being is always derived from the present being. The future can only be created from the possibilities that are present today, which are, by definition, limited.

The Word "God"

We come then to the word **God** itself. Views about the word **God** (or its equivalent in other languages) that have been subscribed to historically may be divided into four major categories, which will be referred to by the following names: theopanism; theosupernaturalism; theonaturalism; and atheonomatism.

A. In **theopanism**, the meaning given the word **God** is of an entity that is not separate from the universe. Theopanism includes among its major concepts pantheism and panentheism. Pantheism is the belief that the universe as a whole is identical with **God**; **God** is nothing other than the integrated complex of beings, forces, and laws that constitute the universe. Mystical versions of pantheism, particularly when **God** is intuited as a perfect simplicity, are also referred to as theopantism. Panentheism differs from pantheism in that in panentheism the universe as a whole, while inseparable from **God**, is understood to be only a part rather than the whole of **God**, as is the case in pantheism. In panentheism, **God** includes the world in his being, but his being extends beyond the universe as well.

B. In **theosupernaturalism**, the meaning given the word **God** is of an entity who is separate from the universe, and who has the power to interrupt through miracles the ordinary or natural course of the universe. Theosupernaturalism includes such concepts as polytheism, henotheism, and monotheism. Polytheism is the belief that there are many **Gods.** In henotheism, there is also an admission that there are many **Gods**, but one **God** alone is considered supreme, or one **God** alone is considered the proper object to obey and worship. Monotheism is the belief that there is one **God** only, and the existence of other **Gods** is denied. **God** is generally viewed in monotheism as a person, the sole creator of the universe, who is conscious of the universe and reveals his will to humankind, and who governs the universe through the exercise of supernatural providence.

C. In **theonaturalism**, the meaning given the word **God** is of an entity that is separate from the universe, and that either creates the natural universe, or is an essential part of the processes that give rise to the natural universe. There are no miraculous interruptions of the processes of nature in theonaturalism; and natural laws and forces entirely govern human and all existence. In theonaturalism, **God** may be conceived of as a person or impersonally. Theonaturalism includes certain forms of deism and hylotheism. The form of deism that is included is the belief that **God** is a person who created the universe, imparted to it motion, and who then took no further interest in it, exerted no influence on natural events, exercised no supernatural providence over humankind, and communicated no supernatural revelation. Hylotheism, the view of the author, is the belief that the word **God** refers to "the enduring possibility of being," which is the permanent ongoing potentiality from which the actual universe is continually being realized.

D. **Atheonomatism** is the view of the word **God** that it has no reality meaning, that is, the word **God** refers to no actual being or reality of any kind. Atheonomatism includes atheism (narrowly defined) and agnosticism. Narrowly defined, atheism is simply the position that there does not exist a supreme, conscious and intelligent being. In other words, atheism is merely a negative belief that primarily denies theosupernaturalism; and in itself, it does not necessarily deny all forms of theopanism or of theonaturalism. Often, however, atheists will insist that the word **God** may be used only to refer to a theosupernatural deity, and if there is no such entity then the word is not to be used at all. Accordingly, atheism of this kind, that denies a reality meaning to theosupernaturalism, and will not permit the use of the word **God** to refer to anything else, is a form of atheonomatism. Agnosticism is also of more than one kind. The form of agnosticism that falls under atheonomatism is the belief that denies the possibility of knowing whether there is a **God** of the theosupernaturalistic kind. Accordingly, since a being of whose existence there is no knowledge cannot be said to exist,—at the minimum one must suspend judgment,—the term **God** has no reality reference. It should be pointed out that while atheonomatism is the position that the word **God** cannot be taken to refer to any real being, because it maintains that there is nothing in reality that corresponds to the name, this does not mean that the word **God** cannot be used by atheonomatists for other, non-referential linguistic purposes. Thus there are atheonomatists who claim the word **God** can serve such very important functions as expressing an exciting emotion, or evaluating and dramatizing the positive aspects of life. For such atheonomatists, these non-referential functions of the word **God** are those served by its use in liturgy.

Having enumerated the four major categories of views relating to the word **God**, we turn now to the Jewish religious enterprise. (The Jewish religious enterprise refers to the religious belief and thought of the long series of related communities that includes the Hebrews, Israelites, and Jews. For convenience sake, the members of all these communities will be referred to as Jews.) The question presents itself: to which of the four aforementioned categories of views on the word **God** have the Jews subscribed? The answer will probably surprise those who would judge the Jewish religious enterprise from present-day appearances, namely, the official or formal services, ritual, and educational curricula of almost all contemporary Jewish religious institutions. For the answer is that Jews, over the ages and including the present, have subscribed to all four categories of views on the word **God**. It is not the case that there is some one meaning of the word **God** or "essence of Judaism" to which every Jewish religious thinker, or every Jewish religious community has in the past and does now subscribe. It is true the notion is widespread that this "essence of Judaism" is belief in "one God," by which is meant that which has been referred to above more precisely as theosupernatural monotheism. This notion that "belief in theosupernatural monotheism" is the essence of all Jewish religious systems, as will be seen, is as untrue of antiquity and the Middle Ages as it is of the present. Yet it is a carefully cultivated myth or fantasy of the contemporary Jewish religious establishment, which not only misstates the past, but by claiming theosupernatural monotheism is a universal traditional Jewish dogma, and therefore obligatory upon all Jews, attempts in addition to control the present.

Source: Alvin J. Reines, "The Word 'God,'"
Polydoxy: Journal of the Institute of Creative Judaism 4, no. 1 (1979).

The Requirement of Evidence

Whether to require evidence as a condition for believing a God-view to be true and, if required, the kind of evidence necessary, are decisions each person makes for himself. Owing to my conception of the finity of the human mind, I believe these decisions are made subjectively and arbitrarily. I have chosen to require evidence as a condition for acceptance of a God-view. The kind of evidence I have decided upon is empirical evidence. In point of fact, the evidence I employ for verifying a God-view is no different from that which I require for establishing the reality of any extramental existent, or that required by the physical sciences to validate their theories. To my mind, there is no reason why verification of a God-view should enjoy privileged epistemological status.

By empirical evidence, I mean a sensum (plural: sensa). A sensum, as defined here, is a datum that appears to immediate awareness as a presentation of one of the five senses. I accept no experiences other than sensa as sources of information regarding the existence of entities in the extramental world (among which is a real God), and no propositions other than those verified by sensa as true of the extramental world. All data other than sensa that appear to immediate awareness I take as sources of information regarding intramental entities that are reducible in their entirety to events within the psyche. Such an intramental datum is designated a selfum (plural: selfa). Selfa constitute the evidence upon which statements relating to one's intramental life are based. Sensa and selfa exist only as long as they are present to awareness. As such, they are the only actual entities that are experienced and will, therefore, be referred to as *being*. What is past is not being and does not exist. That which is termed the *past* exists only as a memory in a selfum.

I will use the expression *misinterpreted selfum* to refer to a selfum that, in my view, has mistakenly been understood as a datum providing information regarding extramental reality. It goes without saying that my designation of an experience as a misinterpreted selfum is a subjective evaluation based upon the decision that only my sensa constitute evidence regarding the not-self. Thus my judgment that a person who claims to have seen an angel has in fact experienced a misinterpreted selfum is based upon my having no sensum relating to such an entity. Similarly, I believe to be a misinterpreted selfum the experience of those who profess a meta-sensum apprehension of a divine presence, because I hold that only sensa relate to extramental reality. I do not believe that theological differences based upon disagreements over whether an experience is a misinterpreted selfum or truly related to extramental reality can be argued. It is true that one can present evidence against the consistency of an ostensible misinterpreted selfum with other experiences, but proof that the datum of some other person's immediate awareness is a misinterpreted selfum cannot be brought.

What is the basis for genuine belief in one God-view and for rejection of another? The only authentic response I know to this question is that the one God-view is considered true and the other false. Although this response would seem to be implicit in the foregoing discussion, I bring it up to underscore this principle: the fact that I am a Jew is in no way relevant to which God-view I accept as true. Authentic belief in a God-view is not created by the merely external circumstance that one happens to be born of parents who chance to be members of a particular religious community; authentic belief is not inherited. Genuine assent to a God-view comes from conviction born of a person's individual truth–process regardless of the beliefs of others. The long theological history of the Jews bears out that this has indeed been the course taken by Jewish religious thinkers. One need only look to the diverse theologies of Ecclesiastes, Maimonides, Spinoza, and Buber to see that this is so. Hence, whether the God-views of Jews in the past or present agree with my theology is irrelevant to my belief; all that is germane is that the evidence for the theology creates within me the conviction of its truth. The corollary of this position is that all one has to do to convert me to his or her theology is to present evidence for it superior to that which exists for my own.

Source: Alvin J. Reines, "Hylotheism: A Theology of Pure Process," in *Jewish Theology and Process Thought*, ed. Sandra B. Lubarsky and David Ray Griffin (New York: State University of New York Press, 1996), 256–258.

God

We come then to our final subject, the word *God*. Inasmuch as no authoritative or dogmatic definition of God can be laid down in a polydoxy—more than one view with respect to the word God is consistent with a polydoxy's essence—the discussion that follows is to be regarded primarily as an explanation of why the author takes the position he does, rather than as a polemic against positions to which others are committed and which possess great value for them. Of course, in explaining why any position is taken, it is inevitable that reasons should be given why other positions have been rejected; negation is an aspect of affirmation. Negation, however, is not the purpose of this exposition, and it is only incidental to the spirit in which it is presented.

Justification and Evidence

All inquiry into the reality and nature of a professed existent begins with an examination of the ways of knowing. Even our brief investigation, therefore, cannot proceed directly to a statement of the reality and nature of God. Rather, as all theology must, it starts with a consideration of the nature of evidence and the justification of belief. What is the evidence, if any, that is necessary to justify belief in a reality called God?

To begin with, let us consider the possibility that no evidence at all is to be required. It is evident that no proof can be brought to determine the question of evidence, inasmuch as that which constitutes a proof is itself dependent upon the same question. No proof, therefore, can be brought that evidence is necessary; the choice of evidence is a starting point of inquiry. One who wishes can without evidence state anything, affirm anything, or believe anything. Such is the way of ipse dixit theology. Having conceded this, however, the choice here is that evidence must be given to justify whatever reality reference is to be assigned the word God. There is no quarrel with those who use their freedom to deny that evidence is necessary, provided that they affirm the freedom of others to withhold serious consideration from any proposed reality meaning of God for which no evidence is given. The word theology literally means "science or knowledge of God," and though the heart may not wish to know, thought must have its reasons. As Maimonides says in laying down the rules of evidence and faith which preface his inquiry into the nature of God:

[B]ear in mind that by "faith" we do not mean that which is uttered with the lips, but that which is apprehended by the [rational] soul, the conviction that the object [of belief] is exactly as it is conceived. If, as regards real or supposed truths, you content yourself with giving utterance to them in words, without conceiving them or believing in them, especially if you do not seek certainty, you have a very easy task, as, in fact, you will find many ignorant people who retain [the words of] beliefs [in their memory] without conceiving any idea with regard to them . . . belief is only possible after a thing is conceived; it consists in the conviction that the thing apprehended has its existence beyond the mind [in reality] exactly as it is conceived in the mind. . . . Renounce desires and habits, follow your reason . . . you will then be fully convinced of what we have said. . . . [*Guide to the Perplexed*, 1, 50]

1. Once the principle is affirmed that subjective evidence is valid, then the subjective evidence of every person is validated. If everyone's subjective evidence is valid, how is a choice to be made between two conflicting statements on the nature of God and religion, both of which are supported by subjective evidence? How does one choose between the God and religion of the Pentateuch, which knows of no Trinity, Messiah, resurrection, or immortality, and the God and religion of fundamentalist Christianity, which affirms the Trinity, a Messiah, and makes afterlife the goal and purpose of human existence? Surely, unless reason and the law of contradiction are to be dismissed, these religions cannot both be correct. It is possible, we may suppose, for a person to claim that her or his subjective evidence testifies to its own validity and tells as well which other subjective evidence is valid. But this seems rather arbitrary and unconvincing. It is equivalent, in fact, to a claim of prophecy. Subjective evidence, then, does not seem to provide a much better criterion for determining truth than no evidence at all. One of the principal reasons for requiring evidence is to judge between truth claims, but the theology of subjective evidence seems to serve this purpose no better than ipse dixit theology.

2. Furthermore, if the believer "is conscious of God Himself," how is it, for example, that the preexilic prophets' and Jesus' concepts

of the nature of God differ so? And why does the Muslim experience Allah; the Christian, Jesus; and the Hindu, Brahma? The analogy between religious cognition and sense perception is surely farfetched. Few will disagree, I am sure, that the tree the prophet sees will answer to Jesus' notion of a tree, and to ours as well, yet for people ostensibly experiencing the same "presence," their notions of deity and religion differ greatly indeed.

3. One of the conclusions of Sigmund Freud's investigations was that the experience of "presence" which some take as meeting with the deity is properly understood as an experience of self objectified and projected outward. How, in this Freudian and scientific age, can it be considered "rational" to accept the mere fact of experiencing a "presence" as consciousness of "God Himself"? Rather, it would appear that one of the prime methodological considerations in a theology competent for our time is the recognition that "presences" per se can well be projections of the unconscious.

4. The concept of God that the experience of "presence" is usually taken to substantiate is theistic absolutism. This is the concept of a being whose nature has consequences for the world we experience. A universe created and governed by an omniscient, omnipotent, and omnibenevolent being may be expected to display the marks of a perfect source. Thus the apprehension of "presence" is clearly not adequate by itself to demonstrate the truth of this concept; it must be proved coherent with the facts of the universe as well. We can all grant that there are those who encounter "presences"; the problem is the world of brute fact. Many of our experiences in the world of brute fact are incoherent with theistic absolutism, the most critical of which is the experience of surd evil. If the facts could be brought into harmony with the concept of theistic absolutism, "presence" theology would have little difficulty in making its point. Yet the medievals, who considered their concept of God supported by indubitable evidence, gave more attention to its congruence with the external world than theologians today whose primary evidence is the ambiguous "presence."

The conclusion from these considerations is that subjective evidence does not convincingly establish a real being, a reality reference for the word God. Before leaving the subject of subjective evidence, however, three points should be stressed. First, repeating the opinion stated earlier, theology based upon subjective evidence is appropriate to Polydox Judaism only if such theology is understood to be nonauthoritative. Second, the use of "presence" is only objected to as primary evidence for a concept of deity; no objection is made to the use of "presence" as corroborative evidence for a divine reality established by objective means, or as a symbol referring to a reality so established. Third, not all forms of theism are established by subjective evidence; the exponents of theistic finitism, for example, appeal in the main to objective evidence.

Objective Evidence Theology

The form of theology to which we now come is the pursuit of a reality reference for God based on objective evidence of the kind earlier classified as theology of the fifth form. For many, the primary difficulty regarding this form of theology is that the objective evidence presently available does not substantiate the concept of theistic absolutism. Their disappointment is understandable, but no rebuttal of truth. Those who require objective evidence employ a strict standard of evidence precisely because they are aware of the human person's infinite strivings and the screen they often place between the person and reality. Genuine religion is to have one's view of the word God shape one's emotions and desires, and not the contrary. Thus, far from being that which religion should avoid, reality objectively determined provides the basis of true religion and ultimate meaningful existence. For authentic response to finitude, which constitutes true religion, must be based upon reality, and ultimate meaningful existence is nothing other than the state such response produces.

Moreover, while subjective theology is consistent with the essence of Polydox Judaism, objective theology is more than consistent; it is also coherent, fitting naturally with the origins and spirit of polydoxy. Polydoxy came into existence as a result of the conclusion that Scripture is fallible, the work, at least in part, of humans. This conclusion was arrived at through critical and objective study, scientific inquiry applied to Scripture. Is it not natural to apply this same method to the theology of Polydox Judaism as well?

Enduring Possibility of Being

There are several theories of truth based upon objective evidence. Since it would take us far afield to enter upon the intricacies of reflection involved in selecting one theory over another, it will suffice for our purpose merely to indicate the one to which the author subscribes. This is the theory that a proposition concerning the external world is true if it is empirically verifiable. This does not mean, as those who generally subscribe to empirical verifiability as the criterion of truth maintain, that there is no knowledge of one's self. That such knowledge is held to be possible is clear, inasmuch as it is the knowledge on which the ontal symbol and authentic response to the conflict of finitude are based. However, empirical verifiability is prescribed as the arbiter of truth concerning the external world, and seeing that God as a real being is a fact of the external world, a theory of truth regarding deity must be one that pertains to knowledge of this world.

A brief formulation of the notion of empirical verifiability can be stated thusly: "A proposition or series of propositions concerning the external world will be true if there are predictable and observable consequences of such a proposition or propositions." Hence the test that a definition of God must meet is empirical verifiability. If there are empirical consequences of the definition, then the proposition *God exists* will be true, and if there are not, the proposition will be meaningless or false. The definition of God I propose, consequently, is the following: *God is the enduring possibility of being.* By *being* is meant selfa (or self-data) and sensa (or sense-data). Inasmuch as being is analyzable without remainder into selfa and sensa, the existence of God is verified whenever selfa and sensa can both be experienced, and the existence of God is disproved when, under equivalent conditions of personal normalcy, selfa are experienced and sensa no longer are. God is disproved as the enduring possibility of being rather than as the enduring possibility of sense experience alone because the person (that is, the continuing self-consciousness that is constructed out of selfa) is evidently dependent upon the external world (sensa and the unobservables reducible to sensa), and with the annihilation of the external world, the inexorable annihilation of the person may be inferred.

Hylotheism

The definition of God as the enduring possibility of being is a concept of God called *hylotheism*. Hylotheism belongs to the class of concepts that may generally be subsumed under the heading of *finite God concepts*. Quite different theologies are grouped together under this heading but they all possess the common characteristic that deity is not regarded as perfect, judging "perfection" by the largely imaginary and arbitrary standard of "possessing every desirable attribute." For the most part, the imperfection attributed to deity in finite God concepts relates to the inability of God to overcome the force of evil. In the view of deity as the enduring possibility of being, the divine imperfection goes beyond this, to the essential nature of the divine existence.

The Possible, the Actual, and Nothingness

Two classes of existence, each with its distinctive nature, can be distinguished: the *possible* and the *actual*. Possible existence suffers this defect: it lacks actuality. As possibility, it is neither a selfum nor a sensum. Yet if the divine existence is to be of lasting duration, it can accomplish this only as possibility. For the actually existent is always limited; nothing unlimited can be experienced or imagined, let alone conceived. Hence to be actual is to be finite. While the finity of every actuality is present in all the spheres of its existence, it is temporal finity that provides the definitive boundary. The actual is finite in time because, as an actuality, it is finite in the power of existence and destined therefore, as an individual, to annihilation. Being thus breeds nothingness; indeed, *nothing* has no meaning except in relation to being. Accordingly, if God is to be of lasting duration, the divine existence must forego actuality for possibility. We find therefore that God is of lasting duration, but possesses only possible existence, whereas being is finite in duration, but possesses actual existence.

Metaphorically speaking, existence, the act of overcoming nothingness, lays down conditions on all that would possess it. As a consequence, nothingness is never entirely overcome. Actual existents temporarily overcome nothingness at the cost of future and total annihilation. God overcomes nothingness by incorporating it into the divine existence, and, in so doing, is emptied of actuality and must forever remain possibility. The divine existence, so to speak, is a compromise between being and nothingness; the ground of being overcomes nothingness to exist as the enduring possibility of being, but in the uneasy victory defect is assimilated into the Godhead.

God and the World

The status of God's existence as the enduring possibility of being leads to a further consequence: God cannot exist without the world. God has no meaning without being; being has no endurance without God. God's existence is not absolute; the enduring possibility of being exists as a correlative of being. The world was not created by an absolute God who arbitrarily willed it so; rather the world exists because the divine existence is unconditionally dependent upon it. Of creation *ex nihilo*, we have no knowledge. In experience, God coexists with finites in a process of continuous interaction. In this process, as we are justified in concluding from the regular and orderly nature of causal sequence, the possibility of future being is derived from present being. In other words, the existence of God is derived from every present moment of being and realized in every future moment. God is the ground of being and being is the ground of God.

God, Humankind, and Covenant

A further consequence of God's nature as possibility is the relation that obtains between God and humankind. In this view of God, where the divine is subject to the conditions of existence, it is the nature of actual entities, by virtue of the finity or encompassing boundary that gives them their existence, to be cut off from the ground of their being. To be actual is to be alone. To be finite is to be severed from the enduring. Hence the relation between God and humankind is one of muted communication. Accordingly, as polydoxy teaches, there exists no infallible or verbal revelation, nor can there be such revelation, because humankind, necessarily and substantially separated from the ground of being, has no sure relation to this ground. Equally, the perfect providence of theistic absolutism, its Messiahs and supernatural eschatologies, have no place in a world where the enduring exists only as a possibility and the actual world is always finite. Yet if God cannot overcome human finity, humans are not power-less. The possibilities that constitute the Godhead can be influenced and even altered by humankind. Every ontal decision that resolves the pain of injustice and poverty increases the possibility of social betterment in the future; every scientific discovery becomes a power for the future. If humans will the good, God conserves all the value that is possible.

This relation of action and passion between humankind and God may be viewed symbolically as a covenant, an ethics of hypothetical necessity: If the human person acts, then God reacts; and, as the human person acts, so God reacts. In the words of the prophet Amos:

> *Seek good, and not evil, that ye may live;*
> *And so the Lord, the God of hosts,*
> *will be with you, as ye say.*
> *Hate the evil, and love the good,*
> *and establish justice in the gate. (Amos 5:14 f)*

This covenant, in which the human person must do the good to receive the good, is to be sharply distinguished from supernatural covenants with deity, in which the person is required to perform some act irrelevant to the good, ritualistic or otherwise, and God, without prior and competent natural causes, miraculously produces the good.

Hylotheism and the Problem of Evil

The absence of an infallible and verbal revelation is only part of the larger problem of evil, the great complex of events and conditions that beset and anguish human existence. Evil comes from events outside the human person and from conditions within. The human person, in attempting to cope with the problems the self and world present, is not only inherently deficient intellectually, lacking certainty in knowl-edge and absolutes in ethics, but is constitutionally deficient emotion-ally and physically as well. These lacks keep the person from perfect and permanent solutions to ultimate problems, and provide constant threats to the very meaning of existence. In no way can evil be accounted for satisfactorily by theological absolutism. This includes not only theistic absolutism, but pantheistic absolutism as well, such as we find, for example, in Spinozism. The Whole that is the Spinozistic substance cannot contain the evils of the world and be coherently pronounced perfect any more than a theistic omniscient, omnipotent, and omnibenevolent Creator can be coherently pronounced perfect. The Whole exists in and through its parts and cannot escape the defects of their nature, just as the absolute Creator is responsible for his creatures and cannot escape the consequences of their acts.

In the theology of divine possibility, there is a coherent explanation of evil. Evil is the inevitable result of the nature of a God that can only exist as possibility and the nature of humans who can only exist as finite. Evil is not willed into existence; it is a necessary concomitant of existence. The choice, figuratively stated, is not between a world with evil and a world without it, but between a world with evil and no world at all.

Thus two principles in the theology of divine possibility serve to explain evil. The first is that all actual being is necessarily finite. Every actual thing will in every way be limited; being does not endure. This does not mean that meliorism is unrealistic and melioration cannot occur—it can and does—but melioration is all that can occur. No final triumph over limitation and nothingness is possible. The second principle is that God, the divine possibility, can only offer for realization in the future the possibilities that reside in the being of the present. God, in other words, is not an independent and absolute agent who can miraculously produce the good *ex nihilo*; the divine existence can present for realization in the future only that which has been made possible in the past. Together, these two principles, that the "present" or world of actualities is always limited, and that the future can only be created out of possibilities derived from a present that is limited, offer an explanation of the pervasive occurrence of evil in the world.

Hylotheism and Polydoxy

The theology of divine possibility is offered as a theology appropriate and coherent with a polydoxy. Out of their freedom polydoxians may accept or reject it. A theology should, however, only be rejected on valid grounds; and there is one objection that is not valid. This objection argues that a theology must satisfy the infinite wishes of humans and provide them with unlimited consolation. This argument is invalid because it is based upon a mistaken conception of theology in particular and of religion in general. The purpose of theology is truth and the purpose of religion is to enable the human person to live authentically with that truth. Hence truth is the only relevant and necessary justification of a theology.

As Maimonides so profoundly taught, a theology is as important for that which it negates as for that which it affirms. The worship of false gods is idolatry, and if a theology should serve to keep humans from idolatry, even though, as in the case of Maimonides' theology, it should tell them nothing of the essence of God, then such a theology will have accomplished a great good. Throughout history, there has been a special fury attached to the deeds of those who have acted in the name of false gods, and who have rationalized through idolatry despotic and tyrannical urges that were solely their own. The theology of divine possibility as a negative theology serves the moral role of denying divinity to any finite, no matter the basis upon which the divinity is claimed, whether through revelation or incarnation. The fact of evil, resulting as it does from the necessary limitations of existence, should not bring us to despair, but to the meaningful awareness that the divine possibility reacts to acts of value and conserves all possible good. Yet there is an austere overtone to the concept of God as possibility. As possibility, God does not produce the concrete realization of human good; this of necessity is left to humankind. Should humans in this critical age fail, then we must be aware with Amos and the author of the Noah story that God does not require for his existence any particular people, species, or world. While it is true that God without any world at all has no existence, the divine enduring possibility does not require any particular world or class of finites for existence. The awesome choice, whether humans are to be included in an existing class of finites, is left at this point in time to humankind itself.

Source: Alvin J. Reines, *Polydoxy: Explorations in a Philosophy of Liberal Religion* (Buffalo: Prometheus Books, 1987), 168–181.

· 12 ·

HAROLD S. KUSHNER

b. 1935

Rabbi laureate of Temple Israel in Natick, Massachusetts, Harold S. Kushner was born in 1935 in Brooklyn, New York. He graduated from Columbia University and was ordained by the Jewish Theological Seminary (JTS) in 1960, where he also earned a doctorate in 1972. During his illustrious tenure at Temple Israel, he received six honorary doctorates, and studied at the Hebrew University of Jerusalem. He taught at Clark University in Worcester, Massachusetts, and in the Rabbinical School of JTS. For six years he was the editor of the Conservative Judaism *magazine. Honored in 1995 by the Christophers, a Roman Catholic organization, Kushner was also recognized in 1999 by Religion in American Life as their clergyman of the year.*

Harold Kushner has published many articles and books on Jewish thought, and is the author of the renowned When Bad Things Happen to Good People, *an international best-seller, published in 1981 after the death of his son Aaron in 1977 of progeria, also known as "rapid aging."*

Kushner was heavily influenced by the naturalistic theology of Mordecai Kaplan (see chapter 2). Like Kaplan, Kushner too, noted that we live in a predictable and orderly world, pointing to God as a force or a process behind it. Furthermore, he added, God cannot be viewed as an object, a "thing," or a "person," not even a super-person, but better as an invisible and intangible power, a quality of relationship. Belief in God simply means assuming that the order and direction of the universe are present to allow for human growth and creativity. Operating through the laws of nature, God, for Kushner, has limited powers. In other words, God cannot create miracles.

According to Kushner, God has not made us perfect but has given us free will to choose between good and bad. Using the forces that surround us as well as those we can draw on from within ourselves, we can become better human beings. In fact, religion encourages us to follow the path of good and stay away from wrongful ways. However, at times, tragedy does strike. And when bad things happen to good people, Kushner adds, they need not blame God for being the culprit. Some misfortunes are caused by bad luck, others by evil people, and many are the result of our being frail human beings. The laws of nature treat everyone alike. God does not, and in fact cannot, interfere. On the contrary, it is when we confront evil in life that we need to turn to God, who gives us the strength to cope with it. To those who face tragedies, what we should offer is sympathy and compassion, not theology.

God Is Not a Thing

If the Second Commandment teaches us anything, it teaches us that *God is not a thing*. We are to make no visual representation of Him, not because it would offend His dignity to have His portrait done poorly, but because He does not lend Himself to pictorial representation. He is totally different from the three-dimensional animal-vegetable-mineral world in whose terms we are accustomed to think. We cannot see Him, not because He is *invisible*, but because He is *intangible*. He has no form, He does not fill space and therefore (as we will have the opportunity to discuss later) the question of His being in one place and not in another is misleading and almost meaningless. God is not a thing—He has none of the physical properties of things.

This is one reason why, as I wrote [earlier], all discussion of God in human, thing-oriented language is bound to be metaphorical and misleading if taken literally. Does God hear prayers and cries? Human beings and animals hear because of the reverberations of sound waves on the organs of their inner ears. If God hears, He certainly doesn't hear that way. Whatever else I believe about God, I can't believe that He has bones and cartilage in His ears the way we do. Does God know our thoughts? Is He pleased or angered by them? For human beings, knowledge involves electrical currents passing between brain cells. Emotional changes involve secretions of the glands. God, removed from the world of "thing-ness," has neither brain cells nor adrenal glands. "God's knowledge," "God's wrath," "pleasing in the sight of God". . . must be understood as poetic metaphors and not taken literally as implying anything about God's nature.

And yet, I would plead for the right to continue using such metaphors, open to misconception as they may be. Our language and conversation would be impoverished beyond repair if our every utterance had to meet the stringent requirements of a logician and linguistic analyst. We permit ourselves to speak of sunrise and sunset, though we know well enough that the sun neither rises nor sets, but that our corner of the earth moves toward it or away from it. The poet Lovelace can write *"When Love with unconfined wings hovers within my gates . . ."* we can send greeting cards with Cupids on them, yet no one suspects us of being pagan animists who really believe that Love is a winged cherub with a bow and arrow. We recognize these as poetic usages that appeal to the imagination. Similarly, we should be free to speak of "God's creating," "God's caring," "God's inspiring the doctor and scientist," without being taken to mean a God who is a Heaven-dwelling Superman, a God who is actually "doing" these things with real hands and real bodily organs. We have no language other than this language by which to speak of God and we must speak of Him.

Let us agree then that we will continue speaking of God and use traditional forms of expression, with the understanding that we are not obliged to take them literally or be held accountable for the strict connotations of the word, as long as these expressions do not lead us astray. Let us give ourselves the same freedom of expression we extend to the weatherman, who is free to speak of sunrise and sunset as much as he wishes—as long as he doesn't base his forecast on the theory that the sun moves around the earth.

If God is not a thing, it goes without saying that He is not a person, nor even a superperson. Despite Michaelangelo God does not resemble anyone's musclebound grandfather. He does not "do what people do, only better." He is a totally different order of reality than we humans are, not just bigger, better, or further away, but completely *different*.

Yet so much of the confusion, so many of the misunderstandings about God stem from this habit of thinking of Him as a pious Superman, subject to no limitation, not even to the laws of Nature. "Why did God do that?" "How could He let it happen?" "Don't you believe that God *told* us this is wrong, and *wants* us not to do it?" Perhaps the greatest step toward a mature understanding of God is the realization that God doesn't "do" things the way a person does them. He doesn't "cause" things to happen in the world, except in a special sense of the word, different from the way we use it about ourselves when we speak of our "causing things to happen" or our "making" things. It would be very pleasant to believe in a God who really did make things happen by the same rational and physical processes that we employ, a God who punished us for what we did wrong and protected us from harm if we deserved protection. But there is so much evidence from real experience contradicting this kind of belief that its proponent would have to spend all his time defending and apologizing for it.

If God is not a person or a thing, if He has neither shape or form and does not take space, what is He? There is probably no completely accurate word in our language, for the reasons we have already mentioned. In order not to mislead, we would need a word used only for God, not for any tangible, earth-bound object and then we would have no basis for understanding that word. As a matter of fact, we have such a word—"God"—and we have difficulty understanding what we mean by it because there are no other things on earth to which we can apply it. But there are, however, words that point in the right direction. God is something like a Force, a Power, a Process, a quality of relationship. God is the name we attach to the fact that we find certain things possible and meaningful in the world and in our lives and the fact that we find ourselves stirred to move in the direction of realizing these possibilities. We call God the force behind our growing and learning, our curiosity to discover and our impulse to share and to help.

The name "God" stands for all those qualities in the world and in ourselves which our religious tradition labels as divine, that is, as comprising full human spiritual development, fashioning Man into what he is at his best and most fully realized. If Truth, Justice, Mercy, Generosity, Love are among the things we need to be genuine human beings, to be, in the Biblical phrase, men "*in God's image*", then the name "God" stands for the existence of these qualities in the world and the existence of a corresponding impulse toward them in every human soul.

The statement, for example, that "God is just" or that "God demands justice of men" doesn't really tell us anything about a being named God. But it does tell us that justice is one of the qualities human beings need to be fully and satisfyingly human. It tells us that we cannot realize our potential greatness as human beings *unless* we practice justice and are part of a just society. And it tells us further that justice is possible in this world, that the world around us and the human soul within us are not constructed so as to mock our strivings for justice from the outset. The same process of interpretation holds for all the other qualities for which the name of God stands. Belief in God is not so much a statement about Somebody living in Heaven as it is an affirmation of the world and the human beings who inhabit it, what they are and what they are capable of becoming. Belief in God means believing that the universe has order and direction, that it encourages human goodness and moral growth and that the impulse each of us feels to be a good person is a reflection of the purposefulness existing in the cosmos at large.

Some years back, a Soviet cosmonaut emerged from his space capsule and announced triumphantly that he had circled the earth several dozen times without bumping into God or any of His angels. He thought he was proving that God didn't exist and that religion was therefore false. Actually, he was only noting that God was not a thing, an object occupying space with which a spaceship might collide. But if we understand "God" to mean, among other things, the Power that awakens in men the curiosity to explore the universe, that plants in them the potential for scientific genius, that gives them the courage to face danger and risk their lives in outer space in an effort to expand the boundaries of human knowledge and mastery of the world, might we not say that the astronauts have "bumped into God" and seen Him "face to face" *more* than the average person?

May I emphasize at this point that God is *no less real* for not being a thing or a person. A force can be real. An idea can have reality; it can affect and change the world by its operation. No one would claim that electricity, heat, fire are imaginary because they are not *things*, but are forces and processes that operate through their effect on other, more tangible objects. Nor would anyone say that love and courage are unreal because you can't keep them in a box and take them out to show people.

Source: Harold S. Kushner, *When Children Ask about God*
(New York: Schocken Books, 1976), 12–17.

God Gives Us Strength

The God I believe in does not send us the problem; He gives us the strength to cope with the problem.

Where do you get the strength to go on, when you have used up all of your strength? Where do you turn for patience when you have run out of patience, when you have been more patient for more years than anyone should be asked to be, and the end is nowhere in sight? I believe that God gives us strength and patience and hope, renewing our spiritual resources when they run dry. How else do sick people manage to find more strength and more good humor over the course of prolonged illness than any one person could possibly have, unless God was constantly replenishing their souls? How else do widows find the courage to pick up the pieces of their lives and go out to face the world alone, when on the day of their husband's funeral, they did not have that courage? How else do the parents of a retarded or brain-damaged youngster wake up every morning and turn again to their responsibilities, unless they are able to lean on God when they grow weak?

We don't have to beg or bribe God to give us strength or hope or patience. We need only turn to Him, admit that we can't do this on our own, and understand that bravely bearing up under long-term illness is one of the most human, and one of the most godly, things we can ever do. One of the things that constantly reassures me that God is real, and not just an idea that religious leaders made up, is the fact that people who pray for strength, hope, and courage so often find resources of strength, hope, and courage that they did not have before they prayed.

I also believe that sick children should pray. They should pray for the strength to bear what they have to bear. They should pray that sickness and its treatment not hurt them too much. They should pray as a way of talking out their fears without the embarrassment of having to say them out loud, and as a reassurance that they are not alone. God is close to them even late at night in the hospital when their parents have gone home and all the doctors have left. God is still with them even when they are so sick that their friends no longer come to visit. The fear of pain and the fear of abandonment are perhaps the most troubling aspects of a child's illness, and prayer should be used to ease those fears. Sick children can even pray for a miracle to restore them to good health, as long as they do not feel that God is judging them to decide whether or not they deserve a miracle. They should pray because the alternative would be giving up all hope and marking time until the end comes.

"If God can't make my sickness go away, what good is He? Who needs Him?" God does not want you to be sick or crippled. He didn't make you have this problem, and He doesn't want you to go on having it, but He can't make it go away. That is something which is too hard even for God. What good is He, then? God makes people become doctors and nurses to try to make you feel better. God helps us be brave when we're sick and frightened, and He reassures us that we don't have to face our fears and our pains alone.

The conventional explanation, that God sends us the burden because He knows that we are strong enough to handle it, has it all wrong. Fate, not God, sends us the problem. When we try to deal with it, we find out that we are not strong. We are weak; we get tired, we get angry, overwhelmed. We begin to wonder how we will ever make it through all the years. But when we reach the limits of our own strength and courage, something unexpected happens. We find reinforcement coming from a source outside of ourselves. And in the knowledge that we are not alone, that God is on our side, we manage to go on.

It was in this way that I answered the young widow who challenged me about the efficacy of prayer. Her husband had died of cancer, and she told me that while he was terminally ill, she prayed for his recovery. Her parents, her in-laws, and her neighbors all prayed. A Protestant neighbor invoked the prayer circle of her church, and a Catholic neighbor sought the intercession of St. Jude, patron saint of hopeless causes. Every variety, language, and idiom of prayer was mustered on his behalf, and none of them worked. He died right on schedule, leaving her and her young children bereft of a husband and father. After all that, she said to me, how can anyone be expected to take prayer seriously?

Is it really true, I asked her, that your prayers were not answered? Your husband died; there was no miraculous cure for his illness. But what did happen? Your friends and relatives prayed; Jews, Catholics, and Protestants prayed. At a time when you felt so desperately alone, you found out that you were not alone at all. You found out how many other people were hurting for you and with you, and that is no small thing. They were trying to tell you that this was not happening to you because you were a bad person. It was just a rotten, unfair thing that no one could help. They were trying to tell you that your husband's life meant a lot to them too, and not only to you and your children, and that whatever happened to him, you would not be totally alone. That is what their prayers were saying, and I suspect that it made a difference.

And what about *your* prayers?, I asked her. Were they left unanswered? You faced a situation that could easily have broken your spirit, a situation that could have left you a bitter, withdrawn woman, jealous of the intact families around you, incapable of responding to the promise of being alive. Somehow that did not happen. Somehow you found the strength not to let yourself be broken. You found the resiliency to go on living and caring about things. Like Jacob in the Bible, like every one of us at one time or another, you faced a scary situation, prayed for help, and found out that you were a lot stronger, and a lot better able to handle it, than you ever would have thought you were. In your desperation, you opened your heart in prayer, and what happened? You didn't get a miracle to avert a tragedy. But you discovered people around you, and God beside you, and strength within you to help you survive the tragedy. I offer that as an example of a prayer being answered.

Source: Harold S. Kushner, *When Bad Things Happen to Good People* (New York: Schocken Books, 1981), 127–131.

Our Sense of Morality

The affirmation of monotheism—that there is only one God—is a moral statement, not a mathematical deduction. If there is only one God and He demands moral behavior, then there can be such a thing as good and evil. (Technically speaking, right and wrong are matters of fact: Who stole the money? Good and bad are matters of morality: Should I take the money?) When there are many gods, as in pagan legends, the issue is not: What is good? The issue is: Which God shall I serve? Which one has the power to protect and reward me? Think, for example, of the conflicts in Homer's *Iliad*, where the gods take sides. What pleases one displeases another. A person offends one of the gods but is under the protection of another, stronger one. The issue is not what is right but who has the might.

The assertion that there is only one God is the assertion that issues of moral behavior are not matters of personal taste. We cannot decide by majority vote that it is all right to steal and lie, any more than we can decide that winters should be mild or cookies more nourishing than vegetables. Bertrand Russell, perhaps the most articulate spokesman for enlightened atheism in our generation, captured the dilemma with which I confronted my Holocaust students in these words: "I cannot . . . refute the arguments for the subjectivity of ethical values, but I find myself incapable of believing that all that is wrong with wanton cruelty is that I don't like it." In other words, it may be hard to persuade someone philosophically that there is a God who sets moral standards for us. We may be more comfortable with the notion "I will do what I believe is good, and I will leave you free to do what you believe is good." But we instinctively feel that there is something lacking in our philosophy when it can be reduced to "Personally, I choose not to torture little children or persecute people because of their race or religion, but if it doesn't bother you to do it, go ahead."

As I see it, there are two possibilities. Either you affirm the existence of a God who stands for morality and makes moral demands of us, who built a law of truthfulness into His world even as He built in a law of gravity (so that if we violate either one, we suffer the consequences). Or else you give everyone the right to decide what is good and what is evil by his or her own lights, balancing the voice of one's conscience against the voice of temptation and need, like some cartoon character with an angel whispering in one ear and a devil whispering in the other.

Some moral philosophers distinguish between two kinds of wrongdoing. There are things which are wrong because people have declared them wrong, like driving over the speed limit or on the wrong side of the road, and there are things which are wrong in and of themselves, like murder or rape. What makes them wrong? Not public opinion (it might be possible to get 51 percent of the population to vote in favor of permitting adultery or letting the poor steal from wealthy corporations); they are just wrong whether people like it or not.

Which brings me to my problem with Clint Eastwood. I have seen only one of his very successful "Dirty Harry" movies, but I remember it clearly. I have never responded to a movie the way I did to that one, with as strong a sense of divergence between my mind and my gut. Throughout the movie, my head kept saying, "Why am I watching this? This is cheap, manipulative trash." But at the gut level, my emotional reaction was "Yeah, go get 'em. Get out the Magnum and blast them away. Don't let those punks get away with it." Intellectually, I found it shallow. Emotionally, I found it compelling and satisfying.

The point is not that the millions of people who go to Clint Eastwood movies are less intellectual and more emotional than I am. The point is that there is something instinctive in me, and I suspect in every one of us, that reacts with a surge of anger to injustice, to the prospect of villains and criminals "getting away with it." It is not an intellectual position, a carefully thought out conclusion about what kind of society I want to live in. It is a gut reaction, an instinctive sense of "That's not right." (I can't tell you how many people have urged me to write a book on the problem of "when *good* things happen to *bad* people.")

Edmund Cahn, former professor of law at New York University, suggests that there is such a thing as a "sense of injustice." We may not be able to define justice, he writes, but we all recognize injustice when we see it, and we all respond to injustice in the same way, the way I responded to the villain in the Clint Eastwood movie, with a feeling of outrage and a sense of "That's not fair." Even little children are capable of saying "That's not fair" (and not only about what happens to them, but also about unfair treatment of friends or even strangers).

This sense of injustice is more than a matter of maintaining a safe society. It is not saying it is wrong to steal because it would be maddening to live in a society where other people could take your belongings. It is not saying we should not murder because if it were all right to murder, the people with the most guns would control the world, and they might not be the best people to do that. It says murder and theft are wrong. Even if you could persuade yourself that the world would be better off if certain people were killed, or if the poor could take what they need from the rich because they need it more, it would still be wrong. Codes of law before the time of Moses were phrased "If a man kills another, this will be his punishment. . . . If a man steals, this is the punishment." The Ten Commandments were the first code to go beyond "If . . . then . . ." and say "You shall not murder! You shall not steal!" not because it is punishable, not because it is illegal, but because it is wrong.

Where does our sense of injustice come from? I would maintain that it comes from God, by which I mean that it is not man-made, not a matter of human consensus, but is built into the world we live in, as part of what makes it a world capable of morality.

Furthermore, just as I believe that our encounter with holiness is something we welcome, so I would maintain that our encounter with the moral dimension of life, the existence of fixed standards of good and evil, is not just something we recognize, like the truth of a geometrical proposition, but something we have reason to be grateful for. I believe we want to be addressed by God. We want to be recognized as moral beings, significantly different from animals because we have eaten from the Tree of Knowledge of Good and Evil. We want to have moral demands made of us, not because we are sure we will live up to them, but because the demands addressed to us make us feel that we are special because we are human.

Source: Harold S. Kushner, *Who Needs God?*
(New York: Summit Books, 1989), 70–74.

Where Is God?

A Christian pastoral worker in Central America, working with insurgents against a repressive government, tells of hearing a woman cry out, "Why is God doing this to us?" and hearing her neighbor answer, "God has abandoned us. If we have not done anything bad, if what we are asking for is not all that much, where is God now?" The pastoral worker had no answer. But it seems to me that there is an answer, and it might be something like this: Where is God when people are tortured and murdered by a tyrannical government? Where was God when a handful of Jews in the Warsaw Ghetto rose in defiance of the Nazi army? Where was God when black people were brutalized by angry mobs and bigoted white sheriffs in the American South? God is found in the courage of the human soul to stand up for human dignity, no matter what the odds, so that no matter how poor, no matter how uneducated or how badly outnumbered, people are willing to risk their lives for what they believe is right. What source, if not God, gives people the power and courage to say, "I may die in the attempt, but I will die one day anyway, so I might as well spend my life in the service of something I believe in." God is not found in happy endings. God is found in the human being's capacity to cherish something as being more valuable than life itself, and in our recognizing that it is precisely that capacity that makes human life precious to begin with.

Where is God when brave people are murdered? The answer might be "God cannot guarantee that you will survive, or even that your side will win sometime soon. He can only promise you this—that if you die, your sacrifice will not have been in vain. Deeds of courage and self-sacrifice are never meaningless. Don't feel that you are a failure when you lose one battle in the service of a cause that deserves to win. Even as a match has the power to light a candle and perpetuate its light before it is consumed by its own flame, even as a candle can chase the darkness from an entire room before it uses itself up in the process of shedding light and warmth, so your dedication will make a difference to people whose existence you may not even know about today." Some problems are too grave to be solved in one lifetime. In those cases, we need God to link one lifetime to another, to join one heroic sacrifice to another, until justice triumphs.

The Jewish activist Natan (Anatoly) Sharansky was imprisoned by the Soviet government on false charges of spying for the United States and sentenced to fifteen years of hard labor. Despite the efforts of the Soviet government to break his spirit, he survived his sentence and came out of prison stronger than he went in, by constantly reminding himself that the Power he relied on was greater than the power of those who kept him in prison. God could not open the doors of his jail cell, but God could keep him free wherever he was. When he lit Hanukkah candles in his cell, when he celebrated Passover by recalling the Exodus of the Hebrew slaves from Egypt, he reminded himself that he was freer than his captors. Only his body was in a Russian prison; his mind, unlike theirs, was not enslaved. When he was finally released and permitted to go to Israel, he told his story in an autobiography, and chose for its title a passage from the Psalm he would recite to himself when things were hardest, *Fear No Evil*.

A person dies, perhaps painfully, perhaps prematurely, and in our anguish we ask, "Where is God?" Where is God? God is found in the incredible resiliency of the human soul, in our willingness to love though we understand how vulnerable love makes us, in our determination to go on affirming the value of life even when events in the world would seem to teach us that life is cheap. God is found in our insistence on finding our way through the valley of the shadow, knowing that there is evil in the world, knowing that some of the time the evil may overpower us, yet fearing no evil, "for Thou art with me."

Source: Harold S. Kushner, *Who Needs God?*
(New York: Summit Books, 1989), 176–178.

RICHARD N. LEVY

b. 1937

A *prolific writer and liturgist of our time, Rabbi Richard N. Levy was born in Rochester, New York, in 1937. After attending public school in Larchmont, New York, he attended Harvard College and graduated in 1959 with a degree in English literature. He then enrolled in the Hebrew Union College–Jewish Institute of Religion (HUC-JIR) and was ordained at the Cincinnati campus in 1964. After serving as a congregational rabbi at Temple Beth Am in Yorktown Heights, New York (1965–1966), he moved to Leo Baeck Temple in Los Angeles as its assistant rabbi (1966–1968). He came to the Hillel Council at UCLA in the fall of 1968 and served as its director until 1975. At that time he assumed the position of executive director of the Los Angeles Hillel Council, a regional center of Hillel, holding that position until 1999, when he became the director of the Rabbinic School at the Los Angeles campus of the HUC-JIR. From 1997 to 1999, he also served as the president of the Central Conference of American Rabbis (CCAR).*

During his tenure as president of the CCAR, Levy realized that Reform Judaism was going through major changes, such as the growing comfort with more traditional practices, the greater role of women in liberal congregations, an enhanced desire to pursue a richer and more diversified religious life, and the experience that many young rabbis bring to their synagogues after the required first year in Israel program. He argued that Reform Jews had become more willing to rethink Jewish practices that have been long ignored or rejected. He therefore set out to create a new structure within which nothing in traditional lore would be closed to Jewish scrutiny and experience. He prepared a first draft and sent it to all his colleagues. After long debate across the country and many emendations, the "Statement of Principles for Reform Judaism," also known as the "new Pittsburgh Platform," passed overwhelmingly at the May 1999 CCAR Convention in Pittsburgh, Pennsylvania. This represents the most recent statement of beliefs and practices of Reform Jews in North America.

A number of sources have nurtured Levy's theological views. Mordecai Kaplan's idea of God as a power actualizing itself in nature has had a deep influence on him. From Buber and Rosenzweig, he learned how God might function as a commander of mitzvot for liberal Jews. Jonathan Omer-Man and Yaffa Eliach introduced him to Kabbalah and chasidut, and how the development of faith in ordinary times could sustain faith in desperate times.

In his own writings, Levy has stressed the idea of connectedness as the background of his theological construct. Reflecting some of the basic mystical teachings of Judaism that all nature is somehow related to each of its components in an intricate and mysterious way, he argues that God represents the ultimate source of all of these connections, even though human beings are incapable of knowing the mind of the Divine. He maintains, furthermore, that our sacred texts represent the substance of the encounter between God and the Jewish people throughout the centuries. Therefore, by studying Torah, we can discover the will of God and the direction that we must take in leading our lives as committed Jews.

The God Puzzle

"I don't believe in God," the young woman said as she sat down in my office. "Do you have to believe in God to be Jewish?"

Before saying "No you don't" to her question—Jewishness is determined by parentage or by conversion—I decided to engage her on her opening statement.

"You say you don't believe in God," I began. "Do you believe that there are connections in the world—between you and other people, you and nature?"

"Of course," she said. "What kind of person would I be if I didn't?"

That answer—that to be human is to believe there are connections in the world—convinces me that most people—perhaps all people—believe in God, whether they acknowledge it or not. All of us feel connected to something, whether to friends or relatives, to an ocean or a lake as we watch its waves, to the mountains as the sun rises or sets over them—and we know that all of us are made up of atoms and molecules that are connected to one another. Not to believe in the interconnectedness of the universe is to fly in the face of what we know about science, the strong emotions we feel for others, and the great and humbling phenomena in nature. Indeed, the term the rabbis used for a nonbeliever was *Apikoros*, probably derived from the Greek philosopher Epicurus, who believed there were no connections between the isolated particles in the universe.

The next step toward recognizing the religious nature of a belief in connectedness is to acknowledge that there is a sum of all the connections in the world, and that another name for the sum of all these connections is God.

A problem with that definition, of course, is that we cannot see all these connections, and while we might acknowledge that all the static elements of the universe are connected, we may be less ready to acknowledge that the events of the universe—the dynamic interrelationships with other people or with nature—are interconnected. Is there a correlation between the events of our lives, between ours and others' lives, between our lives and natural events?

We cannot know the answer to that question, and here is where knowledge and faith diverge. We can *know* that there are connections in the world, and we can call the sum of those connections God—but can this assumption lead us to an affirmation of faith that God is the Source, the Cause, of those connections? I believe it can.

I believe that the world—the interconnections between space and time, which Hebrew translates as *olam*—is like a huge jigsaw puzzle.*

---

*I have been teaching about the jigsaw puzzle image of God for a number of years, unaware until after I wrote this piece that my friend Rabbi Lawrence Kushner also used the metaphor in his *Honey from the Rock*, published in 1977.

But there is one major difference: on the front of the jigsaw puzzle box is a picture of how it will look when we have connected all the pieces. We can consult the picture on the box to see how to construct the puzzle. When God brought us into the world, however, we were not given the picture on the cover. All we have are the disconnected pieces of the puzzle, and part of the purpose of our existence is to figure out how they fit together. If God is the sum of all these pieces, when we begin to see how they relate to each other, we begin to come into the presence of God.

How do we know that the connections we see among the pieces of our life make sense?

I believe we have to *want* to know. We have to *work* at finding out. God told Moses that everything that went into creating the *mishkan*, the tabernacle in the wilderness, was to be called *melachah* (work). In the *mishkan*, which means "dwelling place," the Israelites could experience the dwelling of God in their midst, but they had to build it, using their possessions, their creativity, their skills, their sweat—all so that they could experience the presence of God. I believe we are enjoined to do no less in our days—to turn all our experiences, all our creativity, all our possessions, all our encounters with nature into an awareness of God's presence—and an awareness of *how* God dwells in our midst.

Were you greeted this morning by a beautiful sunrise? Did you take it for granted, or did you stand at your window or on your front step and look at it, watch as the pink and orange rays spread over the rooftops of your street, and realize that the Creator of Light was giving you a gift of light? You may even have responded, *Baruch atta Adonai Eloheynu melech ha-olam, oseh ma-asei v'reisheet*, Praised are You, Adonai our God, ruler of the *olam*, who does the deed of Creation. You may know the physics behind the sunrise, but your prayer gives you a statement of faith—that the way the molecules combine to bring its color to your eyes is caused by the *Ribono shel Olam*, the Source of Time and Space.

But what if your encounter with the world is an unpleasant one—with someone tailgating you on the expressway or elbowing you out of the way of the closing subway door? You can say the same *berachah* for the patience, the empathy even, that that hurrying person could have taught you, had you asked yourself, "What can I learn from this unpleasant encounter?"

Unpleasant encounters with God's creations, of course, are much more challenging tests of our ability to see God's presence in our lives than encounters with sunrises, oceans, and mountains. Developing the faith that God is the Source of connections requires a lot of work—particularly when we feel abused by someone. Most of us tend to label these events as random human failings—he was in a hurry so he tailgated, she pushed her way through the subway line more aggressively than I did. But if we are struggling to move from the *knowledge* that God is the sum of connections to the *faith* that God is the cause of at least some connections, we will not be satisfied with a random interpretation of events. If we are determined to see how the pieces of the jigsaw puzzle fit together, we will insist on asking, "What can I learn from this event?" "Why did this happen to me now?" To strive to see *everyone* we encounter as a potential teacher is to live in a much more highly aware, spiritually conscious plane than most of us do.

Is it a denial of our free will to assert that there is a relationship between events? Rabbi Akiba argued that life is not a question of free will *or* a divine plan, but a paradoxical dialogue between them both: "Everything is seen (by God), and free will is given" (Pirkei Avot 3:19).

An example. Some years ago, my office received a call from a stranger who was stranded at a gas station and needed money. I stopped what I was doing, drove to the gas station, gave the man some money, and pulled out into the street. Suddenly I heard behind me the crack of one car plowing into another, and then that car hit me. I was not injured, but the irony of the situation rattled me. Here I had gone out of my way to do a *mitzvah*, an act of *tzedakah*—and instead of realizing Rabbi Azzai's teaching in Pirkei Avot (4:2) that one *mitzvah* draws another with it, my act had negative consequences. I thought about this for some time, asking myself: Why did this happen to me? What was I to learn from it? After a while, the answer that came to me was that I had felt a little too much self-satisfaction in the minor act of *tzedakah* that I had done, and that I could understand the accident to be a little comeuppance. Did that mean that God had caused the accident? If so, was that God's reason? If I believed I knew the answer to either of those questions, I would be adding the sin of arrogance to that of self-satisfaction. Of course we cannot *know* the mind of God. But if we are trying to develop the *faith* that the events of our lives can show us part of the invisible picture on the cover of the jigsaw puzzle box, we can interpret the events as a teaching that the Source of All Teaching has presented to us as a gift—a gift as valuable as a sunrise, even though the teaching comes through our mind or our intuition rather than through the (usually) more reliable five senses. But just as we use intuition to guide our understanding of our relations with human beings, why should we not rely on it in our relations with God as well? In the messianic time, we shall find out whether our intuitions were correct; for the present, if they help us feel accompanied by God as we live our lives, that should be sufficient.

But—the inevitable *but*, the intimidating *but*, the *but* that often closes off any further discussion of the role of God in our lives—what can we possibly learn from the senseless death of a child, the heartless killing of an upstanding citizen, the ghastly murders of six million of our people in the Shoah?

There is no answer, many people say. We shall never understand those things. Better not to ask—better, even, not to open the question of the role God can play in our lives.

I cannot accept that. If we allow the sicknesses that are spreading in the world, the cruel acts that abound, the unspeakable cruelty that has befallen our people, to silence our work on the *mishkan* of God's presence in the world, then not only have we given Hitler a victory he does not deserve, not only have we capitulated to atheism, but we have declared that the millions of Jews throughout the centuries who staked their lives and their deaths on *faith* were misguided, naïve, and—because they could not argue their faith with proofs based on knowledge—they were wrong.

I will not do that. Jacob was given a new name, Israel, because his destiny was to wrestle with God and with human beings, and to prevail. It is not easy to search for the picture of the world-puzzle in the pieces that make up our lives—but we cannot surrender before we begin.

How shall we wrestle with death? Why does God permit the death of a child? Kohelet, the biblical book of Ecclesiastes (3:2), declares: *et la-ledet ve-et la-mut*, there is a time to be born and a time to die. Jewish law has understood that verse to mean that God determines when our time to die comes—it is the proof text for the belief that we may not hasten anyone's death. *Everyone* has an *et la-mut*—a time to die—and that is part of our problem. We have never really adjusted to the fact that, after Eden, we ceased being immortal. Who are we to decide what is a person's proper life span? When I conducted my first funeral for a baby who died at the age of a year, I tried to suggest to the grieving family that, in some mysterious way we could not know, it was possible to have faith that this sweet little boy had fulfilled his calling in the precious few months he lived on earth. Did it comfort the family? Probably not on the day of the funeral. But I hope, as time passed, that they came to understand what they and others had learned from his short time on earth, and that the work they had put into bringing him into the world and sustaining him was not in vain.

The Bible emphasizes over and over that, *because* death is part of our existence, we are to live life as joyfully, as much in the presence of God, as we can. We can transform death from the invasive, violent destruction of life into the act of culmination of life by filling our lives full of sunrises with their blessings, of joyful awakenings, of eating and loving and celebrating and giving *tzedakah* with no expectation of any reward beside the awareness of helping to build a *mishkan* for the presence of God in all the days we are granted on earth.

The book that helped me make the most sense out of the Holocaust was Yaffa Eliach's *Hasidic Tales of the Holocaust*. Don't be misled by the title—it is not fundamentally about Hasidim, but about all religious people who are able to see the presence of God in the normal events of their days. *Because* these people had grown accustomed to feeling themselves in God's presence during ordinary times, they could also feel themselves in God's presence when the times became extraordinary—when they were herded into the ghettos and into the extermination camps. Some of them survived, others were killed—but they all knew that God is present in death as in life. They, like we, had offered the Mourner's Kaddish, praising God for the beauty of life that is beyond praise, even as they mourned the end of one after another bearer of such a life. If such people could feel that the *mishkan* lived in the ghetto and the extermination camp, how can we say that it is impossible to see God's presence now? How can we say that the agony of a baby's death or a teenager's collision or a strong young woman's cancer wipes out the possibility of faith that there is some connection between those tragedies and a world of sunrises and soaring mountains?

When the Central Conference of American Rabbis passed the Statement of Principles for Reform Judaism in May of 1999, we offered some assistance to Reform Jews—and others—seeking to find the presence of God in difficult times. For a generation, the Reform Movement had proclaimed that each Reform Jew was autonomous, free to find whatever meaning and purpose in the world each of us might, with our tradition as a guide. The Pittsburgh Principles suggest another model—not the lonely, autonomous individual struggling unassisted to see where God is present in the world, but a model which invites "all Reform Jews to engage in a dialogue with the sources of our tradition, responding out of our knowledge, our experience and our faith. Thus we hope to transform our lives through *kedushah*, holiness."

The Principles present a world in which God's presence is accessible in a myriad of ways—"in moments of awe and wonder, in acts of justice and compassion, in loving relationships and in the experiences of everyday life." And we in turn can "respond to God daily," for belief in God is not a one-way, autonomous journey, but an ongoing dialogue with a God who—if we have trained our intuitions sufficiently—we can sense is calling us. Our response, the Principles remind us, can come through prayer, study, and the observance of *mitzvot* between God and ourselves, and among each other. This work of looking for God in all these moments through the doing of all these *mitzvot*—of not merely working with the homeless but stepping back to feel God's presence working there as well, not merely giving *tzedakah* but stepping back to experience our giving back to God what God has given to us, of not merely praying that our loved ones heal but stepping back to experience God working alongside us—this hard work will help us "strive for a faith that fortifies us through the vicissitudes of our lives—illness and healing, transgression and repentance, bereavement and consolation, despair and hope." And this kind of faith will also sustain our belief that, "in spite of the unspeakable evils committed against our people and the sufferings endured by others, the partnership of God and humanity will ultimately prevail."

The Principles state that "we affirm the reality and oneness of God." To be human, to experience the interconnectedness of things, is to believe in God. Our task as Reform Jews is to strive to encounter God's reality in as many ways as we can, to put together as many pieces of the puzzle of that reality as we can, so that more and more of God's oneness, God's active role in the relationships of all of our lives, will become apparent to all. In this way, we will help to realize the creation of the *mishkan* of God's *kedushah*, God's holy, palpable presence in our days and the days of our children, soon and in our time.

Source: Richard N. Levy, "The God Puzzle," *Reform Judaism* 28
(Spring 2000): 18–22.

When We Study Torah, Is God the Teacher?

One of the more penetrating criticisms leveled at Jewish religious education is that too often it is not religious. Its curricula may teach Jewish history, language, customs, and creativity, but too often it does not convey the way these studies manifest the working of God in the life of the Jewish people and of Jewish individuals. The absence of the religious, spiritual, element in Jewish education is often cited as one of the reasons that more young Jews than we would like become attracted to Christian or cult groups that seem to take God more seriously than we do. At the same time we also know that many Jewish parents become quite agitated if it appears that their children's teachers are taking God too seriously.

Nonetheless, I daresay a majority of us would like to help our students, of all ages, make God more a part of their lives. We would like to help them feel that God is real, that God cares for them, and that God is present in the life of the Jewish people. We would even like to feel some of those things more strongly ourselves. The most accessible way to help children and adults to feel addressed by God (at least in a classroom setting) would seem to be through the texts of our tradition. But is it? We may not all agree. If we grant for the moment that the Jewish encounter with God is expressed in its own words through the *Chumash*, the Prophets, and the Writings of the written Torah, and through the Midrash, Mishna, Gemara, Responsa, Codes, stories, and contemporary (if less traditional) literature of the oral Torah—can our students, still children in most cases, understand these texts? Most of them cannot read Hebrew. Although an accurate English translation may be fine for adults, children may find it almost as difficult to comprehend as the Hebrew. Yet to give them a children's version prevents them from receiving a direct experience of the tradition at all.

Most of us would agree that *direct* experience is generally better than second-hand, mediated experience. Desirous of giving our people the best in all things, we would wish to give them the "real" thing, the encounter between God and the Jewish people in its own words. Still, if direct versus mediated experience were the only issue, we could talk briefly about the best versions of texts, and bring our discussion rather dryly to a close.

But we are speaking not only about a pedagogical problem of reading. We are also speaking about the place of the text in the Reform tradition—a topic that sends us back to the very assumptions with which we rather cavalierly began. Do we really believe that texts form the substance of the encounter between God and the Jewish people? Does the Reform movement believe that notion? Given Reform's traditional belief in progressive revelation (despite Professor David Ellenson's preference for the term "ongoing revelation"), one could argue that the texts of the past must always give way to those of the present. Because both the written and the oral Torah are filled with time-bound, long-supplanted ideas (old myths and metaphors, practices long held in disrepute), expressions of contemporary ideas and practices would seem much more in accord with Reform philosophy. Indeed, before we discuss the role played by the study of texts in recovering the direct experience of God and Israel, we must properly ask: Do we know what the experience of Israel with God has been? Does any text represent the substance of the encounter between God and Israel? Is any text the word of God?

Cultural Masterpiece or Divine Creation?

Most of us were raised on the documentary hypothesis as the primary answer to this question: The texts we have may represent the inspiration of God (a process rarely defined), but that inspiration took concrete form in the oral traditions of different groups of Israelites and eventually collected in the documents edited by J (the tradition preferring the name *YHWH, Adonai*), by E (the tradition preferring the name *Elohim*), by D, the Deuteronomist, and by P, the final, Priestly redactor. According to these theories, the Bible is a human product, the brilliant epic of an ancient people, a cultural masterpiece, to be studied because it shows the marvelous creativity of ancient Jews who believed in God, who even felt inspired by God. However, it is not the direct record of encounters between God and the Jewish people. The Bible is itself a mediated document, the reflections—generations later—of the way in which real people, or people portrayed metaphorically, might have interpreted the world. Contradictions, repetitions, and anachronisms appearing in the text can easily be attributed to different redactions.

This view of the Bible, of course, is far from the traditional Jewish one. As described at the beginning of the midrash to Genesis (Bereshit Rabba 1.1), the Rabbis believed that God created the Torah before creating the world and that the world itself was an actualization of the blueprint of Torah. God offered the Torah once to the world, they argued, in the seven mitzvot commanded to Adam and Eve and again to the children of Noah (see Bereshit Rabba 16.6 and Sanhedrin 56a-b), but humanity as a whole was unable to live even by the seven commands. So God tried again, choosing two individuals, Abraham and Sarah, in the expectation that their teaching would raise up generations of a people who could live by the Torah. When there were enough of us, encamped at Sinai shortly after God revealed the divine power at the Red Sea, God delivered the Torah (now with many more mitzvot) to that segment of humanity which was the children of the patriarch Israel, in the hope that we might one day share it with the human race.

Moses tried to write down as much of what God told him as he could; but being human, he could write only so much, only the *rashei perakim* (the chapter headings) of the total Torah, leaving the rest to be filled in by the oral discussion of subsequent generations of scholars. While one may say that to study the Torah written down by Moses is also to study a mediated document, the tradition holds that what Moses wrote down was what God wanted Israel to hear. Therefore, the written text is as close as humans can come to a direct, verbatim record of God's teachings to the Jewish people, and ultimately, to all people.[1]

That view—that the Torah really did come down to us from God—I daresay, makes most of us very uncomfortable. "That's Orthodox!" many of you will say. But, of course, it is not. It predates the division of Western Jewry into Reform, Orthodox, Conservative, and Reconstructionist. For all its insistence on individual choice, the Reform movement has perversely removed many ideological choices from its adherents by excising a number of traditional beliefs that a century ago seemed to contradict popular rational, Western ideas. In censoring such beliefs so violently (divine authorship of Torah, the possibility of resurrection, of a messiah, and of angels, and many others), it acted against its own liberalism. It discouraged, even intimidated, its followers from responding to those beliefs in a manner consistent with their own study and their own experience. The belief in the divine authorship of Torah, of course, is not only a part of Jewish tradition inherited by all Jews—whatever they may do with that particular part of their heritage. It is also a crucial part of the tradition, for the belief that the Torah is the word of God gives authority to the mitzvot. It gives a compelling argument for obeying one very important mitzvah, that of *Talmud Torah*, Torah study: God wants us to know what God has said to us. Torah study, written and oral, is the surest way of knowing the will of God and the direction in which we, children of God, are to lead our lives.

If Torah is but a cultural masterpiece, knowledge of it may further our people's ethnic pride, but it will not further their spiritual development. Indeed, parts of it may even make them a bit embarrassed at their ethnic heritage: so many wars this people celebrated, so much animal sacrifice, so much concern over how the tabernacle should be constructed, so much scheming and plotting among brothers, so many restrictions upon women. If Torah is a cultural masterpiece, it is a selective masterpiece, and, along with many congregations, we have to expurgate whole books (Leviticus, for example) or the last 16 chapters of Exodus, or the genealogies, or the curses, or . . .

J, E, D, and P have no claim on us. Their words surely are time-bound, no more compelling an insight into God's will than—well—than our own. The end result of viewing Torah as the selective process of editing by generations of human scribes is to elevate the editing, and not the words: If J could edit, so can I; if P can edit, so can U. Thus, the final redactor of Torah becomes any individual's likes and dislikes, based on views having nothing to do with the Torah at all. Many of our teenage students have already discovered this form of editing, as they rebel against our attempts to have them take the Torah seriously.

Does this mean that the only way text study can be a religious enterprise is to accept Moses as the author? And what does that do for post-Torah literature and the oral law? The Midrash was also edited. The Mishna and the Gemara were edited. Jewish histories and literatures were the product of individual inspirations! Is only the Torah of Moses legitimate to teach? And since we do not believe Moses wrote it down, does that mean we cannot teach it? In other words, if we deny Moses, must we also deny God?

The Possibility of God

It is revealing that Spinoza, perhaps the earliest critic of Mosaic authorship, did not deny God. True enough, he argued that much of the Torah was of human authorship, but he insisted that the "universal truths" were divine. He identified the probable redactor as Ezra, rather than the anonymous P-priests who were Ezra's contemporaries.[2] In affirming the historicity of Ezra, Spinoza suggests that Torah did not originate from the people itself, percolating up from the popular soul. It did, indeed, come from outside, in the person of a great religious figure who not only felt himself to be inspired by God, but who was recognized by others to have been so inspired, and whose clear inspiration, in turn, inspired the people to accept the Torah as the word of God.

Others who felt themselves inspired by God were the Rabbis of the tannaitic period who divided the Torah into 54 weekly sections. They did so with such exquisite sensitivity that the key words which gave their names to the *parashiyot*, in a phenomenal number of cases, not only introduce their section but describe its contents as well. As they taught the text they had so insightfully divided up, the Rabbis tried to understand what God could have meant in each difficult passage. They asked why God had permitted what seems so clearly a contradiction, why God seemed to be saying the same thing over and over again. The results of their struggle are the jewels we know as Midrash, the prisms of clarity we know as Mishna.

We forget sometimes that these works were the products of a religious struggle—a struggle to discern no less than the mind of God. Had they believed they were interpreting only the minds of anonymous priests, or J-scribes in an eleventh-century court, it is very doubtful that they would have produced the Midrash and Mishna which form the basis for the legal and philosophical traditions on which Judaism is based. Even to such a bitter skeptic as Spinoza, it was inconceivable that the essential part of the Torah could have been anything other than the product of the mind of God. Similarly, the Rabbis believed that it was God's mind they were probing. This belief inspired them to arrive at the brilliant interpretations they have handed down to us.

But was their belief true? Before answering this question, we must ask another: How do we determine the truth of belief? Divine authorship of Torah is a belief; documentary, human, authorship of Torah is also a belief. Spinoza and the Protestant critics who followed him have adduced much good intrinsic evidence for multiple authorship of the Bible. It is clearly not an illogical, irrational belief. The belief in divine authorship, however, led to the creation of that marvelous literature called Midrash, which enables us to transform repetitions and contradictions into stunning poetry. Surely, a belief that produced such a magnificent literature and that formed the basis for the equally magnificent halachic literature of Mishna and Gemara, must have a claim on truth as well. Nor should one overlook the fact that, until the nineteenth century, the majority of Jews believed that the Torah was divine. They based their lives and their fortunes on it. Despite overwhelming odds, they survived in the world, while one after another, the polytheists and the idolators who had oppressed them were swallowed up into history. While it may not be the sole truth, divine authorship is at least a hypothesis that should have no less a claim on our attention.

The tradition has never said that the Torah is an insight into Moses' mind. Moses was an instrument, whom God has wanted us to believe received the Torah from the divine hand. But there have been others who received and transmitted it as well. Moses himself, a talmudic fantasy runs (Menachot 29b), wanders into Akiba's classroom in the second century. He understands not a word of the Torah Akiba is teaching, but is ultimately reassured when God tells him it is the Torah that Moses received on Sinai. Moses senses, the story seems to say, that Akiba was an instrument of God's word just as he himself was, and that much more important than the person who transmitted it was its common source in the divine. The chain of transmission includes many P-priests and J-scribes too, not as editors, but as transmitters. They are not to be particularly singled out as authoritative, but are part of the chain of those in direct touch with God which Moses began, and for whom Moses stands as a symbol, as the first chapter of Avot describes.

Study of Torah—whether we are Reform, Conservative, Orthodox, or Reconstructionist Jews—can be seen as the study of God's will as the Jewish people has preserved it, and the study of God's desires for humanity as those desires have been revealed to the Jewish people. Christians and Moslems—and other peoples as well, I believe—have preserved other aspects of God's will, other perceptions of God's desires for human actions. We need not argue whether ours are better or worse, only that they are ours—not ours to keep to ourselves, but ours to share with others.

And the responsibility to share them is very frightening. For it suggests that Moses and Ezra and P-priests and Akiba are not the only agents of transmission of God's will. Everyone who teaches Torah assists in that transmission, as well. The early Reform movement loved to quote Exodus 19:6: *Ve-atem tihyu li mamlechet kohanim*, "You shall be a realm of priests to Me," you shall act as priests to Me. But what if we teach Torah wrong? What if we do not understand a word or phrase here and there? What if we do not know the critical theory explaining this or that contradiction, if we have never learned the midrash that explains this or that omission? Paradoxically, one of the arguments for the divine origin of Torah may be our very fear of it. It causes a kind of unconscious trembling before God that has been passed through the generations, which leads many of our leaders and laypeople—and even ourselves—to a "text anxiety" much more profound than the "math anxiety" so many of us have for other reasons. But this "text anxiety" only leads us and our students further away from God when it prevents us from studying texts with them.

How much we could convey of God's presence if we passed out a text, and said: "It's taken me a long time to be able to study a passage of Bible or Midrash or Talmud with you—I've been afraid of it. I've never understood why I've been afraid of it. Maybe because, unbeknownst to me, I really have believed that God might be speaking to me, to us, out of this text, and I wouldn't know how to respond. Perhaps when we study it together, we can all give each other strength and insight, and see together whether this passage will help us find out what God wants us to do."

I think one reason teachers refrain from saying things like this to their students is their concern lest students laugh at them. But if we could really believe such a statement, I think we would all find that as we were speaking, the room suddenly would become very still.

Torah Responses from God

I believe we encounter God's desires as revealed in the text at two times: when we study and when we read from the Torah in the worship service. It is instructive to note the place of the Torah reading in the morning service: after the *Shemoneh Esrei*. This great prayer, during the week, lets us ask God for knowledge and repentance, pardon and healing, a good year and a better society, and so on. Then the Rabbis used to pause for their own silent prayers, a practice the Reform movement happily reinstituted. So we plead for our needs, and then we listen.

And what happens next? The reading of the Torah. It is as though the Rabbis were saying to us, "Listen for the answer to your prayers in Torah." Listen to the Torah reading not as a recitation of a great cultural masterpiece, but as a revelation—not only to the Jewish people as a whole, but to those of us hearing it in this synagogue, to me personally, who has just poured out my heart in prayer. Perhaps we may also learn something from Franz Rosenzweig's teaching of the difference between *Gesetz*, the Torah commanded to the whole people at Sinai, and the *Gebot*, the individual mitzvah being heard directly by this one Jew at this time and place. The Torah reading may reveal not only the eternal message of God to the Jewish people, but also the response of God to this one Jew crying out to God here, today.

Suppose that this Monday morning when I *davened* the prayers for healing, *Refa-einu*, and the prayer that God might listen to me, *Shema Koleinu*, I knew that one of the ways to discover whether God was listening to me was by my listening for God. So, supposing that this morning, I paid extra-close attention to the Torah portion, which at the time of this writing happens to be *Va-eira*, Exodus chapter 6. And when the reader comes to verse 5, God is quoted as saying, "And I have also heard the moaning of the children of Israel whom the Egyptians had put in bondage, and I recalled my covenant, and so I say, 'I will bring you out from under the burdens of the Egyptians.'" The text continues with the rest of the promises, which eventually give rise to the four cups of wine at the *Seder*. And the passage read on this morning concludes, "And Moses said this to the children of Israel, but they did not listen to him because of their *kotser ruach* (literally, 'shortness of breath') and their hard labor."

If I were listening hard for God's response to my prayers, I might have heard in this Torah reading the comforting message that God's covenant with us is always present, that the power capable of freeing us from the burdens of our lives is always at work—as sure, as predictable, as the four cups we shall drink at Pesach. However, because I am so short of breath all the time, I am more conscious of my own burdens than I am of the signs of redemption, memory, and caring in the world outside my own life. And I might even smile that delicious, spontaneous smile of recognition of something wonderfully true, and resolve to look more closely for signs of redemption and caring when I walk out of the service into the world.

That is not J, E, and P speaking to me, nor is it a cultural masterpiece. I have been able to listen because I have heard it before—not only last year at the time for this *parasha*, but millennia ago at Shavuot, when I, like all the other Jews not yet present, stood at Sinai and heard the Torah spoken into the collective mind of the Jewish people—a view enshrined in Reform theology by its adoption as the Yom Kippur morning Torah reading. As a result, when I am in trouble, when I feel myself in the straits of my own *Mitsrayim*, now I, as an individual, can hear those words again as a direct address to me, and I must figure out what I need to do with the answer I have been given.

But the Torah not only formulates God's answer to our prayers; even more powerfully, as the source of mitzvot, it also articulates God's initiating call. The mitzvot clearly pose many problems to Reform Jews: As long ago as the Pittsburgh Platform of 1885, we relegated major areas of the mitzvot to time-bound irrelevance—*kashrut*, *talit*, and *tefilin*—suggesting that God's "continuing revelation" was now manifest through Western diet, modes of dress, language, and even worship. This extreme interpretation of what could be a profound doctrine is similar to the elevation of the editing process of Torah over the words of Torah. Any individual becomes as qualified as any other to pick and choose among the mitzvot. The basis for the choice may be no more than the individual's own needs and convenience. Individuals who want to grow spiritually, however, do not want to be the sole determiner of their religious lives, as though it did not matter to any reality beyond themselves which path they took.

But if Torah is the word of God, then Torah speaks to us, either in response (as in the Torah reading) or as a call (in Torah study). What "continuing revelation" must mean is just that—a revelation. Torah calls us to something, tells us: "There are standards for that which you need to do; it *matters* to God what you do." Torah pushes a bit of darkness away from the light of God's purpose and asks us to continue the process, calling us to push away more and more darkness by the acts we do in response to the call.

Mitzvah: Response to Divine Request

The reader may have noticed that I said, "Torah asks us to continue the process," and not, "Torah (or God) commands us." Mitzvah means "command." But to understand Torah as a call suggests that the call comes in a manner befitting the relationship we have with God. Two of the important ways in which Jews have traditionally related to God are as a child to a parent and as a lover with a spouse. (Younger people may prefer the analogy of a best friend.) From human relationships we know that a child relates most closely with a parent and a lover relates most closely with the beloved, in hearing not a demand, but a request: As my wife puts it, "This is something I want you to do that is very important to me." One may say "No," to such requests—but the act of saying "No," or as Rosenzweig put it, "Not yet," also is a response.

In all these cases, heeding the call of a mitzvah becomes an act of love, responding to the call *Ve-ahavta et Adonai Elohecha*, "You shall love Adonai your God," just as, two prayers earlier, *Ahava rabba ahavtanu*, "A great love has God loved us."

How is that love most profoundly manifest? The *Ahava Rabba* asks that the God who taught our ancestors the laws of life might also show how much God loves us, however unworthy we may be, by teaching us Torah, as well (*techoneinu utelamedeinu*). We are encouraged, when we study Torah, to feel ourselves invited to sit at God's study table, while the Author of the universe says, in a tone pitched differently for each of us, "This is a law that will help you live out more fully the direction of your life. This is a mitzvah by which you can further the harmony of the universe. I would like you very much to do it."[3]

Mitzvah as loving request reminds us again of Franz Rosenzweig's distinction between the two kinds of Torah—the entire tradition that has a claim on us all and the individual mitzvah that speaks to each of us differently, at different times, out of the darkness. But it is not we who choose—it is the text, and the God behind it, who chooses us. This is a text study that asks, "What do you hear in this mitzvah?" This is an encounter with a text that says, "Listen to the self in you that stood at Sinai when you first heard this mitzvah: What do you hear that self saying to you? What does your self today hear in it?"

Questions from the Tales of God

And because we are liberal Jews, because we know that not only the halachic texts call us but the aggadic ones as well, we shall learn more and more to listen for the call in the great stories of the tradition. For not only is there a mitzvah not to destroy the earth; there is also a call in the story of the Flood as well. If, indeed, revelation continues through the ages, we need to listen not only to an ancient fable, but also to a call that speaks amid the noise of missiles being put in place, amid the growing terror at what flood of fire may await us if we, like Noah's generation, let violence roar away unchecked for too long.

When I was taking Jewish education courses years ago, we were told to find a contemporary "motivation" for teaching a particular story, as though to entice children into the arcane text by gilding it with modern gloss. I am suggesting just the opposite. I am suggesting that God knew that violence would not end once Noah's family began to repopulate the earth. One of the reasons the Flood story was placed in the Bible is that it might awaken us to analyze our own times and to discover what sort of ark might be appropriate in the world in which we find ourselves.

Many of us grew up assuming that the women in Genesis were rather shrewish, conniving, and manipulating. But if this were so, why have they been so revered by the tradition as *imoteinu*, our mothers? Why did the Rabbis regard them as prophets, possessed of insights into God's will which their sainted husbands often lacked? Rebecca, doubled over by the struggles of the twins in her womb, asks: *Lama zeh anochi*? "What purpose am I to discover in this agony?" (Gen. 25:22). And God tells her. Contrary to the natural commands of mother love, she is to make sure that her elder son serves her younger. As we read the text verse by verse, questions arise before us: Does Rebecca call to us as a model woman? Does Isaac call to us as a model father?

If we believe it is God, and not just Jewish creativity, that speaks in these stories—we believe it, no matter whether our students do or not—such questions matter because they are questions from the Divine. They are calls to us to probe our own motherhood and fatherhood, and to see in the Rebecca and Isaac in ourselves a revelation of God the mother and God the father that may be a contribution to the continuing revelation that will shed more and more light on the nature of truth itself.

And the embarrassing parts of Torah—the wars, the bloody offerings, the nasty struggles, the cruel punishments—how does God speak in them? If we refuse to expurgate them from the Torah because we believe that God in some obscure way is calling to us through them, then perhaps they are like the embarrassing members of our family on whom we cannot turn our backs because we know that they have something very important to tell us about ourselves. Because, behind the veil of their complicated lives, we know they hold a mystery to part of who we are, of what we are.

In us, as in our forebears, there is violence and vengeance. There is the aching yearning to reach across the corporeal boundary that keeps us from the incorporeal God, as our ancestors did with animal or meal offerings. Through fire, they made the journey from the visible world to the invisible. All these mysteries that the ancients knew about the heart of God we can recover through the texts they have preserved against great odds, beneath great suffering—*for us*. They preserved them not so much because they wanted us to honor them, but because they wanted us to hear the voice of God they heard, clearer than they heard it, or at least in an echo of what they heard. If we do not teach the embarrassing texts, the difficult beliefs, we shall be unfaithful both to our vocation as teachers and to our calling as liberals, for we shall be preventing our people from hearing the voices it is their right, their inheritance, to hear.

We are religious educators, spiritual educators, if you will—educators of the spirit. In the words preserved for us by Moses (whomever he was), by P-priests, R-rabbis, and S-skeptics, by our own grandparents; in the words that now rest within our hands to transmit to the teachers and skeptics of generations yet to come, in those same words we, too, can hear the voice of the Spirit that hovered over the waters once and said—to the universe and to each one of us—"Let there be light."

Source: Richard N. Levy, "When We Study Torah, Is God the Teacher?" *Journal of Reform Judaism* (Winter 1985): 40–51.

Notes

1. Compare the debate between the school of Akiba and the school of Ishmael as to whether the Torah was given in the idiomatic way in which humans speak (*dibera Torah bileshon benei Adam*, Ishmael's view) or whether God intended some specific meaning in each seemingly unnecessary word or particle (see, for example, *Sifrei* to Numbers, Piska 12, on *hikaret tikaret*).

2. See Baruch Spinoza, *A Theological-Political Treatise*, chapters 4 and 8.

3. Is this a metaphor or a picture of reality? I do not know the answer. On the principle of *mitoch shelo lishmah ba lishmah*, if we begin by experiencing our study *as though* God were teaching us, we may gradually be vouchsafed the direct experience of God's teaching us. Whether that experience will be the product of our own imagination or of an act of God, only the Messiah (another metaphor?) will be able to tell us for sure. But why should we be so concerned with this issue? If in the middle of a moment we suddenly feel ourselves hugged, there is a reality to the experience whether our eyes see the arms or not. God works inside us as well as outside—our bodies are not barriers to God's presence.

· 14 ·

JUDITH PLASKOW

b. 1947

Author, teacher, and one of the first feminist theologians of our time, Judith Plaskow was born in 1947 in Brooklyn, New York, and grew up on Long Island. Her family belonged to a Reform Jewish congregation. After her college studies at Clark University, from which she received her B.A. degree in 1968, she then concentrated on Protestant theology at Yale University, graduating with a doctoral degree in 1975. The greatest influence on her theological thinking came from a fellow graduate student, Carol Christ, then a Protestant and now a Goddess feminist. Other prominent feminist writers who shaped the development of Plaskow's theology included Valerie Saiving, Rosemary Ruether, and Mary Daly.

Plaskow has taught at various universities and has been professor of religious studies at Manhattan College since 1990. She has held important leadership positions within her academic field. She played a major role in the creation of the Women and Religion section of the American Academy of Religion and served as president of that organization from 1997 to 1998.

Plaskow has written widely and lectured on feminist theology in many parts of the world. Her articles and essays have appeared in numerous journals, including Journal of the American Academy of Religion, Tikkun, Sh'ma, Menorah, *and* Reconstructionist. *In 1983, she co-founded the* Journal of Feminist Studies in Religion *and served as co-editor for its first ten years.*

For a long time, Plaskow has been interested in metaphors that are traditionally used to describe God and finds them inadequate. She notes, for example, that for the most part, these metaphors are male oriented, authoritative and hierarchical in nature, and marginalize women. The terms, "ruler," "king," or "father" may have been appropriate in a patriarchal setting, but not for the modern times, where women play a major role in our society. Plaskow therefore suggests terms for God that not only reflect our egalitarian society but also eliminate the sense of hierarchy and dominance, such as "source," "fountain of life," "Shekhinah," "companion," "lover." These terms do not ignore the fact that God, who is unknown to us, is still "Other" (as, for example, described by Emmanuel Levinas [1906–1995]) and remains a mystery that we cannot resolve, especially as it relates to the question of evil in the world. Similarly, she points out, any term used for God that assumes a dominating role for the divinity ends up condoning dominance, for terminology applied to God often reflects our aspiration to become as godly as possible. Therefore, for instance, if God were to be viewed as a "ruler," those who speak in God's name would end up relating to those disenfranchised in society in an authoritarian and discriminatory way. And this becomes a special threat to women today, who are often denied equality in society. Finally, the belief that God is all-powerful, she asserts, often encourages human passivity at a time when we need to stress human responsibility.

Facing the Ambiguity of God

Much feminist work on God-language, including my own, has focused on particular aspects of God to the neglect of others. Feminist characterizations of the sacred have emerged largely out of two central experiences: coming to self-awareness in community with other women; and claiming the healing power of connection to the natural world. These experiences have generated a rich array of images for God focusing on female, natural, and non-hierarchical metaphors. Such images depict God as source, wellspring and fountain, mother and womb of life. God is Shekhina, Goddess, all that seeks life; earth, moon, lover, friend—and so on.

It is entirely legitimate and even essential for a new community finding its voice to speak and write about God by drawing upon its own most fundamental experiences. In a profoundly misogynistic culture that has ruthlessly exploited the natural environment—and that has linked women with the natural world on many levels of practice and discourse—feminist metaphors for God elucidate long-buried dimensions of divinity. These metaphors are not just political correctives to dominant modes of seeing and being; they arise from and refer to real discoveries of the sacred in places we had long stopped looking to find it.

Insofar as feminist metaphors represent a deliberate attempt to capture particular aspects of experience, however, they are also necessarily partial. In a discussion in the *Journal of Feminist Studies in Religion* (Spring 1989), Catherine Madsen and a number of respondents criticized the "niceness" of God in feminist theology. Madsen argued that once God becomes Goddess or acquires female characteristics, she is connected too exclusively with the so-called female virtues of nurturing, healing, and caretaking, and is cordoned off from the savagery of the world. A "nice" female God does not take us sufficiently beyond traditional images, Madsen argued—any more than a "Queen of the Universe" undoes the hierarchical nature of traditional male imagery.

A number of feminist writers and religious thinkers have begun to articulate a fuller and more complex account of the divine than the notion of a "nice" female God allows for. But I basically agree with Madsen that the ambiguity of God has not received enough attention in feminist discourse. Rereading the story of Nadab and Abihu in this year's annual cycle of Torah readings, I was struck by the extent to which the God who devoured Aaron's sons for offering "strange fire" (Lev. 10:1) is largely absent from feminist imagery. This God, the same who killed Uzzah for putting out his hand to steady the ark (2 Sam. 6:6-7), and who wanted the assembled Israelites not to come too close to the base of Sinai lest they die (Exod. 19:12-13), seems to me to point to a profoundly important dimension of human existence. Unless the God who speaks to the feminist experiences of empowerment and connection can also speak to the frightening, destructive, and divisive aspects of our lives, a whole side of existence will be severed from the feminist account of the sacred.

The question of God's ambiguity is not the same as the classical problem of theodicy. Theodicy is a problem only if one accepts a series of propositions about the nature of God, most of which are irrelevant to my own understanding. Theodicy assumes not only that God is perfectly good and all powerful; it assumes that God's omnipotence is that of a person who acts and interacts as supreme ruler of history. According to this view, if God deliberately chooses not to intervene in a particular evil, then either there must be a higher theological explanation, or God must be blamed.

I do not believe in a God who stands outside of history and manipulates it and who therefore can be charged with our moral failures. The stories of Uzzah and Nadab and Abihu seem to me to present a somewhat different problem. Their deaths are not so much an expression of divine injustice as they are of divine unpredictability. These stories confront us not with a choice between God as good or evil but with the irrationality and ambiguity of the sacred. To use Madsen's term, the God of these stories is not "nice." S/he is not neat, sanitized, containable, or controllable. S/he does not easily fit our categories or conform to our expectations. But neither, of course, does the world that God created.

The God of these stories is an ambiguous God—the Goddess as energy of the universe, responsible for life and death and rebirth. S/he is a God who creates forms of startling fragility and beauty and also brings forth monstrosities that frighten and overwhelm us. S/he is the God who makes dry land rise up out of the waters and then washes it away with tidal waves and volcanoes. Creativity by its very nature seems profoundly ambiguous. The power of invention has yielded all the fruits of civilization, but the same power has also brought forth our civilization's horrors.

The ambiguity of life is a truth we all know on the small scale as well as the large. The experience of empowerment so central to feminism may allow women to make considered and important choices, but it does not guarantee that we will always choose rightly. Many movements for liberation generate new forms of tyranny or infighting; many women have been hurt in the name of feminism. In the same way, the Egyptians lost their lives when the Israelites walked safely through the Red Sea; the Palestinians lost their homeland when the Jews found one. On the other hand, it is not just projects begun with good intentions that often go awry. Choices made from selfish motives or dictated by circumstance sometimes lead to unanticipated good or open up new possibilities we could never have imagined. "Were it not for the evil impulse," said Rabbi Nahman B. Samuel, "man would not take a wife, or beget a child, or engage in business."

These truths do not absolve us from responsibility for the consequences of our choices, but they do point to ambiguity, contradiction, and paradox as fundamental aspects of our experience. One of the things I have always most valued about the Jewish tradition is its refusal to disconnect God from the contradictory whole of reality. "I form light and create darkness, I make weal and create woe—I, the Lord do all these things," Isaiah announces (I Isa. 45:7). This has always seemed to me a far more religiously satisfying perspective than a theology that would close off huge areas of our experience and declare them devoid of sacred power. I do not know how a monotheist can choose to find God in the dry land and *not* in the tidal wave that destroys it—or only in our power to choose life and not also in our power to *choose* (see Deut. 30:15 and 19).

Yet I certainly understand why I and other feminists have not raced to deal with this aspect of God. It is not unique or central to feminist experience; and in addition, it is difficult and painful. More than this, however, the ambiguous God threatens to bring us back to the images of domination we see as so problematic in the tradition. I and many other feminists have pointed to the destructiveness of hierarchical images of God such as Lord and King, images that draw upon and in turn justify oppression in society. But what if God as Lord points not simply to the manipulative ruler of history, the cosmic patriarch who authorizes numerous forms of oppression, but also the nonrational and unpredictable dimension of experience, the forces we cannot control or contain? How do we name the power in the world that makes us know our vulnerability, that terrifies and overwhelms us? Can we name this power without invoking images of Otherness? Can we jettison the Lord of history without also losing the Lord of contradictory life? Can we name the ambiguous God without resorting to the tra-

ditional metaphors that have rationalized oppression and denied the
humanity of women?

I do not know the answers to these questions, but they bring me to
a new place of wrestling my tradition. If I read the traditional liturgy
from the perspective of God's ambiguity, then I suddenly see it in a new
and ambiguous light. Kaddish, for example, is not simply a hymn to
God's sovereignty; it is a hymn to God's sovereignty said precisely at the
moment when I most deeply know my lack of power to preserve those
I love. It is an acknowledgement of my own impotence exactly when I
know myself as impotent. But should I pray to this contradictory God?
Or should I pray *against* him or her? If I acknowledged God's ambiguity directly rather than burying it in images of praise would that make
the ambiguity any easier to worship? Do I have to change "who creates
weal and woe" to "who creates all things" in order to be able to say the
words? And how do I continue to pray to the God who empowers me
when I have confronted the equivocal nature of all power?

Source: Judith Plaskow, "Facing the Ambiguity of God,"
Tikkun 6, no. 5 (Sept./Oct. 1991): 70, 96.

God: Some Feminist Questions

An extraordinary passage in *Pesikta Rabbati* (21.6) describes the many
guises in which the one God has appeared to the children of Israel.
God spoke to the Israelites on Mount Sinai not "face to face" (Deut.
5:4) but "face after face." "To one he appeared standing, and to one
seated; to one as a young man and to one as an old man." Showing
them a plurality of aspects, each appropriate to some part of the divine
message, God revealed a threatening face and a severe face, an angry
face and a joyous face, a laughing face and a friendly face.

This midrash at once points the way out of the feminist dilemma
of God-language and simultaneously illustrates its most trying
aspect. It acknowledges the legitimacy, indeed the necessity, of plural
ways of perceiving and speaking about the one God. It asserts that
multiple images of God are not contradictions of monotheism but
ways in which limited human beings apprehend and respond to the
all-embracing divine reality. And yet while the passage authorizes

theological and liturgical inventiveness, the many faces of God it describes are only male ones. God is an old man or a young man, a man of war or a man of wisdom, but never a woman.

This unyielding maleness of the dominant Jewish image of God is not the end of the feminist critique of God-language, but it is its beginning. The absence of female metaphors for God witnesses to and perpetuates the devaluation of femaleness in the Jewish tradition. The God-language of a religious community is drawn from the qualities and roles the community most values, and exclusively male imagery exalts and upholds maleness as the human standard. It belies the biblical insight that God created human beings, male and female, in God's image. It denigrates women's lives and experiences as resources for knowing the sacred.

Transforming Meaning not just Old Terms

As this language has become increasingly alienating to large numbers of women, those committed to shaping a living Jewish spirituality and theology have looked for ways to change it. They have sought a richer and wider range of images for speaking about and to the sacred. The *Pesika Rabbati* passage seems to suggest that of those who saw God on Sinai "face after face," it was only the men who recorded and passed down their experiences. Feminists have taken on the task of recovering and forging a female-language for God—female not simply in its metaphors but in its mode of religious apprehension and expression.

But if feminist attempts to find a new vocabulary for God began in the concern with gender, they have not resulted in a uniform response to the oppressiveness of traditional language. Rather feminist explorations of God-language have gradually opened up deeper dimensions of the problem of God. Early feminist efforts to make God a mother and give her a womb, to praise her as birthgiver and nourisher, performed important functions. They validated women's sexuality and power as part of the sacred. They pressed worshippers to confront the maleness of a supposedly sex-neutral liturgy. Yet at the same time, these efforts often left intact images of dominance and power that were still deeply troubling. If the hand that drowned the Egyptians in the Red Sea was a female hand, did that make it any more a hand feminists wanted to worship?

The issue of the maleness of God-language has thus ineluctably moved to the question of the nature of the God feminists want to pray to. Where do Jewish women find God in our experience, and what do we find there? What images most powerfully evoke and express the reality of God in our lives?

The Guises of the Empowering Other

While these questions lend themselves to unanimity even less than the issue of gender, there is a theme that seems to sound strongly through a range of feminist discussions of God-language: the need to articulate a new understanding of divine power. If the traditional God is a deity outside and above humanity, exercising power over us, women's coming to power in community has generated a counter-image of the power of God as empowerment. Many Jewish feminist arguments about and experiments with God-language can be understood to revolve around the issue of how to express this new image and experience of power in a way that is Jewishly/feministly authentic.

For some Jewish feminists, for example, it is nonpersonal imagery for God that most effectively captures a conception of divine power as that which moves through everything. Metaphors for God as source and fountain of life evoke the deity that is wellspring of our action without tying us to gendered language that channels and confines. For other feminists, the question of divine power lends new interest to the continuing debate about the viability of the image of *Shekhinah* in a feminist Judaism. This image, which at first seemed to promise such a clear Jewish way to incorporate female language into theology and liturgy, also has been resisted by many feminists as part of a system that links femaleness to immanence, physicality and evil. In the context of the quest for new metaphors for power, however, this image of deity provides an interesting resource for feminist thinking about a God who dwells in the world and in the power of human relation. For still other feminists, it is incorporation of the names of goddesses into feminist liturgy that best conveys multiple images of female power, images that may have had power to our foremothers and that thus

connect us in community to them. Use of these images does not constitute polytheism any more than do the multiple images of *Pesikta
Rabbati*. Rather, these images fill out the traditional record, exploring
and recovering faces of God that have been forgotten or expunged.

The Old/New Search for the Ineffable

These forays into new imagery are experimental and tentative, and
there are many Jews for whom some or all of them will seem shocking
or foreign. Yet if we attend to the roots and intention of these lively
experiments, we can find in feminist experience a potentially powerful
resource for the revivification of Jewish religious language. The feminist experience is one of finding in community both a sense of personal identity and power and the power and knowledge of God. This
experience may not be so different from that of the early Israelites who
found together in community both a new national identity and connection with the God who gave it. From a feminist perspective, the
problem with traditional Jewish God-language is that the initial experience of empowered community found expression in images that
established hierarchy within the Jewish community and that margin-
alized or excluded half of its members. The challenge to women as we
seek to name the God we have experienced "face after face," is to find
a language that carries through the experience of divine power in community and that evokes the living presence of God in the whole Jewish
people.

Source: Judith Plaskow, "God: Some Feminist Questions,"
Sh'ma 17 (Jan. 9, 1987): 38–40.

Towards a Feminist Understanding of God

Recognizing, then, that the becoming of new images is in its early
stages, I would suggest that there are (at least) two kinds of Jewish
feminist God-naming that need to be taken together to produce a picture of God that reflects the experience of egalitarian community. The
first kind of God-language is anthropomorphic language. Modern
Jewish thinkers who have emphasized the importance of a lived rela-

tionship with God have tended to speak about God in philosophical language, avoiding anthropomorphisms that might objectify God and thus undermine the immediacy of relation. Similarly, some feminists have sought to solve the problem of traditional male metaphors by using nonimagistic, or at least nonpersonal language. Some women have preferred to fill in names like "God" or "the Eternal" with new experiences, rather than create new images that would reify certain aspects of experience. Others have avoided personal imagery because it necessarily reinforces traditional anthropocentrism and because it implies that God is separable from the world.

But while it is certainly true that anthropomorphic images can be dangerous, supporting patterns of dominance or substituting for the experiences they claim to communicate, such images also appeal to places in our nature that cannot be reached by abstract philosophical discourse or direct designations like "God" and "the Eternal." Even nonpersonal images, though they are important to feminist God-language, are not themselves sufficient, I would argue, to evoke the God of community. Nonanthropomorphic language threatens to leave intact old anthropomorphic images that can continue to coexist with and subvert neutral language. For the English speaker, it is quite possible to avoid pronouns for God and to refer to God as the Eternal or source of life and still picture that eternal source as male. Only deliberately disruptive—that is, female—metaphors can break the imaginative hold of male metaphors that have been used for millennia. For the Hebrew speaker, who has available nonpersonal female images, it is still difficult to convey the presence of God in community while excluding those images that come most directly from the web of interpersonal relations that constitute community. We are roused to remember the God of community and to value and create certain kinds of communities precisely by those images that most vividly evoke our real experiences of community. Just as feminists are struggling to find communal structures that do not involve hierarchy, so we need to find ways of speaking about God's presence in community that do not invoke metaphors of domination. Failing to use the images that emerge from our real-life struggles, we banish as a source of religious expression central aspects of our lives.

To my mind, then, feminists cannot avoid the use of anthropomorphic imagery. Indeed, incorporating the appreciation of diversity that should characterize all feminist God-language, this kind of imagery would include a wide range of metaphors, from purposely disquieting female images, to female and nongendered images that express intimacy, partnership, and mutuality between humans and God. It may be important, for example, to use for a time images like Queen of the Universe and Woman of War in order to jar worshipers, precipitate discussion, and raise questions about the meaning and effects of the imagery we use. What is the source of our attachment to male imagery? Is the image of a monarch—male or female—one we want to affirm? Do women need to claim the warrior within ourselves, and are there images of warrior that are not images of violent destruction? While metaphors of queen and warrior are problematic and will not constitute the lasting contribution of feminism to Jewish God-language, they have an important bridge role to play in presenting images of female religious power to a community that has denied women this attribute. Other, perhaps more enduring, images will try to combine female metaphors with a changed conception of God or use nongendered language drawn from human community. Sallie McFague, in her book *Models of God*, devotes extensive discussion to images of God as lover and friend. These images, along with companion and cocreator, might well be taken up by Jewish feminists and developed conceptually and liturgically.

Images of God as lover and friend are present in the Jewish tradition, but they are greatly overshadowed by father and king and rarely appear in the liturgy. In midrashic parallels to the passage in *Pesikta Rabbati* that describes God's different guises, God as a young warrior at the Red Sea is identified with the lover of the Song of Songs who, at the moment of liberation, comes to Israel as her beautiful bridegroom. Although the image of God as lover-bridegroom later disappears, it and father-judge are the central rabbinic metaphors for the love of God. In McFague's rendering, the image of God as lover validates the erotic element in spirituality and affirms the value of that which is loved. Unlike images of king, judge, and (one side of) father, which promise enduring love *despite* a community's sins, the notion of God as lover proclaims that God loves Israel *because of* who Israel is.

The idea that we are loved for what is most valuable in us, that God sees our worth even when we cannot, is far more conducive to human empowerment and accountability than the idea that we are loved despite our worthlessness. In traditional Jewish usage, of course, God as valuing lover is the comely young man wooing (the subordinate) Israel as his bride. Feminist use of the image of God as lover would need to bring through this patriarchal model of love relations, envisioning the lover as both female and male Israel is not "she"; *it* is a community of women and men, all of whom can be lovers and loved of God. The astonishingly mutual imagery of the Songs of Songs presents both male and female lovers as pursuer and pursued. There is no reason why, with this book as a model, only the male should be identified with God—except, of course, for the androcentric context of the history of its interpretation.

The image of God as friend also appears in rabbinic discussion and finds its way into the Yom Kippur liturgy in the multiple metaphors of *Ki Anu Amekhah*. A striking contrast with symbols of God as Other, this image of free and reciprocal connection is a profound metaphor for the covenantal relation. As McFague sees it, the image of God as friend points to a common vision or commitment that brings friends together and that both unites them and turns them to the world. While friendship often implies an exclusive element, it is also possible for people of different backgrounds and abilities to join in friendship around a common undertaking. Friendship is a human possibility, moreover, irrespective of gender and across gender lines. Indeed, McFague suggests, since all of life is relational, friendship is possible even across ontological boundaries: We can be friends of the earth and friends of God.

Closely related to the image of friend is the image of companion. While both images are ambiguous, and they are often used interchangeably, they can also represent different aspects of the experience of relation. If friendship entails a unique bond between two people that distinguishes their relationship from more casual connections, a companion is simply one who travels on the same way. The image of companion thus lacks the passion and specialness of friendship, but it provides the same sense of equality with a more communal metaphor. One can image many companions linked together by some shared task, laboring side by side for the achievement of their ends. Such companionship may be brief or can last throughout a lifetime, lightening shared work with the pleasure of human connection. Metaphors of God as friend and companion capture in different ways the closeness of God's relationship to Israel and the sense of striving toward a common goal. They suggest that God and Israel are mutually related and accountable as they join in the shared project of sanctifying and repairing the world.

Another, somewhat more awkward, image that suggests the shared responsibility of God and Israel has both feminist and Jewish roots. At the Grailville conference at which the participants used many "ing" words for God, they also suggested the term "cocreator" as evoking important aspects of their week together. The prefix "co," which might in fact be used with a range of images, conjures the sense of personal empowerment and mutual responsibility that emerges out of speaking and acting in community with others. The feeling of possibility that comes with seeing the limits placed on women and envisioning a life beyond them fosters a sense of significant participation in the larger project of world-creation, a project that God and human beings share. To name the self and name the world in new ways is to enter with God into the act of creation. Insofar as human beings are cocreators with God, God is also a cocreator. Creation is not a discrete event completed by God in six days but a process that continues in dialogue with human beings who can carry forward or destroy the world that God has brought to be. This image of God as cocreator strongly accords with the sense of the Jewish mystical tradition that human beings are responsible for fulfilling the work of creation, uniting the separated aspects of divinity through the power of the deed.

These images of God—lover, friend, companion, cocreator—are more appropriate metaphors for the God of the covenant than traditional images of lord and king. Defining God's power not as domination but empowerment, they evoke a God who is with us instead of over us, a partner in dialogue who ever and again summons us to responsible action. Rather than reminding human beings of our frailty and nothingness, they call us to accountability as partners in a solemn compact that makes demands on us to which we can respond. It is not as we are subjugated, as we feel our worthlessness and culpability, that we can act most responsibly and effectively, but as we know our own value, mirrored in the constancy of God as friend and lover who calls us to enter into the task of creation. Responding responsibly, we do so not because otherwise we are guilty, but because—as the Kabbalistic tradition reminds us—what we do or leave undone as cocreators makes a difference in the world.

Imagining God as friend and cocreator begins to name aspects of the deity lost in metaphors of domination, but it still provides only one stratum of a feminist understanding of God. Human beings become cocreators with God only after we come into being as part of a much larger web of existence—a web we now have the power to destroy but which we did not conceive or create. Moreover, the images I have suggested are still primarily dyadic; and while they can be applied to community, they do not in the first instance take us beyond the interpersonal plane. Anthropomorphic images must thus be supplemented by a second kind of language that can evoke the creative and sustaining power of God present throughout the world and in ever-widening circles of relation. This stratum of language will encompass an even wider range of images than the first—from natural and impersonal metaphors to conceptual terms that express God's relation to all being and becoming.

Images of God as fountain, source, wellspring, or ground of life and being remind us that God loves and befriends us as one who brings forth all being and sustains it in existence. As cocreators with God for the brief span of our lives, we are responsible not just to the community of our fellow persons with whom we especially share the sense of God's presence, but to the larger community of creation that God also loves and befriends. Metaphors of ground and source continue the reconceptualization of God's power, shifting our sense of direction from a God in the high heavens who creates through the magical word to the very ground beneath our feet that nourishes and sustains us. As a tree draws up sustenance from the soil, so we are rooted in the source of our being that bears and maintains us even as it enables us to respond to it freely. Images of God as rock, tree of life, light, darkness, and myriad other metaphors drawn from nature, teach us the intrinsic value of this wider web of being in which we dwell. The God who is the ground of being is present and imaged forth in all beings, so that every aspect of creation shows us another face of God.

More conceptual images for God also have a role in feminist discourse. The traditional image of God as place (*makom*) evokes both the presence of the world in God and the extraordinary presence of God in particular places. As Rabbi Jose b. Halafta said, "We do not know whether God is the place of His world, or the world is His place." Lacking personal communal images to refer to God, we can use this richly ambiguous term to point to community as a special place of God's self-manifestation. Community is a place we find ourselves in God; God dwells in this place. Also relevant here is the image of Shekhinah, which like the term God itself, cuts across the layers of anthropomorphic and nonpersonal language. Addressed in myriad personal guides, the Shekhinah is also the presence of God in the place called the world and the one who rests in a unique way in the midst of community.

There are, of course, many other metaphors that can be and have been evoked as part of the feminist naming of God. The images I mention here are just some of those that might convey the presence of God in a diverse, egalitarian community, replacing images of domination with a different understanding of the divine/human relation. Moreover, insofar as these images reflect the experience of a distinct community, they comprise only one of many communal namings of the experience and nature of the sacred. The connection between these different namings remains an important question, particularly as it pertains to the continuing place of traditional images of God in a feminist Judaism.

Certainly, the particular metaphors that emerge out of feminist experience are not meant to replace all other metaphors for God. Feminist metaphors call attention to important neglected aspects of the experience of God in community, and in doing so relativize and modify traditional metaphors by placing them in a different and larger context. Many traditional images of God can be altered in connotation or meaning by being seen in conjunction with feminist metaphors and with the changing social context out of which these metaphors arise. The image of God as father, for example, in a transformed social and metaphoric nexus, is potentially simply a parental image, shedding its implications of patriarchal domination and control. The image of God as judge confronts us when we fail to live up to our own ideals of diversity and mutuality, thus remaining an important counterpart to friend and source of being. But while feminist metaphors are nonexclusive, the experience of God in diverse, egalitarian community is also normative from a feminist perspective and as such functions as a criterion for selecting and rejecting images of divinity. Traditional images like god and king, for example, evoke by definition relations of domination. Since it is difficult to imagine how such images could be transformed by context, they need to be seen as injurious reflections and supports of a hierarchical social system, and excised from our religious vocabularies.

The rejection of all metaphors of domination raises, finally, a question frequently asked of feminists: What becomes of the Otherness or "Godness" of God when the primary feminist metaphors for God are warm and intimate ones? If God is friend and lover—albeit also ground and source of being—does this not somehow make God less God, less utterly more than us in every way? This question can be answered only by distinguishing among very different meanings of the concept of Otherness. The sense of Otherness I have been criticizing throughout this chapter is the notion of God as a dominating sovereign manipulating the world from outside it and above. I have argued that metaphors that depict God as Other in this sense mirror and sustain destructive social relations that ought never to be sanctified by any religious usage. But rejecting such metaphors does not entail abandoning God's "moreness"; it simply challenges us to imagine that moreness in nonhierarchical terms. Just as a community is more than the sum of its members, for example, without necessarily controlling or dominating them, so God as the ultimate horizon of community and source of unity is more than all things—also without needing to control or dominate them. A second meaning of Otherness found frequently in this book refers to peoples or aspects of reality seen as different from and less than some dominant group, the nonnormative Other in a hierarchical system. Feminist God-language does not simply reject this sense of Otherness, but seeks actively to address and undermine it through finding divinity in what has hitherto been despised. In imaging God as female, as darkness, as nature, and as a myriad of other metaphors taken from realms devalued and spurned, we reexamine and value the many forms of

Otherness, claiming their multiform particularity as significant and sacred.

The third meaning of Otherness points to God as mystery and adversary—the presence of God experienced not as friend but as devouring fire, and the relationship of God to the terrible aspects of human existence. Feminists, although we continually confront human evil in the form of patriarchy and other destructive structures of hierarchical relation, have not yet fully addressed the theological question of evil as a feminist issue. This side of God, which we cannot neglect without introducing a fundamental dualism into our conception of the world, can be expressed through images of waning and death, pain and struggle, all of which are aspects of a complex and changing reality. God as source can also be experienced as abyss; God as friend can also appear as enemy. But while we must speak about God as other in this sense, it is unnecessary to do so using images of hierarchical domination. The hierarchies in our world are human creations. The God who brings to birth and destroys, gives forth and takes away, judges my limitations and calls me to struggle, is terrifying not for God's distance, but precisely for God's nearness. That which is awesome, painful, or evil appalls or bewilders me not because it is far away, but because it is all around and as near as my own heart. This otherness is not incompatible with the intimacy of feminist metaphors, but is found alongside and within them as their difficult counterparts and companions.

We are left, then, with a picture of God as a God of many faces— as many as the 600,000 souls that stood at Sinai and the complexities and conflicts of Jewish and human existence. At the center of this picture stands the Jewish/feminist experience of a God encountered in the midst of community—a God revealed as the community and those within it discover their destiny and understand that destiny as part of a larger universe of action and response. This God is male/female lover, friend, companion, cocreator, the one who, seeing what is best in us, lures us to be the most we can become. This God is ground and source of all life, creating, holding, sustaining the great web of existence and, as part of it, the human companions who labor to make the world a home for the divine presence. This God is the God of Israel, the God the nascent community experienced and acknowledged behind the wonderful events at the Red Sea. This is the God the people stood before at Sinai, coming to their identity as a people, responding with the myriad laws, institutions, and customs that have given form and substance to their communal life. This is the God to whom they found themselves tied in a covenant, reciprocally binding through good times and bad: friend, holy terror, persistent goad.

Jewish feminists, in seeking to name this God of our experience, search for images of God that convey God's power and presence in community, at the same time trying to undo that community's hierarchical distortions. Selecting metaphors for God that acknowledge the differences within a covenantal community, we are also aware of the many covenants and greater differences that lie beyond our particular naming. As feminists, as Jews, we come to respond to and speak of God in certain characteristic ways. So every community in its uniqueness imagines the power that surrounds and sustains it. The naming of God and Israel that would turn God into Israel's God and Israel into "his" chosen people is part of the dualistic, hierarchical misnaming of God and reality that emerges out of and supports a patriarchal worldview. In speaking of the moving, changing ground and source, our companion and our lover, we name toward the God known in community that cherishes diversity within and without, even as that diversity has its warrant in the God of myriad names.

Source: Judith Plaskow, *Standing Again at Sinai: Judaism from a Feminist Perspective* (San Francisco: Harper and Row, 1990), 159–169.

· 15 ·

MARGARET MOERS WENIG

b. 1957

A rabbi and academician, Margaret Moers Wenig was born in New York City in 1957. She earned her B.A. degree from Brown University in 1978 and her rabbinic ordination from the Hebrew Union College–Jewish Institute of Religion (HUC-JIR) in 1984. She served as the rabbi of Beth Am, the People's Temple, in New York City, from 1984 to 2000 and has been on the faculty of the HUC-JIR, New York campus, since 1985, teaching liturgy and homiletics. She has also run workshops for Christian clergy in continuing education programs at Union/Auburn Seminary in New York and in the United States Navy.

Wenig's undergraduate honors thesis, on Mishnah Bikurim, *has been published in sections, within larger works, by her teacher Jacob Neusner and his students William Scott Green and Richard Sarason. When she was a member of the Brown University Women's Minyan, she also co-edited* Siddur Nashim: A Sabbath Prayer Book for Women *in 1976, which uses feminine imagery for God. Her sermons and articles have been published in many journals, including* Reform Judaism, The Reconstructionist, Journal of Feminist Studies in Religion, The Living Pulpit, *and* National Bulletin on Liturgy, *as well as in other anthologies. Rabbi Wenig's sermon "God Is a Woman and She Is Growing Older" won a Harper Collins Best Sermons Award in 1991 and has appeared in numerous publications, twice in German translation, and was aired on Chicago Public Television and on cable TV's Odyssey channel.*

Wenig uses the sermonic form as a vehicle to delve into the theological issue of God. Acknowledging that God is ultimately unknowable, even unfathomable, she accepts the reality of God as given and prefers to use feminine imagery to describe the Divine. This pattern is not unknown among many Jewish thinkers who have tried to understand God through the prism of their own limited human ability, and most do so by speaking metaphorically of the Divine either in masculine or, in a few occasions, in feminine terms. Even though the Bible and rabbinic literature emerged out of a patriarchal society that viewed God primarily in male terms, there are some biblical sources that seem to contain female allusions to God, primarily in II Isaiah (e.g., Isa. 46:3; 49:15; 66:9, 13). This is clearly the case with the Jewish mystical literature, the Kabbalah. God is not only referred to as male in the Kabbalah, but also as having female characteristics manifested through the Shechinah, a Hebrew feminine term that refers to one of the divine emanations closest to humanity. Wenig has not developed a thorough and systematic view of God, yet her insightful sermon "God Is a Woman, and She Is Growing Older" is based on the powerful image of the Divine as a woman getting older, endowed with all the love and care of an ideal mother.

God Is a Woman, and She Is Growing Older

Who or what is God? Where shall we look for God's Presence? Our sages and philosophers are by no means unanimous in their response. But they do concur on one matter: God is ultimately unknowable. God is the Hidden One (*El Mistater*), the one who conceals His Face (*Hester Panim*), or the Infinite, Unmeasurable One (*Ein Sof*)— unknowable, unfathomable, indescribable.

Yet these same sages also dare to try to capture our people's experience of God in images we do know and can comprehend. The Kabbalists go so far as to sketch God's form: the Primordial Man (*Adam Kadmon*). They associate each of God's attributes with a specific part of His body: head, arms, legs, torso, even male genitals. *Midrashim* give us images of God weeping at the sight of Egyptians drowning, laying *tefilin* each weekday morning, or studying Torah with Moshe Rabbenu. Our liturgy shows us God as an immovable Rock (*Tzur Yisrael*); as a shield (*Magen Avraham*); as the commander of a host of angels (*Adonai Tzeva'ot*). On the Days of Awe, the *machzor* focuses upon the images of God as Father and God as King (*Avinu Malkenu*).

All these images are metaphors or allusions—never meant to be taken literally, merely meant to point us toward something we can imagine but never really see.

Imagine now that God is a woman, and she is growing older. . . .[1]

She moves more slowly now. She cannot stand erect. Her hair is thinning. Her face is lined. Her smile is no longer innocent. Her voice is scratchy. Her eyes tire. Sometimes she has to strain to hear. Yet she remembers everything.

On Rosh Hashanah, the anniversary of the day on which she gave us birth, God sits down at her kitchen table, opens the Book of Memories, and begins turning pages; and God remembers.

"There is the world when it was new and my children when they were young. . . ." As she turns each page she smiles, seeing before her, like so many dolls in a department store window, all the beautiful colors of our skin, all the varied shapes and sizes of our bodies. She marvels at our accomplishments: the music we have written, the gardens we have planted, the skyscrapers we have built, the stories we have told, the ideas we have spun.

"They now can fly faster than the winds I send," she says to herself, "and they sail across the waters which I gathered into seas. They even visit the moon which I set in the sky. But they rarely visit me." Pasted into the pages of her book are all the cards we have sent to her when we did not bother to visit. She notices our signatures[2] scrawled beneath the printed words someone else has composed.

Then there are pages she would rather skip. Things she wishes she could forget. But they stare her in the face, and she cannot help but remember: her children spoiling the home she created for us, brothers putting each other in chains. She remembers seeing us racing down dangerous roads—herself unable to stop us. She remembers the dreams she had for us—dreams we never fulfilled. And she remembers the names, so many names, inscribed in the book, names of all the children she has lost through war and famine, earthquake and accident, disease and suicide. . . . And God remembers the many times she sat by a bedside weeping that she could not halt the process she herself set into motion.

Tonight, *Kol Nidrei* night, God lights candles, one for each of her children, millions and millions of candles illuminating the night, making it bright as day. Tonight God will stay awake all night, turning the pages of her book.

God is lonely tonight, longing for her children, her playful ones. Ephraim, her darling one. Her body aches for us.[3] All that dwells on earth does perish. But God endures, so she suffers the sadness of losing all that she holds dear.

God is home tonight, turning the pages of her book. "Come home," she wants to say to us, "Come home." But she won't call, for she is afraid we will say, "No." She can anticipate the conversation: "We are so busy," we'd apologize. "We'd love to see you, but we just can't come tonight. Too much to do. Too many responsibilities to juggle."

Even if we don't realize it, God knows that our busyness is just an excuse. She knows that we avoid returning to her because we don't want to look into her age-worn face. She understands that it is hard for us to face a god who disappointed our childhood expectations: She did not give us everything we wanted. She did not make us triumphant in battle, successful in business, and invincible to pain. We avoid going home to protect ourselves from our disappointment and to protect her. We don't want her to see the disappointment in our eyes. Yet, God knows it is there, and she would have us come home anyway.

What if we did? What if we did go home and visit God this Yom Kippur? What might it be like?

God would usher us into her kitchen,[5] seat us at her table, pour two cups of tea. She has been alone so long that there is much she wants to say to us. But we barely allow her to get a word in edgewise, for we are afraid of what she might say, and we are equally afraid of silence. So we will fill an hour with chatter—words, words, so many words—until finally, she touches her finger to her lips and says, "Sha. Be still. Shhh."

Then she pushes back her chair and says, "Let me have a good look at you." And she looks. And in a single glance, God sees us as both newly born and dying: coughing and crying, turning our head to root for her breast, fearful of the unknown realm which lies ahead.

In a single glance she sees our birth and our death and all the years in between. She sees us as we were when we were young: when we idolized her and trustingly following her anywhere,[6] when our scrapes and bruises healed quickly, when we were filled with wonder at all things new (a new dress, a driver's license, the new feelings in our body when we first allowed a friend to touch it). She sees us when we were young, when we thought there was nothing we could not do.

She sees our middle years, too, when our energy was unlimited, when we kept house, cooked and cleaned, cared for children, worked, and volunteered; when everyone needed us, and we had no time for sleep.

And God sees us in our later years, when we no longer felt so needed; when chaos disrupted the bodily rhythms we had learned to rely upon. She sees us sleeping alone in a room which once slept two.

God see things about us we have forgotten and things we do not yet know. For nothing is hidden from God's sight.

When she is finished looking at us, God might say, "So tell me, how are you?" Now we are afraid to open our mouths and tell her everything she already knows:[7] whom we love; where we hurt; what we have broken or lost; what we wanted to be when we grew up. We are afraid to speak now, lest we begin to cry. . . .

So we change the subject. "Remember the time when . . . ," we begin. "Yes, I remember," she says. Suddenly we are both talking at the same time, never completing a sentence; saying all the things the greeting cards never said:

"I'm sorry that I . . ."
    "That's all right, I forgive you."
"I didn't mean to . . ."
    "I know that, I do."
"I was so angry that you hit me."
    "I'm sorry that I ever hurt you."

"But you wouldn't listen to me."
"You're right, I wouldn't listen. I should have. I know that now, but at the time I had to do it my way."
    "I know," she nods. "I know."

We look away from her now, our eyes wander around the kitchen. "I never felt I could live up to your expectations," we say. "I always believed you could do anything," she answers.

"What about your future?" she asks us. We stammer out an answer for we do not want to face our future. God hears our reluctance and understands.

After many hours of sitting and drinking tea, when at last there are no more words to say or to hear, God begins to hum:[8]

And we are transported back to a time when our fever wouldn't break and we couldn't sleep, exhausted from crying but unable to stop. She picked us up and held us against her bosom and supported our head in the palm of her hand and walked with us. We could hear her heart beating and hear the hum from her throat:

Ah yes, that's where we learned to wipe the tears.[9] It was from her we learned how to comfort a crying child, how to hold someone in pain.

Then God reaches out and touches our arm, bringing us back from our nostalgia, bringing us back to the present and to the future. "You will always be my child," she says, "but you are no longer a child. Grow old along with me. The best is yet to be, the last of life for which the first was made."[10]

We are growing older as God is growing older. How much like God we have become.

For us, as well as for God, growing older means facing death. Of course, God will never die, but she has buried more dear ones than we shall ever love.

In God we see, "tis a holy thing to love what death can touch."[11] Like her we may be holy,[12] loving what death can touch, including ourselves, our own aging selves.

God holds our face in her two hands and whispers, "Do not be afraid.[13] I will be faithful to the promise I made to you when you were young.[14] I will be with you. Even to your old age I will be with you. When you are gray-headed, still I will hold you. I gave birth to you. I carried you. I will hold you still.[15] Grow old along with me. . . ."

Our fear of the future might be tempered now by curiosity: The universe is infinite. Unlimited possibilities are arrayed before us. Though the sun rises and sets just as the day before, no two days are the same. We can greet each day with eagerness, awakening to wonder. What shall I learn today? What can I create today? What will I notice that I have never seen before?

It has been a good visit. Now we are tired and need to go to sleep. Before we leave, it is our turn to take a good look at her. The face which time has marked looks not frail to us now, but wise. For we understand that God knows those things only the passage of time can teach: that one can survive the loss of a love; that one can feel secure in the midst of an ever-changing world;[16] that there can be dignity in being alive, even when every bone aches.

God's movements seem not slow to us now—but strong and intent, unlike our own. We are too busy to see beneath the surface. We speak too rapidly to truly listen. We move too rapidly to feel what we touch. We form opinions too quickly to judge honestly.

God moves slowly and with intention. She sees everything there is to see, understands everything she hears, and touches all that lives.

Now we understand why we were created to grow older. Each added day of life, each new year makes us more like God, who is ever growing older. That must be the reason we are instructed to rise before the aged and see the grandeur in the faces of the old.[17] We rise in their presence as we would rise in the presence of God, for in the faces of the old we see God's face.

Looking at her, we are overwhelmed by awe (though embarrassed to say so). This aging woman looks to us now . . . like a queen: her chair a throne, her house dress an ermine robe, and her thinning hair, shining like jewels on a crown.

Yom Kippur we sit in the house of prayer, far from home, holding in our hands pages of greeting cards bound together like a book, thousands of words we ourselves have not written. Will we merely place our signatures at the bottom and drop the cards in the mail box?

God would prefer that we come home. She is sitting and waiting for us as she has waited every Yom Kippur, waiting ever-patiently[18] until we are ready. She will leave the door open and the candles burning, waiting patiently for us to come home.

Perhaps this Yom Kippur we will be able to look into God's aging face and say, "*Avinu Malkenu*, our Mother our Queen, we have come home."

Notes

1. *Anim Zemirot*, a *piyyut* included in the *Musaf* service on Shabbat, described God as a young man, a warrior, and an old man:

> They saw thee in both old age and young age,
> With the hair of thy head now gray, now black . . .
> Age in judgment day, youth in time of war . . .

I thank Rabbi Sharon Kleinbaum for calling this *piyyut* to my attention.

2. ". . . Thou openest the Book of Memories (*Sefer Hazichronot*) and it reads itself; every man's signature is contained in it." From the *Unetaneh Tokef* prayer on Rosh Hashanah and Yom Kippur.

3. From the *Zichronot* section of the Rosh Hashanah *Musaf Amidah*:

> I remember the loyal love of your youth, the affection of your bridal days, how you followed Me through the wilderness, through a land unsown. I will keep the promise I made to you in the days of your youth; I will make an eternal promise to you. . . . Is not Ephraim my dearest child, my playful one? I often speak of him. I remember—yes, I remember him. My heart longs for him, My womb aches for him (Jeremiah 2:2; Ezekiel 16:60; Jeremiah 31:19).

4. See, for example, *Adam yesodo* from the *Unetaneh Tokef*, "Man's origin is dust and dust is his end . . . But You are the King, the everlasting God."

5. In "A Short Amidah," Syd Lieberman offers the image of sitting in a kitchen drinking *schnapps* with God. (*Siddur Kol Haneshamah*, p. 184)

6. See note 3.

7. Psalm 139 (*Union Prayerbook* II, p. 157); and the *UPB II* translation of *Mah nomar lefanecha* and *Atah yodea razei olam*, from the *Selichot* section of the Yom Kippur liturgy (p. 148).

> What shall we say before Thee, who art on high, and what shall we recount unto Thee, who dwellest in the heavens? Dost Thou not know all things; both the hidden and the revealed? Thou knowest the secrets of eternity and the hidden thought of every living being.
> Thou searchest the innermost recesses and probest the deepest impulses of the heart. Naught is concealed from Thee nor hidden from Thine eyes.

8. This *niggum* begins the *vidui zutta* (*Ashamnu, bagadnu* . . .), *Zumra Lo III*, p. 198.

9. Hannah Senesh begins her poem "To My Mother" with the words "Where have you learned to wipe the tears?"

10. Robert Browning, from his poem "Rabbi Ben Ezra."

11. "tis a holy thing . . .," from a poem by Rabbi Chaim Stern.

12. "You shall be holy, for I *Adonai* am holy," from the Torah reading for Yom Kippur afternoon in the Reform tradition (Leviticus 19:2b).

13. From a prayer added to the Mourner's *Kaddish* during Rosh Hashanah *Musaf* and *Minchah*:

Be not afraid of sudden terror, nor of the storm that strikes the wicked. . . . Even to your old age I will be there. When you are gray-headed, still I will sustain you; I have made you. I will carry you; I will sustain you and rescue you (Proverbs 3:25, Isaiah 8:10, 46:4).

14. See note 3.
15. See note 13.
16. Al Carmines wrote in his song "Many Gifts, One Spirit":

God of change and glory
God of time and space
When we fear the future
Give to us Your grace.
In the midst of changing ways
Give us still the grace to praise.

17. *Mipnei sevah takum vehadarta penei zaken* ("rise before the aged and see grandeur in the faces of the old"). From the Yom Kippur afternoon Torah reading in the Reform tradition (Leviticus 19:32).
18. *Erech apayim* ("ever-patiently"). Central to the *Selichot* service recited prior to Rosh Hashanah is the name of God revealed to Moses on Sinai: *"Adonai, Adonai, El rachum vechanum, erech apayim"* (Exodus 34:6).

I am grateful to my colleagues and friends Dr. Janet Walton and Rabbi Judy Shanks for their constructive criticism of early drafts of this sermon.

This sermon was written for the three women who raised me: Mary Moers Wenig, Anna Wenig, and Molly Lane, and for the older women of Beth Am in whose face I have seen God's face.

Source: Margaret Moers Wenig, "God Is a Woman, and She Is Growing Older," in *Introduction to Judaism: A Sourcebook*, ed. Stephen J. Einstein and Lydia Kukoff, rev. ed. (New York: UAHC Press, 1999), 190–196; first published in *Best Sermons V*, ed. James W. Cox and Kenneth M. Cox (San Francisco: Harper Collins, 1992), 116–128.

Sof Davar: CONCLUSION

*T*he search for the Divine is a lifelong endeavor. As we continue to grow older and mature, we develop new images of God based on life experiences. The list of our priorities changes with time and place. Our quest for meaning and purpose remains alive throughout our lives, and we can find these in God, who, as Paul Tillich argues, is the ground of our existence, our ultimate concern. However, limited as we are, we will never be able to fathom what or who God is or is truly like. We all project our own imperfect images of God onto the universe.

As thinking and feeling individuals, we often ask ourselves: Why am I here? What is the purpose of my life? How do I deal with my limitations? But that is not a new question. It was raised already by the Psalmist when he asked, "Adonai, what is man that You should care about him, mortal man, that You should think of him?" (Ps. 144:3; cf. 8:5). Though limited and destined to die, we are still given some understanding of the universe and increasing ability to resolve many of the issues we face daily. We are determined to spend our lives looking for answers and at times find them in whatever God concept we arrive at as the best possible framework through which we can understand our existential condition. Belief in the reality and existence of God is a leap of faith. But that is the best we can do at any particular stage in our life. With years, this image changes, because our needs, our perspectives, and our purpose in life undergo continual mutations.

Not all of us are theologians who can come up with constructs that incorporate all the ramifications of our basic premises into an integrated whole. But we all seek meaning for the questions of existence. If one approach does not work, we look for another that best represents our personality and needs.

Like others, I too went from stage to stage in my theological development. I consider myself more of a researcher and teacher than a systematic theologian. I like to look for legitimate options and make them available to my students and readers as viable and authentic responses to matters of life and death. As an individual I have had to struggle with questions of existence and looked for explanations that made sense to me. I gave up my childhood notion of classical theism, because my logical mind and inquisitive nature would not yield the conclusions I was asked to accept. I find mysticism appealing but not totally compatible with my rationalistic tendencies. I am not satisfied with the claim of the religious humanists that God, as the highest images of ourselves, is capable of answering our queries. Also, I cannot conceive of a theology that looks at the universe from the divine perspective. I believe theology starts with our own questions and ends with our tentative answers.

I am more attracted to the views of the religious naturalists who maintain that there is energy that sustains the universe. Based on observation and analysis, I see a certain order in the world around us and conclude, much like some of the medieval thinkers and even a few early rabbis, that this order implies an ordering mind or, in my case, an ordering power and energy that stands for God. The laws of nature, I argue, are simply a manifestation of this universal energy that makes it possible for me to exist. And for this, I am very appreciative and express my thanks to God through prayers of gratitude and works of loving-kindness that benefit my family and community. I do affirm the freedom of the human will and can live with the realization that I don't have all the answers for the tension that exists between the realities of good and evil, because I do not know all the inner workings of the universe. In the spirit of Spinoza, I say that if we knew how the world operates, we could predict our next move. But alas, this is not within our ability. So, we live in an imperfect world and with limited abilities to understand the mysteries around us, while desperately looking for meaning and purpose in our daily struggles.

I hope the images portrayed in this book will enlarge the scope of our views on God, and lead the reader who is looking for answers to appropriate any of these positions, or even other views that remain beyond the scope of this collection, as a possible explanation for the mysterious workings of the world. My attempt is not meant to be exclusive or limiting. As all teachers, I, too, am interested in widening the perspective of my readers so that they may find their niche within the contemporary theological discourse. If I have achieved even part of my goal, my efforts hopefully would have been worthwhile.

BIBLIOGRAPHY

Borowitz, Eugene B.
  Choices in Modern Jewish Thought. New York: Behrman House, 1983.
  Jewish Spiritual Journeys, edited by Lawrence A. Hoffman and Arnold J. Wolf. New York: Behrman House, 1997.
  Liberal Judaism. New York: UAHC Press, 1984.
  Renewing the Covenant. Philadelphia: Jewish Publication Society, 1991.

Buber, Martin
  Between Man and Man. Translated by Ronald Gregor-Smith. New York: Routledge Classics, 2002.
  "The Holy Way." In *On Judaism*, edited by Nahum N. Glatzer, 108–110. New York: Schocken Books, 1995.
  I and Thou. Translated by Ronald Gregor-Smith. New York: Scribner, 2000.

Fackenheim, Emil L.
  Quest for Past and Future: Essays in Jewish Theology. Bloomington: Indiana University Press, 1968.
  Paths to Jewish Belief. New York: Behrman House, 1961.
  What Is Judaism? Syracuse, N.Y.: Syracuse University Press, 1999.

Fromm, Erich
  The Art of Loving. New York: Perennial Classics, 2000.
  Psychoanalysis and Religion. New Haven: Yale University Press, 1958.
  You Shall Be as Gods. New York: Henry Holt and Co., 1991.

Gittelsohn, Roland B.
  Little Lower than the Angels. New York: UAHC Press, 1955.

"A Naturalist View." In *The Theological Foundations of Prayer: A Reform Jewish Perspective. Papers Presented at the UAHC 48th Biennial*, edited by Rabbi Jack Bemporad, 43–52. New York: UAHC Press, 1967.
Wings of the Morning. New York: UAHC Press, 1969.

Heschel, Abraham Joshua
"The Divine Pathos." In *God in the Teachings of Conservative Judaism*, edited by Seymour Siegel and Elliot Gertel, 114–121. New York: Rabbinical Assembly, 1985.
God in Search of Man. New York: Noonday Press, Farrar Straus and Giroux, 2000.
Man Is Not Alone. New York: Noonday Press, Farrar Straus and Giroux, 1997.

Kaplan, Mordecai M.
Judaism without Supernaturalism. New York: Reconstructionist Press, 1958.
The Meaning of God in Modern Jewish Religion. New York: Reconstructionist Press, 1994.

Kushner, Harold S.
When Bad Things Happen to Good People. New York: Schocken Books, 1981.
When Children Ask about God. New York: Schocken Books, 1976.
Who Needs God? New York: Summit Books, 1989.

Levy, Richard N.
"The God Puzzle." *Reform Judaism* 28 (Spring 2000): 18–22.
"When We Study Torah, Is God the Teacher?" *Journal of Reform Judaism* (Winter 1985): 40–51.

Plaskow, Judith
"Facing the Ambiguity of God." *Tikkun* 6, no. 5 (Sept./Oct. 1991): 70, 96.
"God: Some Feminist Questions." *Sh'ma* 17 (Jan. 9, 1987): 38–40.
Standing Again at Sinai: Judaism From a Feminist Perspective. San Francisco: Harper and Row, 1990.

Reines, Alvin J.
"Hylotheism: A Theology of Pure Process." In *Jewish Theology and Process Thought*, edited by Sandra B. Lubarsky and David Ray Griffin, 256–258. New York: State University of New York Press, 1996.
Polydoxy: Explorations in a Philosophy of Liberal Religion. Buffalo: Prometheus Books, 1987.
"The Word 'God.'" *Polydoxy: Journal of the Institute of Creative Judaism* 4, no. 1 (1979).

Rubenstein, Richard L.
After Auschwitz: History, Theology and Contemporary Judaism. 2nd ed. Baltimore: Johns Hopkins University Press, 1992.
"The Symbols of Judaism and the Death of God." In *God in the Teachings of Conservative Judaism*, edited by Seymour Siegel and Elliot Gertel, 231–234. New York: The Rabbinical Assembly, 1985.

Schachter-Shalomi, Zalman
   The First Step. With Donald Gropman. New York: Bantam Books, 1983.
   Paradigm Shift: From the Jewish Renewal Teachings of Reb Zalman Schachter-Shalomi, edited by Ellen Singer. Northvale, N.J.: Jason Aronson, 1993.

Schulweis, Harold M.
   Evil and the Morality of God. Cincinnati: Hebrew Union College Press, 1983.
   Finding Each Other in Judaism. New York: UAHC Press, 2001.
   For Those Who Can't Believe. New York: Harper Collins, 1994.
   "From God to Godliness." In *God in the Teachings of Conservative Judaism,* edited by Seymous Siegel and Elliot Gertel, 237–240. New York: Rabbinical Assembly, 1985.

Wenig, Margaret Moers
   "God Is a Woman, and She Is Growing Older." In *Introduction to Judaism: A Sourcebook,* edited by Stephen J. Einstein and Lydia Kukoff, rev. ed., 190–196. New York: UAHC Press, 1999. First published in *Best Sermons V,* edited by James Fox, 116–128. San Francisco: Harper Collins, 1992.

About the Editor

Rifat Sonsino is rabbi emeritus of Temple Beth Shalom in Needham, Massachusetts. He had previously served congregations in Buenos Aires, Philadelphia, and Chicago. Rabbi Sonsino teaches in the Theology Department at Boston College.

A graduate of the Hebrew Union College–Jewish Institute of Religion, Cincinnati campus (1966), he holds a degree in law from the University of Istanbul (1959) and a Ph.D. from the University of Pennsylvania in Bible and ancient Near Eastern studies (1975). He has served as editor of the *Central Conference of American Rabbis Journal* (1999–2001) and is the author of numerous articles on Bible and Jewish thought. His publications include *Motive Clauses in Hebrew Law* (1980) and *Six Jewish Spiritual Paths* (2000). He has also co-authored two books with Rabbi Daniel B. Syme, *Finding God: Selected Responses* (1986; revised in 2002) and *What Happens After I Die? Jewish Views of Life after Death* (1990).

He and his wife, Ines, have two children, Daniel and Gabriela Sonsino, and Deborah and Ran Seri, and are proud grandparents of Ariella Sonsino and Abraham Seri.